Jacques de Werra (éd.)

La résolution des litiges de propriété intellectuelle
Resolution of Intellectual Property Disputes

llectual p®operty - p®opriété intelle©tuelle
opriété intelle©tuelle - *intelle©tual p®operty*

Jacques de Werra (éd.)

La résolution des litiges de propriété intellectuelle

Resolution of Intellectual Property Disputes

Contributions de Joost Pauwelyn, Pierre Véron, Edouard Treppoz, Julie Bertholet/Pierre-Alain Killias, Torsten Bettinger, Bernard Hanotiau et Sarah Theurich

Actes de la Journée de droit de la propriété intellectuelle du 8 février 2010

UNIVERSITÉ DE GENÈVE
FACULTÉ DE DROIT

BRUYLANT

L.G.D.J

Schulthess
ÉDITIONS ROMANDES

Information bibliographique de la Deutsche Nationalbibliothek
La Deutsche Nationalbibliothek a répertorié cette publication dans la Deutsche Nationalbibliografie; les données bibliographiques détaillées peuvent être consultées sur Internet à l'adresse http://dnb.d-nb.de.

ISBN 978-3-7255-6154-4 Schulthess Médias Juridiques SA, Genève · Zurich · Bâle
ISBN 978-2-8027-3064-4 Bruylant, Bruxelles
Diffusion en France Éditions Juridiques Associées / LGDJ, Paris

www.schulthess.com
www.bruylant.be
www.lgdj.fr

Avant-propos

Le présent ouvrage, qui constitue le deuxième volume de la série propriété intellectuelle – *intellectual property* (www.pi-*ip*.ch), réunit les contributions rédigées à l'occasion de la Journée de droit de la propriété intellectuelle (www.jdpi.ch) qui a eu lieu le 8 février 2010 et avait pour thème « La résolution des litiges de propriété intellectuelle / *The Resolution of Intellectual Property Disputes* », cette journée ayant été organisée en collaboration avec le groupe suisse de l'Association Internationale pour la Protection de la Propriété Intellectuelle (AIPPI Suisse) et le Centre d'arbitrage et de médiation de l'Organisation Mondiale de la Propriété Intellectuelle qui en sont remerciés ici.

Cette journée avait pour objectif de faire le point sur la question des modes de règlement judiciaire ou extra-judiciaire (notamment par l'arbitrage) des litiges de propriété intellectuelle sur le plan international, régional (européen) et national. Le choix de cette thématique – qui ne porte pas sur l'analyse du droit matériel de la propriété intellectuelle – s'est imposé, sachant qu'il ne saurait y avoir de protection efficace des droits de propriété intellectuelle sur le plan *matériel* qu'à la condition que des *procédures* de résolution des litiges permettent d'assurer une telle protection, ceci valant à tout niveau (international, régional et national).

Pour introduire ce sujet, il a paru logique de s'arrêter tout d'abord à la résolution des litiges de propriété intellectuelle sur le plan international et interétatique, en faisant ainsi le point sur la mise en œuvre de la protection internationale du droit de la propriété intellectuelle résultant de l'Accord sur les aspects des droits de propriété intellectuelle qui touchent au commerce (ADPIC) et sur les différends interétatiques ayant éclaté dans ce cadre, ce que le Prof. Joost Pauwelyn s'est attaché à faire en examinant l'impact de l'ADPIC quinze ans après sa mise en œuvre (p. 1).

Passant à un plan régional et plus spécifiquement européen, Me Pierre Véron a ensuite dressé le tableau de l'évolution des modes de résolution judiciaire des litiges de propriété industrielle au sein de l'Union européenne, ce qui a permis d'en révéler les complexités et les finesses et d'esquisser les développements à venir (p. 53). Le Prof. Edouard Treppoz s'est pour sa part attelé à la délicate tâche de présenter la thématique complexe du droit international privé du droit de la propriété intellectuelle dans une perspective française et également européenne, en s'intéressant particulièrement aux questions épineuses qui se posent dans des environnements dématérialisés comme Internet (p. 75).

La question de l'efficacité des mécanismes de résolution des litiges de propriété intellectuelle se pose naturellement aussi en droit interne, ceci valant tout particulièrement pour la Suisse. A ce propos, l'attention se concentre actuellement sur la mise en œuvre du nouveau Tribunal fédéral des brevets qui est destiné à entrer en fonction en 2011 et dont il a dès lors paru nécessaire de présenter les traits essentiels ce qui a été fait grâce à la plume de Me Julie Bertholet et de Me Pierre-Alain Killias (p. 101).

Force est de constater qu'en matière de propriété intellectuelle comme dans d'autres domaines du droit des affaires, les parties peuvent souhaiter résoudre leur litige en dehors des tribunaux étatiques, en recourant à des modes alternatifs de résolution de leurs différends. Il n'est à cet égard plus nécessaire de démontrer que des raisons légitimes peuvent justifier que les opérateurs du marché s'intéressent aux moyens extrajudiciaires de résolution de leurs litiges, qu'il s'agisse de la confidentialité, de l'expertise des organes et institutions intervenant dans ce contexte, ou encore de la facilité d'exécution d'une décision rendue dans un tel cadre.

C'est probablement à propos des litiges relatifs aux noms de domaine sur Internet que l'utilité des modes alternatifs de résolution des différends en matière de propriété intellectuelle a été démontrée de manière la plus éclatante, de par le succès phénoménal rencontré par l'Uniform Domain Name Dispute Resolution Policy (UDRP) institué par l'Internet Corporation for Assigned Names and Numbers (ICANN) depuis 1999, l'UDRP étant devenu en quelques années le mode classique (et dès lors plus véritablement alternatif) de résolution des litiges en matière de noms de domaine. Même si l'UDRP est connu (et ne mérite dans cette mesure plus de présentation détaillée), force est de constater que la création à venir de nouveaux types de noms de domaine (nouveaux *generic Top level domains*, gTLDs) est susceptible de générer d'autres types de conflits avec des droits de propriété intellectuelle de tiers, pour lesquels se pose également la question de la création de modes alternatifs de résolution des litiges appropriés, ce qui fait l'objet de l'article de Me Torsten Bettinger (p. 129).

Parmi les modes alternatifs de résolution des litiges, l'arbitrage occupe naturellement une place de choix, mais le recours à ce moyen classique de résolution des conflits, particulièrement dans le contexte de contrats commerciaux internationaux, suppose que la question litigieuse soit arbitrable, ce qui n'est pas sans poser de difficulté en matière de propriété intellectuelle. Aussi a-t-il paru utile de traiter de la question de l'arbitrabilité des litiges de propriété intellectuelle dans une perspective de droit comparé, ce à quoi s'est livré le Professeur Bernard Hanotiau dans sa contribution (p. 155).

Or, l'offre de modes de résolution alternative des litiges de propriété intellectuelle suppose l'existence d'organes susceptibles de gérer efficacement ces litiges. Dans ce contexte, force est de constater que le Centre d'arbitrage et de médiation de l'Organisation Mondiale de la Propriété Intellectuelle créé en 1994 s'est désormais profilé comme un acteur important sur la scène internationale. Outre la gestion des litiges proprement dite (notamment en matière de noms de domaine pour lesquels il joue un rôle moteur), le Centre a en effet développé une expertise qui se manifeste notamment dans la création de mécanismes de résolution des litiges adaptés à différends types de litiges et de secteurs commerciaux, ce qu'expose Sarah Theurich, collaboratrice du Centre, dans sa contribution (p. 175).

En fin de compte, cet ouvrage illustre la nécessité de prêter une attention soutenue à la mise en place de mécanismes, ordinaires ou alternatifs, de résolution des différends visant à permettre de régler efficacement et équitablement les litiges de propriété intellectuelle. A cet égard, par la diversité des thèmes qu'il aborde (allant de la résolution des différends entre Etats à celle des litiges relatifs aux noms de domaine sans omettre le droit international privé de la propriété intellectuelle, la création de juridictions nationales spécialisées et l'arbitrage), il rappelle que l'analyse de l'efficacité de la résolution des litiges suppose d'adopter une vision décloisonnée de la question, cette efficacité dépendant en effet d'une diversité de facteurs qui ne relèvent pas d'une seule branche du droit. Cette diversité contribue assurément à l'intérêt de la thématique, mais représente également un défi à relever.

Cet ouvrage n'aurait naturellement pas pu être publié sans la diligence des auteurs des articles qui le composent qui nous ont remis leurs travaux avec une grande célérité. Qu'ils en soient vivement remerciés ici. Notre gratitude s'adresse enfin à notre assistant M. Sevan Antreasyan pour sa précieuse collaboration à l'édition de l'ouvrage.

Genève, juillet 2010 Jacques de Werra

Sommaire

Table des matières

The Dog That Barked But Didn't Bite: 15 Years of Intellectual Property Disputes at the WTO

Joost Pauwelyn

Le contentieux de la propriété industrielle en Europe: état des lieux, stratégies et perspectives

Pierre Véron

Les litiges internationaux de propriété intellectuelle et le droit international privé

Edouard Treppoz

La création de juridictions spécialisées : l'exemple du Tribunal fédéral des brevets

Julie Bertholet & Pierre-Alain Killias

ICANN's New gTLD Program: Applicant Guidebook and Dispute Resolution

Torsten Bettinger

L'arbitrabilité des litiges de propriété intellectuelle

Bernard Hanotiau

Designing Tailored Alternative Dispute Resolution in Intellectual Property: the Experience of WIPO

Sarah Theurich

Table des abréviations

AB	Appellate Body (Organe d'appel)
ADPIC	Accord sur les Aspects des Droits de Propriété Intellectuelle qui touchent au Commerce, annexe 1C de l'Accord de Marrakech du 15 avril 1994 instituant l'Organisation mondiale du commerce
ATF	Recueil officiel des arrêts du Tribunal fédéral suisse
BaK	Basler Kommentar (Commentaire bâlois)
BGH	Bundesgerichtshof (Allemagne)
CCE	Revue Communication – Commerce Electronique
ccTLD	Country code top-level domain
CJCE / CJUE	Cour de Justice des Communautés Européennes / Cour de Justice de l'Union Européenne
C.P.R.	Canadian Patent Reporter
CPC	Code de procédure civile fédérale suisse du 19 décembre 2008
DAG	Draft Application Guidebook (on how to register new gTLDs)
EC	European Communities
EIPR	European Intellectual Property Review
EWCA	England and Wales Court of Appeal
EWHC	High Court of England and Wales
FAO	Food and Agriculture Organization of the United Nations (Organisation des Nations Unies pour l'alimentation et l'agriculture)
FF	Feuille Fédérale (Suisse)
GRUR	Gewerblicher Rechtsschutz und Urheberrecht
gTLD	Generic top-level domain
ICANN	Internet Corporation for Assigned Names and Numbers
ICC	International Chamber of Commerce

IIC	International Review of Intellectual Property and Competition Law
INTA	International Trademark Association
IPR	Intellectual Property Review
IPRG-Kommentar	Zürcher Kommentar zum IPRG : Kommentar zum Bundesgesetz über das Internationale Privatrecht, Daniel Girsberger et al. (éd.), Schulthess, Zurich 2004
JCP E	La Semaine juridique Entreprise et affaires
JCP G	La Semaine juridique Edition générale
JDI	Journal du Droit International
JdT	Journal des tribunaux (Suisse)
J.Q.	Jugements du Québec
J.T.	Journal des tribunaux (Belgique)
LPM	Loi fédérale suisse du 28 août 1992 sur la protection des marques et les indications de provenance, RS 232.11
Message LBI	Message concernant la modification de la loi fédérale suisse sur les brevets et l'arrêté fédéral portant approbation du Traité sur le droit des brevets et du Règlement d'exécution du 23 novembre 2005, FF 2006, p. 1
Message LTFB	Message concernant la loi fédérale suisse du 7 décembre 2007 sur le tribunal fédéral des brevets, FF 2008, p. 382
Pasin.	Pasinomie – Collection complète des lois, décrets, ordonnances, arrêtés et règlements généraux qui peuvent être invoqués en Belgique (publiée par Bruylant)
Prop. Int.	Propriétés intellectuelles
Prop. Ind.	Propriété industrielle
RDTI	Revue du Droit des Technologies et de l'Information
Rev. Crit. DIP	Revue Critique de Droit International Privé
R.J.Q.	Recueils de Jurisprudence du Québec
RLDI	Revue Lamy Droit de l'Immatériel
RS	Recueil Systématique du droit fédéral suisse
RSPIDA	Revue suisse de droit de la propriété intellectuelle et du droit d'auteur (jusqu'en 1996)

RTDCom	Revue trimestrielle de droit commercial et de droit économique
TF	Tribunal fédéral suisse
UDRP	Uniform Domain Name Dispute Resolution Policy
UNCTAD	United Nations Conference on Trade and Development (Conférence des Nations Unies sur le Commerce et le Développement)
US UTSA	United States Unfair Trade Secrets Act
WHO	World Health Organization (Organisation Mondiale de la Santé)

The Dog That Barked But Didn't Bite: 15 Years of Intellectual Property Disputes at the WTO

Joost Pauwelyn[*1]

Hope as well as fear was running wild when in 1995 the multilateral trading system incorporated the protection of intellectual property (IP) rights. As one author put it, « the [IP] component of the WTO [World Trade Organization] Agreement represented a revolution in international intellectual property law ».[2] This article provides a reality check 15 years after the fact with a particular focus on how the WTO performed in terms of settling IP disputes under the Agreement on Trade-Related Aspects of Intellectual Property Rights (TRIPS).[3] It compares conventional expectations associated with the creation of TRIPS and WTO dispute settlement to (Chapter II & III) the number and types of TRIPS disputes actually filed and decided, (Chapter IV & V) institutional and substantive decisions and interpretations reached by WTO Panels and the Appellate

* Professor of International Law, Graduate Institute of International and Development Studies, Geneva.

1 This article will also be published in the Journal of International Dispute Settlement, volume 1, issue 2 (2010). The author would like to thank the conference organizers and participants as well as Lauro Locks, Hannu Wager, Jayashree Watal and Werner Zdouc for comments on an earlier version. Thanks also to Miguel Burnier who provided excellent research and editorial assistance.

2 Jerome Reichman, The TRIPS Agreement Comes of Age: Conflict or Cooperation with the Developing Countries?, 32 Case W. Res. J. Int'l L. 441 (2000), at p. 442.

3 For earlier overviews, see Hannu Wager & Matthijs Geuze, WTO Dispute Settlement Practice Relating to the TRIPS Agreement, Journal of International Economic Law Vol. 2 No. 2, at 347 (1999); Hannu Wager & Matthew Kennedy, WTO Dispute Settlement and Copyright: The First Seven Years, in Paul Brügger (ed.), ALAI COPYRIGHT – INTERNET WORLD, REPORT ON THE NEUCHÂTEL STUDY SESSION, Lausanne / Berne, Groupe Suisse de l'Association Littéraire et Artistique Internationale 2003, 223-249; and Adrian Otten, The TRIPS Agreement Ten Years On, 2006, paper on file with the author.

Body in their application of the TRIPS agreement and, finally, (Chapter VI) the status of implementation of adverse WTO rulings under TRIPS.

The article offers a number of hypotheses that may explain these descriptive results centered on (Chapter VII.A) the rather unique features of WTO dispute settlement, (Chapter VII.B & VII.C) the TRIPS Agreement itself as compared to other trade agreements and (Chapter VII.D) an escalating cycle of IP-skepticism, due in no small part to the hard-line position taken by many IP industries themselves, and culminating in the 2001 Doha Declaration on TRIPS and Public Health which confirmed and slightly expanded TRIPS flexibilities in the context of the access to essential medicines debate.

The core message of this article is that based on 15 years of operation both the hopes and fears traditionally linked to TRIPS and WTO dispute settlement, not just in 1995 but to this day, were and continue to be largely exaggerated. TRIPS as conventionally portrayed by many is in this sense « the dog that barked but did not bite ». A *caveat* to this core message is, however, that it says something about the role and impact of formal dispute settlement under TRIPS, less about the broader changes brought about by the TRIPS agreement, in particular, sweeping (and often costly) legislative amendments in many developing countries, monitoring through the TRIPS Council and bargaining « in the shadow » of TRIPS[4] both to weaken and to strengthen global IP protection (be it in the Doha Declaration on TRIPS and Public Health, certain preferential trade agreements, WIPO or the WHO).

I. Conventional Hopes and Fears Triggered by TRIPS

To get a sense of what was expected from the incorporation of TRIPS into the 1994 Agreement Establishing the WTO, which entered into force on 1 January 1995 (TRIPS became binding, at least on *developed* WTO members, one year later), we must go back to why and how IP found its way into the multilateral trading system in the first place. What originated in a desire to more forcefully address trade in counterfeit trademark goods (the original General Agreement on Tariff and Trade

4 See Jerome Reichman & David Lange, Bargaining Around the Trips Agreement: The Case for Ongoing Public-Private Initiatives to Facilitate Worldwide Intellectual Property Transactions, 9 Duke J. Comp. & Int'l L. 11 (1998).

(GATT 1947) provided an exception to restrict trade in counterfeits[5]; it did not impose an obligation to block counterfeit goods) ended with a fully-fledged IP agreement as the third of three WTO pillars, besides trade in goods covered in GATT 1994 and trade in services addressed in the General Agreement on Trade in Services (GATS).

The resulting TRIPS agreement which incorporates selected provisions from existing IP conventions administered by WIPO (such as the Berne Convention for the Protection of Literary and Artistic Works and the Paris Convention for the Protection of Industrial Property) had three core objectives:

(i) expand minimum IP standards to a broader universe of markets to include, in particular, emerging economies,
(ii) add to existing WIPO conventions by strengthening the *domestic* enforcement of IP rights, and
(iii) facilitate the *international* settlement of IP disputes in the face of moribund WIPO mechanisms which, in practice, were or could not be relied on.[6]

The first goal (universal minimum standards) was achieved by making TRIPS part of the WTO's so-called « single package » which means that all WTO members, without exception (currently 153), are bound by the TRIPS agreement and the minimum standards it sets out for most IP rights (ranging from copyright and trademarks to patents and industrial designs) with no reservations possible.[7] The second goal (strengthen domestic enforcement) was translated into Part III of TRIPS which prescribes both civil and criminal procedures and remedies for the domestic enforcement of IP rights within WTO member countries, as well as disciplines on provisional and border measures, including an obligation to restrict importation of counterfeit trademark or pirated copyright goods. The third goal (effective international enforcement of IP rights) was pursued by subjecting TRIPS to the standard WTO dispute settlement system which provides for compulsory and automatic settlement of trade disputes without blocking or veto rights for defending parties

5 See GATT Article XX(d).

6 The Berne Convention, for example, provides for the settlement of disputes at the ICJ (Art. 33), but this provision is subject to reservations and has, in practice, not led to any ICJ case, the same goes for the Paris Convention (Art. 28).

7 See Part II of TRIPS.

and is backed-up with trade sanctions in case of continued non-compliance.

The above, third goal is the central focus of this article and was highly instrumental in reaching a final TRIPS deal : It embodied a trade-off between the United States and other WTO members (especially developing countries) whereby the United States agreed to stop unilaterally enforcing U. S. IP rights backed-up by unilateral trade sanctions under what is known as « Special 301 », in exchange for multilaterally controlled and enforced IP standards made binding on all WTO members. Indeed, pursuant to Article 23 of the WTO's Dispute Settlement Understanding (DSU), which Article 64 of TRIPS makes applicable also to TRIPS disputes, all WTO members (including the United States) must now have « recourse to, and abide by, the rules and procedures » of the multilateral DSU whenever they « seek the redress of a violation » of any WTO covered agreement instead of enforcing their TRIPS rights unilaterally.[8]

What then were the main hopes and fears expressed in relation to this new TRIPS framework ? On the « hope » side, IP industries in developed countries (think of, especially, U. S. and European pharmaceutical companies, software giants and the multi-billion movie, music and publishing industries), that is, the TRIPS *demandeurs*, as well as many commentators, expected a major boost in the depth and width of worldwide protection of IP rights with a new centralizing and enforcement role for the WTO and its dispute settlement system.

On the « fear » side, conversely, many developing countries and NGOs[9] expected merciless WTO enforcement of ever stricter IP rights with little or no room left for national policy space or social objectives in an organization, originally GATT now the WTO, reputed for its trade or economics-first approach.[10] Indeed, one of the few opinions both

8 Note that this has not meant the end of « Special 301 ». It is still used as a preliminary procedure that may result in triggering a TRIPS case before the WTO as well as to address IP issues not regulated in TRIPS (and therefore not subject to Article 23 of the DSU).

9 See, for example, LAURENCE HELFER, Regime Shifting in the International Intellectual Property System, 7 Perspectives on Politics 39-44 (2009), at p. 40 : « Civil society groups feared that TRIPs would undermine the rules and objectives of the human rights, public health, biodiversity, and plant genetic resources regimes in which they carried out their advocacy work ».

10 See, for example, JAYASHREE WATAL, Intellectual Property Rights in the WTO and Developing Countries, London / The Hague / Boston, Kluwer, 2001, at

proponents and critics of TRIPS shared was that the WTO would see a flood of TRIPS disputes (imagine: close to 130, now 153, countries would be bound by TRIPS), especially by *developed* against *developing* members (the latter being forced to introduce new IP legislation on, *inter alia*, pharmaceutical patents and IP enforcement)[11], and an active role for the WTO and its dispute settlement branch in the interpretation and further development of an IP-friendly jurisprudence, without veto rights for defendants and harsh trade sanctions when countries refuse to comply.[12]

Other, more subtle fears voiced by TRIPS critics (some pro IP, others IP-skeptics) were (i) that the WTO as a trade organization would not be appropriate or not have the expertise to handle IP disputes[13], (ii) that major turf battles and inconsistencies would emerge between the WTO and WIPO (whose conventions were now partly transplanted into the WTO), or (iii) that the WTO, as a new and eager actor on the IP scene with enforcement powers that WIPO lacked would first eclipse and ultimately lead to the demise of WIPO.[14]

p. 363 referring to « a strong and widespread perception that the TRIPS agreement is against the interests of developing countries » and arguing that « [t]he focus for the *demandeurs* [of stronger IP protection] in the immediate future is likely to be on implementation of and dispute settlement under TRIPS rather than on further development ».

11 See Jerome Reichman, The TRIPs Agreement Comes of Age: Conflict or Co-operation in the Post-Transitional Phase ?, in Intellectual Property: Trade, Competition, and Sustainable Development (World Trade Forum Series, vol. 3) 115-139 (Thomas Cottier & Petros C. Mavroidis eds.), The University of Michigan Press, Ann Arbor, 2003, at p. 125: « Seasoned observers already expect the number of dispute settlement actions to increase exponentially once the developing countries lose their immunities, and the coalition of intellectual property owners can hardly wait to bring test cases ».

12 See, for example, Nuno Pires de Carvalho, The TRIPS Regime of Patent Rights, 2nd ed., The Hague, Kluwer, 2005, p. 416-7: « One could indeed expect that the WTO DSM would be flooded with settlements of disputes in the area of the TRIPS due to Members› abundant failures in complying with its obligations ... the implementation of the TRIPS Agreement is an extremely complex task, not only from a technical aspect, but also politically ».

13 This was a critique voiced especially by old-hands in WIPO who were apprehensive of the new powers bestowed on the WTO and feared an undermining of WIPO as the focal point of international IP protection.

14 See Watal *supra* note 10.

II. Reality Check 1: Number of TRIPS Disputes Actually Filed

Fast-forward 15 years and reality is quite different. Let us first look at the raw numbers.

Between 1 January 1995 and 1 January 2010, 402 disputes were filed under the WTO dispute settlement system (the first step of which is a « request for consultations »). Of these 402 disputes, 27 (or 6.7 per cent) raised a TRIPS issue (often in combination with claims under other WTO agreements). In one dispute or request for consultations, several WTO agreements may, and are often, invoked (depending on what one counts as an agreement, there are currently around 20 different WTO agreements). If one adds all claims under these different agreements (again, several such claims are often joined into one single dispute), the share of claims under TRIPS is around 3 per cent.

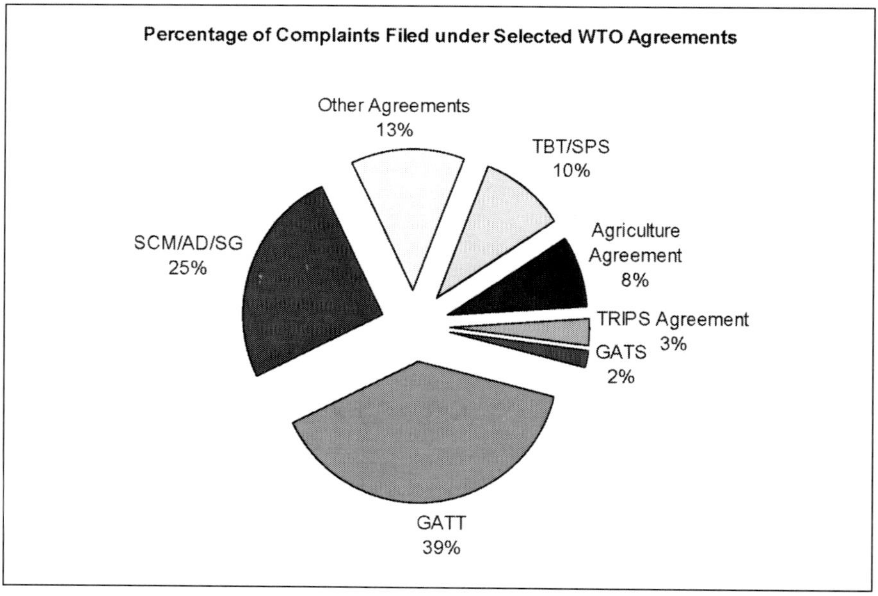

Many disputes formally filed at the WTO do not move beyond consultations and are settled by mutual agreement. On average, the percentage of cases that do move to the second stage of the mechanism, that is, examination by a three-member, *ad hoc* appointed « Panel » is around 53 per cent. Of the 27 TRIPS disputes filed, however, only 9 ended before a Panel (that is, 33 per cent). Once a Panel has examined the dispute, either party can appeal issues of law to the (in 1995 newly) established « Appellate Body », a permanent quasi-judicial organ with 7 members (only 3 of which decide an individual case), appointed each by the consensus of all WTO members for a 4 year period (renewable once). Of all WTO Panel reports issued so far, around 70 per cent were appealed. Of the 9 Panel reports that addressed TRIPS claims, only 3 were appealed (that is, once again, 33 per cent).

Three more numbers are interesting. Firstly, of the 27 TRIPS cases filed between 1995 and 2010, only 9 were disputes brought by developed against developing countries (10, in contrast, were between the United States and the EC; the others involved Australia, Canada or Japan; not a single South-South dispute was brought so far). Similarly, of the 9 Panel reports under TRIPS, only 4 were North-South disputes and of the 3 Appellate Body reports under TRIPS, only 1 was between a developed and developing country (the very first *United States v. India – Patent* case).

Secondly, the United States was by far the most active complainant (17 of the 27 complaints, only 5 of which reached a Panel). At the same time, 4 complaints were also filed against the United States (two of which were decided by a Panel). The most frequent defendant in TRIPS disputes so far was the EC or its member states (10 out of 27 disputes).

Thirdly, following a general trend of gradually less WTO disputes per year (a number that since 2005 seems to have stabilized at between 12 and 20 WTO disputes per year, compared to a maximum of 50 cases filed in 1997 alone), 23 of the 27 TRIPS disputes filed so far were lodged during the first five years of TRIPS (at an annual rate of between 3 and 6 cases). Since 2000, however, maximum 1 TRIPS case per year was filed and during five years not a single TRIPS case was brought (that is, in 2002, 2004-6 and 2009).

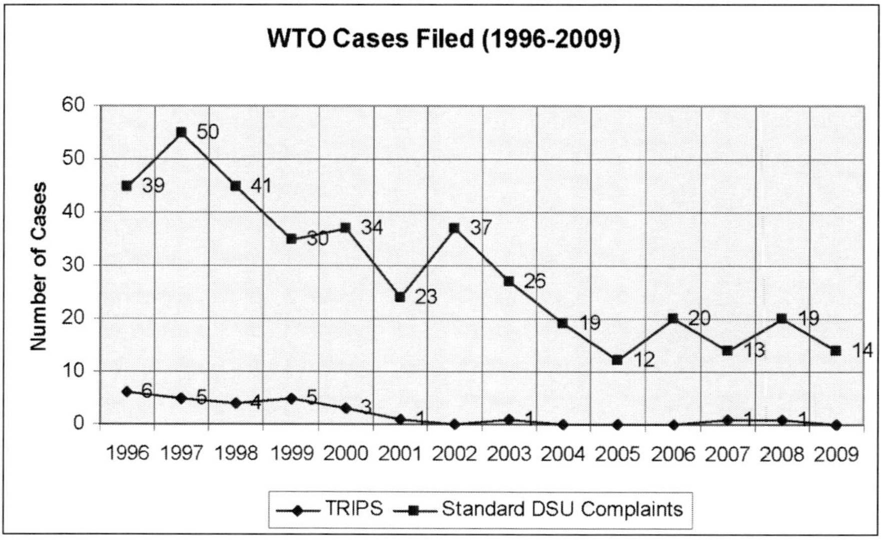

These raw numbers lead to the following five observations:

First, the flood of IP disputes expected by some did not materialize. It is hard, if not impossible, to say whether 27 TRIPS cases out of a total of 402 WTO disputes (or 3 per cent of all claims under around 20 WTO agreements being TRIPS claims) is low, high or about right. For one thing, what benchmark should be used: share of IP in worldwide GDP ?; share of IP royalty streams compared to total trade flows ?; total number of TRIPS violations out there (but how to obtain that number ?) compared to the number of TRIPS disputes actually filed, etc. What we can say, however, is that 4 TRIPS cases in the last 9 years (2001-2010) would hardly strike anyone as a flood of IP cases or major IP activity in WTO dispute settlement.[15]

Secondly, the onslaught of IP enforcement by developed against developing countries did not materialize. Only 9 of the 27 TRIPS disputes (and 4 of the 9 TRIPS Panels) were North-South cases. Rather

15 Note, however, that claims under the WTO's equally new agreement on trade in services (GATS) stand at 2 per cent of total claims (as compared to 3 per cent for TRIPS). Although this number is even lower it may nonetheless be less surprising: Whereas TRIPS imposed genuinely new obligations on many countries, especially developing members, very few developing countries made specific commitments under GATS and, more generally, where WTO members did make GATS commitments they are normally only a confirmation of the status quo (that is, standstill commitments that only confirm liberalization that already took place).

than China or India, the EC was by far the first target of TRIPS complaints so far (10 out of 27 complaints).

Thirdly, TRIPS disputes have a higher settlement rate than average WTO disputes (67 per cent versus 47 per cent, given that on average 53 per cent of WTO disputes move to the Panel stage, compared to 33 per cent for TRIPS disputes).

Fourthly, TRIPS Panels have a lower appeal rate than average WTO Panels (33 per cent versus 70 per cent).

Fifthly, rather than a gradually increasing number of TRIPS disputes over time, we have witnessed a relatively booming start with 6 and 5 cases in, respectively, 1996 and 1997, leveling off to a mere trickle of maximum 1 TRIPS dispute filed in the last 9 years (and none at all in 2002, 2004-6 and 2009). This downward trend is in line with a general trend in WTO dispute settlement but may still be somewhat of a surprise when it comes to TRIPS. Whereas TRIPS became binding on developed countries as of 1 January 1996 (compared to other WTO agreements one year earlier), developing countries as well as economies in transition (e.g. former Communist countries) had to abide by most TRIPS obligations only as of 1 January 2000 and, in certain cases (e.g. where developing countries did not recognize product patents for pharmaceuticals pre-TRIPS, as in the case of India, a major producer of generics) only as of 1 January 2005.[16] Yet, no spike in cases was seen in either 2000 or 2005 (only 3 TRIPS disputes filed in 2000 compared to 5 in 1999; and not a single case filed in 2005 and 2006). Similarly, whereas China joined the WTO in 2001 and is widely seen as a problem child when it comes to IP protection, so far, only two TRIPS disputes were filed against China (one in 2007, *China – IP Rights*, leading to an un-appealed Panel report adopted in 2009; another in 2008, *China – Financial Information Services*, which was settled in the same year).

16 For least-developed countries, TRIPS was extended by the TRIPS Council in November 2005 until 1 July 2013. As regards the protection and enforcement of patents and rights in undisclosed information with respect to pharmaceutical products, least-developed countries have until 1 January 2016 (Decision of the TRIPS Council of 27 June 2002, IP / C / 25, supplemented by a General Council waiver of 8 July 2002 (WT / L / 478) for the Article 70.9 obligations concerning exclusive marketing rights).

III. Reality Check 2: Types of TRIPS Disputes Ultimately Decided

Besides the numbers, lessons can be drawn also from the substantive types of TRIPS claims filed. If one looks only at the TRIPS disputes eventually decided by WTO Panels and the Appellate Body, two features are striking: First, the low number of disputes that are centered on traditional IP questions and could not have been decided without TRIPS; Second, the overwhelming systemic (as opposed to immediate commercial) nature of the cases filed. The table below lists the 9 Panel reports and 3 Appellate Body reports that made findings under TRIPS issued to date.[17]

PANEL REPORTS making TRIPS findings	**APPELLATE BODY REPORTS making TRIPS findings**
1. India – Patent (US) *Sep. 1997 (DS50)*	India – Patent (US) Dec. 1997 *(WT / DS50 / AB / R)*
2. Indonesia – Autos (EC, Japan, US) *Jul. 1998 (DS64)*	
3. India – Patent (EC) *Aug. 1998 (DS79)*	
4. Canada – Pharmaceutical Patents (EC) *Mar. 2000 (DS114)*	
5. US – Copyrights (EC) *Jun. 2000 (DS160)*	
6. Canada – Patent Term (US) *May 2000 (DS170)*	Canada – Patent Term (US) *Sep. 2000 (WT / DS170 / AB / R)*
7. US – Havana Club (EC) *Aug. 2001 (DS176)*	US – Havana Club (EC) Jan. 2002 *(WT / DS176 / AB / R)*
8. EC – Trademarks & Geographical Indications (US / Australia) *Mar. 2005 (DS290)*	
9. China – IP Rights *Aug. 2009 (DS362)*	

17 Complainant(s) are in brackets, followed by date of adoption by the WTO's Dispute Settlement Body (DSB); panel and Appellate Body reports are adopted on the same day.

First, the large majority of disputes (6 out of 9) were not centered on traditional, substantive IP questions and / or could have been decided without TRIPS. Rather, they fell in one of three categories. First, disputes that did not centrally focus on TRIPS at all: *Indonesia – Autos* addressed, and ultimately rejected, trademark-related claims under TRIPS, but was centered rather on discrimination under GATT and TRIMs in connection with tax and customs benefits enjoyed by certain car producers within Indonesia.

Second, disputes that addressed questions of phase-in rather than substantive IP law: Both *India – Patent* cases faulted India for not having certain minimum protection systems in place (so-called « mailbox » and « exclusive marketing rights ») before TRIPS entered into force for India, in violation of TRIPS Articles 70.8 and 9. In *Canada – Patent Term* Canada was found to violate TRIPS Article 33 by not providing 20 years of patent protection from the date of *filing* for patents issued before 1989 but still running after 1996, the date of entry into force of TRIPS for Canada. The Appellate Body confirmed that 17 years of protection from the date of *issuance* of the patent is not good enough.

Third, disputes, though addressing substantive IP matters, centered on traditional trade discrimination the crux of which was, or could have been, handled without TRIPS: *EC – Trademarks & Geographical Indications* (GIs) centered on special EC conditions and procedures for GIs located *outside* the territory of the EC which the Panel found discriminatory under both GATT and TRIPS. No other TRIPS violations were found. In *US – Havana Club*, the only findings of violation addressed certain « extra hurdles » imposed by the United States for trademarks and trade names held by certain Cuban and other foreign nationals which the Appellate Body concluded to be discriminatory under TRIPS. However, this finding of discrimination might have been possible also under GATT, in the absence of TRIPS.[18]

18 See FREDERICK M. ABBOTT AND THOMAS COTTIER, Dispute Prevention and Dispute Settlement in the Field of Intellectual Property Rights and Electronic Commerce: US – Section 211 Omnibus Appropriations Act 1998 (‹ Havana Club ›), *in* Transatlantic Economic Disputes – The EU, the US, and the WTO (Ernst-Ulrich Petersmann and Mark A. Pollack, eds., Oxford, Oxford University Press, 2003), at p. 431 : « We should note at the outset that this is not a case primarily addressing intellectual property … The prime issue … was whether section 211 of the Omnibus Appropriations Act of 1998 which bans protection and recognition of trademarks and trade names in connection with Cuban business relations,

This leaves us with only three disputes decided at the WTO between 1995 and 2010 centered on traditional, substantive IP questions (rather than trade discrimination) which could not have been decided without TRIPS (shaded in grey in the table above), none of which reached the level of the Appellate Body.

First, *Canada – Pharmaceutical Patents (DS114)*: In this case, the EC challenged exceptions under Canada's patent law allowing for the use and production of patented inventions by, for example, generic drug producers, *before* the end of the 20 years patent term to carry out experiments and tests so as to meet Canadian regulatory requirements (the so-called « regulatory review provision », also referred to as the « Bolar exemption » in the United States), or to manufacture and store products for sale *after* the 20 years patent term eventually expires (the so-called « stockpiling provision »). Both exceptions aimed at ensuring market access for generics immediately following patent expiry. The Panel excused the « regulatory review provision » under TRIPS Article 30, but concluded that the « stockpiling provision » does not meet the three-step test exception of Article 30 and violates TRIPS Article 27.

Second, *US – Copyrights (DS160)*: In this dispute, the EC challenged exceptions under US copyright law permitting, under certain conditions, the playing of radio and television music in public places such as bars, shops and restaurants, without the paying of a royalty under either the so-called « homestyle exemption » (which allows small restaurants and retail outlets to amplify music broadcasts without authorization of the owner of the copyright provided that they use only homestyle equipment) or the much broader « business exemption » (which allows the amplification of music broadcasts by food service and drinking establishments and by retail establishments provided that their size does not exceed a certain square footage limit). The Panel, seemingly following the split-it-in-the-middle approach of *Canada – Pharmaceutical Patents*, excused the « homestyle exemption » under TRIPS Article 13, but concluded that the « business exemption » does not meet the three-step test exception of Article 17 and violates TRIPS Article 9.

Third, *China – IP Rights (DS362)*: In this most recent TRIPS ruling the United States challenged, first, China's denial of copyright to works, such as books, movies or CDs, that have not, or not yet, passed China's

is compatible with the TRIPS Agreement. It is a case more closely related to security and embargo policies affecting not only Cuban, but also European interests ».

censorship or content review system. This claim was upheld by the Panel, which left China's censorship system untouched, but found that such system offers no excuse to deny copyright in particular to materials that have failed content review. Second, the United States also contested China's methods of disposal of goods confiscated by customs authorities for IP infringement including donation to social welfare bodies, buy-back by the right holder and auction. This second claim was only very partially upheld in so far as China allows for the auctioning off of confiscated goods after « the simple removal of the trademark unlawfully affixed » in violation of TRIPS Article 59. Thirdly, the United States challenged the volume and value « thresholds » China imposes (e. g. minimum 500 pirated CDs or DVDs) before criminal procedures and penalties are triggered against wilful trademark counterfeiting or copyright piracy. The Panel rejected this claim on the ground that the United States had not demonstrated that the thresholds allow for counterfeiting or piracy « on a commercial scale » as required in TRIPS Article 61.

It must, however, be noted that the Appellate Body in *US – Havana Club* did make the important finding that TRIPS covers not only trademarks but also trade names[19] (contrary to what the original Panel had concluded) and clarified what IP protection under TRIPS is *not* about (namely, confiscation of a trademark in one country, Cuba, and what this means for *ownership* and registration of that trademark in another country, the United States). That said, the US violations ultimately found in *US – Havana Club* concerned rather traditional trade-related discrimination; not minimum standards of IP protection or enforcement. Similarly, the *EC – Trademarks & GIs* Panel offered important clarifications as to the scope of Article 17 relating to trademarks exceptions (discussed below). That said, the violations ultimately found rested on traditional trade-related discrimination which could have been reached without TRIPS.

A second feature that is striking when looking at the type of TRIPS disputes decided so far at the WTO is that most controversies arose not in the context of, or as a result of, a specific IP dispute as between two or more companies (the notable exception being *US – Havana Club* which, behind the scenes, pitted France's Pernod-Ricard against the American

19 Generally speaking a « trade name » is descriptive of a manufacturer or a dealer and applies to business and its goodwill, whereas a « trademark » is applicable only to vendible commodities and services.

rum producer Bacardi[20]). Instead, most disputes challenged general IP laws or regulations in the defending country and did so not with one or more particular companies in mind, but for systemic reasons both to force the specific country to align its legislation with TRIPS and, in some cases even more so, to send a signal to, and set a precedent for, *all* WTO members as to the scope of their TRIPS obligations.

The phase-in cases referred to earlier drew a line in the sand for all developing countries as to the required legal predictability of the « mailbox » and « exclusive marketing rights » they must set up or ensure even before the full entry into force of TRIPS (the two *India – Patent* cases) and firmly established the scope of TRIPS *ratione temporis* (*Canada – Patent Term*). There was no immediate commercial interest or specific company behind the US and Australian challenge of the EC's system of protection of geographical indications (GIs). Indeed, not a single GI based in the territory of either the United States or Australia had been applied for, let alone denied, by the EC. Instead, the dispute was filed for systemic reasons as part of a broader battle (fought also in the ongoing Doha Round negotiations) where the EC is a strong promoter of GIs and the US, Australia and certain other major agricultural exporters regard GIs as disguised protectionism and want to stem the spread of GI protection not only in the EC but also in other WTO members (in particular developing countries) who may still be on the fence. In this sense, the case was as much a signal toward the entire WTO membership as it was a challenge against specific EC legislation.[21] The *Canada – Pharmaceutical Patents* case addressed an ongoing, general debate in many

20 See ABBOTT & COTTIER, *supra* note 18, at p. 439 : « the respective governments have transformed a fairly ordinary commercial trademark dispute between two well-financed private enterprises into a matter of high politics, with attendant invocation of national (or regional) political interests ».

21 See MICHAEL HANDLER, The WTO Geographical Indications Dispute, 69 Modern Law Review 70-80 (2006) at p. 77-79 : «… what is perhaps most striking about the outcome of the dispute is how little practical impact it is likely to have. Australia and the US's complaints were not instituted because particular producers from these countries had been denied access to the EC's GI registration scheme. In fact, it was acknowledged in the dispute that no Australian or US party had *ever* sought to obtain registration … the complainants› greater concern with the ‹ equivalence and reciprocity › conditions in the [EC] Regulation … was that they represented a clandestine attempt to impose European standards of GI protection for foodstuffs throughout the world … The WTO dispute proceedings can thus be seen as a tactical, retaliatory response by Australia and the US to the EC's expansionist agenda and the protectionism that they believe it represents ».

WTO members as to whether the 20 year patent term should be « shortened » to allow for early preparation and screening of generics to comply with increasingly burdensome regulatory approval procedures for pharmaceutical products, and whether or not such « regulatory review » or « Bolar » exemption should be compensated with patent protection beyond 20 years as not only for the generics producer but also (and even more so) for the original patent holder regulatory approval takes many years thereby reducing the effective patent term for the patent holder from 20 to sometimes less than 10 years. *US – Copyrights* was originally triggered by the Irish Music Rights Organization (IMRO) under the EC trade barriers regulation at the request of, especially, Irish songwriters who were not getting royalties for music played in Irish pubs spread across the United States. At the same time, the non-payment of royalties was clearly not only a problem for Irish composers. On the contrary, the major victims of the US exceptions were the US music and broadcasting industry itself, which actively supported the complaint against its own government. Moreover, the United States was not the only country providing for such exceptions. Most other countries, including EC member states themselves, had similar (albeit mostly narrower) exceptions. Indeed, rather than an EC-US dispute, or a commercial dispute between two companies, the *US – Copyright* case was one between right holders (composers) and users (bars and restaurants) irrespective of their national location. Finally, little explanation is needed to realize that the US complaint in *China – IP Rights* was aiming at a broad, systemic concern of under-enforcement of IP rights in China and at sending a WTO-wide signal to other countries listed by the United States as not making serious enough efforts to crack down on counterfeiting and piracy (think of Ukraine or Brazil).

It goes without saying that when such systemic complaints are won, a strong warning signal is sent to the entire WTO membership, and IP industries, in turn, may feel encouraged to push for new and perhaps more daring disputes. Conversely, if such complaints are lost (as more often than not was the case so far), the opposite signal is sent to both the WTO membership and IP industries. This brings us to the substance of WTO dispute rulings under TRIPS which, on balance, are a far cry from the activist, pro-IP jurisprudence that IP industries may have hoped for in the early 1990 s.

IV. Reality Check 3 : Substantive Rulings by WTO Panels and the Appellate Body

It is notoriously difficult to assess whether a treaty has been expansively or restrictively interpreted, especially based on a limited sample of just 9 Panel rulings and 3 Appellate Body reports. Much depends on one's personal starting point (generally for or against IP protection) and subjective assessment of what the TRIPS agreement says or should be saying. That said, few, if any, will question that WTO jurisprudence under TRIPS so far is not the hard-line, pro-IP approach that many may have hoped for or feared in the mid 1990 s. This finds support in WTO rulings clarifying (A) what TRIPS does *not* cover, (B) the relatively flexible scope of TRIPS exceptions, and (C) the limited extent of IP enforcement obligations under TRIPS.

A. Crucial rulings on what TRIPS is not about

The three phase-in disputes discussed earlier (the two *India – Patent* cases and *Canada – Patent Term*) did confirm the importance of legal certainty and predictability when it comes to IP protection. The Appellate Body in *Havana – Club* did « expand » the scope of TRIPS to include trade names and in several disputes (in particular, *EC – Trademarks & GIs* and *US – Havana Club)* the importance and bite of TRIPS non-discrimination disciplines was confirmed.

More importantly, however, in a move that for some may have shattered hopes, for others alleviated fear, WTO jurisprudence to date has clarified what TRIPS is *not* about. First, as noted earlier, in *US – Havana Club*, the Appellate Body made clear that questions of ownership and prior confiscation of trademarks are *not* covered by TRIPS, thereby confirming the limited scope of TRIPS disciplines in the field of trademarks. Whereas the EC advocated a system of mutual recognition whereby registration of a trademark in one WTO member (Cuba) ought to be respected in other WTO members (United States) irrespective of questions of confiscation and ownership, the Panel and Appellate Body found that TRIPS Article 2.1 (which incorporates Article 6*quinquies* of the Paris Convention) only requires that if domestic law *otherwise permits* registration of the trademark (and, *in casu*, US law did *not* so permit), the trademark must be registered « as is » (*« telle quelle »*), that is, in exactly the same *form* as that presented to the authority upon registration. In other words, TRIPS imposes only very minimal harmonization in the field of trademarks as it leaves intact the right of WTO members to determine the conditions for the filing and registration of trademarks by domestic legislation except as regards the *form* of the trademark.[22] In an important interpretative move, the Appellate Body found that « if Article 6*quinquies* A(1) were interpreted too broadly, the legislative discretion reserved for Members under Article 6(1) would be significantly undermined ».[23]

Second, in *Indonesia – Autos*, also addressing trademarks, the Panel found that TRIPS non-discrimination provisions as invoked by claimants are limited to questions of « acquisition » or « maintenance » of trademarks and do not cover an Indonesian rule which states that, to benefit from certain advantages, one must use a new brand name owned by an Indonesian company or citizen. The Panel also rejected that this rule was a « requirement » on the « use » of a trademark in the sense of TRIPS Article 20 since nothing obliged right holders to apply for the benefits, making the rule one to which applicants submitted themselves voluntarily in order to gain certain advantages (hence, not a « requirement »). Similarly, the Panel on *Canada – Pharmaceutical Patents* found that Canada's patent exemptions were available for all products subject to regulatory approval (not just pharmaceuticals) and that, as a result, discrimination against a particular « field of technology » (*in casu*, pharmaceuticals) contrary to TRIPS Article 27.1 required the submission of concrete evidence of *de facto* discrimination which the EC had not provided. In a contested ruling[24] the Panel added that TRIPS Article 30 exceptions are *not* available to justify discrimination contrary to Article 27.1 (or, put differently, that even measures justified as exceptions under Article 30 have to be non-discriminatory in line with Article 27.1). This move could be seen as a restrictive interpretation. However, the

22 See Robert Howse & Damien J. Neven, United States – Section 211 Omnibus Appropriations Act of 1998 : A Comment, The WTO Case Law of 2002, Cambridge University Press, pp. 179-219 (2005), arguing at p. 179 that also on economic grounds « the case for coordination across jurisdictions is less compelling for trademarks than other forms of intellectual property ».

23 AB Report, para. 139. Article 6(1) of the Paris Convention provides : « The conditions for the filing and registration of trademarks shall be determined in each country of the Union by its domestic legislation ».

24 See Frederick M. Abbott, Bob Hudec as Chair of the Canada-Generic Pharmaceuticals Panel – The WTO Gets Something Right, 6 Journal of International Economic Law 3, 733-737 (2003).

Panel made it difficult enough to find discrimination under Article 27.1 – which it defined as « *unjustified* imposition of differentially disadvantageous treatment »[25] – that there would hardly seem to be much need to seek refuge under Article 30 exceptions. Put differently, what some might justify under the Article 30 exceptions, the Panel would find « justified » under Article 27.1 in the first place and, on that basis, not even find « discrimination ».[26]

Third, although the Panel on *China – IP Rights* was not asked to rule on the TRIPS compliance of China's censorship system as such, the Panel made clear that as much as TRIPS rules on trademarks do not address *ownership*, TRIPS rules on copyright do not prevent *censorship*. Referring to Article 17 of the Berne Convention[27], the Panel found that « the right of a government ‹ to control, or to prohibit › the ‹ circulation, presentation, or exhibition › of any work or production clearly includes censorship for reasons of public order ».[28] Although this should temper hopes of attacking China's censorship regime under TRIPS or WTO rules more broadly[29], the Panel nonetheless found that censorship is

25 Panel Report, para. 7.94, emphasis added.

26 The Panel defined TRIPS Article 27.1 « discrimination as to the place of invention, the field of technology and whether products are imported or locally produced » as including both de jure and de facto discrimination but defined the latter rather narrowly, namely: « de facto discrimination is a general term describing the legal conclusion that an ostensibly neutral measure transgresses a non-discrimination norm because its actual effect is to impose differentially disadvantageous consequences on certain parties, and because those differential effects are found to be wrong or unjustifiable » (para. 7.101). This means that under the very definition of « discrimination », the regulating country can come up with justifications for any differential treatment and, on that ground, avoid a violation of Article 27.1 so that it does not even need to rely on the exceptions in Article 30. As the Panel noted, « Article 27 does not prohibit bona fide exceptions to deal with problems that may exist only in certain product areas » (para. 7.92).

27 Article 17 of the Berne Convention provides: « The provisions of this Convention cannot in any way affect the right of the Government of each country of the Union to permit, to control, or to prohibit, by legislation or regulation, the circulation, presentation, or exhibition of any work or production in regard to which the competent authority may find it necessary to exercise that right ».

28 Panel report, para. 7.126.

29 See JOOST PAUWELYN, Squaring Free Trade in Cultural Goods and Services With Chinese Censorship: The WTO Appellate Body Report on China – Audiovisuals, Melbourne Journal of International Law, volume 11, issue 1, 2010; and TOMER BROUDE & HOLGER HESTERMEYER, The First Condition of Progress – The Limits of International Trade Law as a Promoter of Freedom of Speech, Research

one thing (and generally permitted); denial of copyright another (and, in this case, a TRIPS violation).

B. Crucial rulings on TRIPS exceptions

Besides clarifying what TRIPS is *not* about, WTO jurisprudence to date has proven to be less than activist or IP-hard-line in a second way, namely: by offering a nuanced (and, according to some commentators, even too liberal[30]) view on TRIPS exceptions. WTO rulings on the scope of general exceptions to copyright (TRIPS Article 13), trademarks (TRIPS Article 17) and patents (TRIPS Article 30) are no doubt the WTO's most important contribution to the refinement and interpretation of international IP law to date. One prominent commentator, for example, expressed the view that the *US – Copyright* decision « may significantly advance the development of a truly supra national law of copyright ».[31] Some of these exceptions, which are in many ways similar[32], have been around for over a century, were highly contested in diplomatic and academic circles and have now for the very first time been interpreted by WTO Panels. Quite tellingly, none of these rulings have,

Showcase: Poster Session, 103rd Annual Meeting of the American Society of International Law, 27 March 2009.

30 See, for example, David J. Brennan, The Three-Step Test Frenzy – Why the TRIPS Panel Decision Might be Considered *Per Incuriam*, Intellectual Property Quarterly, Issue 2 (2002), p. 212.

31 Jane C. Ginsburg, Toward Supranational Copyright Law? The WTO Panel Decision and the ‹ Three-Step Test › for Copyright Exceptions, 187 Revue Internationale du Droit d'Auteur 3 (2001), p. 3.

32 TRIPS Article 13 (copyright) provides:

Members shall confine limitations or exceptions to exclusive rights to certain special cases which do not conflict with a normal exploitation of the work and do not unreasonably prejudice the legitimate interests of the right holder.

TRIPS Article 17 (trademarks) reads:

Members may provide limited exceptions to the rights conferred by a trademark, such as fair use of descriptive terms, provided that such exceptions take account of the legitimate interests of the owner of the trademark and of third parties.

TRIPS Article 30 (patents) stipulates:

Members may provide limited exceptions to the exclusive rights conferred by a patent, provided that such exceptions do not unreasonably conflict with a normal exploitation of the patent and do not unreasonably prejudice the legitimate interests of the patent owner, taking account of the legitimate interests of third parties.

however, reached the Appellate Body which means that their longer term impact remains questionable.

That WTO rulings on TRIPS exceptions are at least nuanced and not consistently biased in favor of IP protection is confirmed rather superficially by their outcome. In both *Canada – Pharmaceutical Patents* and *US – Copyrights* the Panel accepted at least one of the two limitations as meeting the relevant TRIPS exception (respectively, the « regulatory review provision » and the « homestyle exemption »). In *EC – Trademarks & GIs*, the Panel ruled in favor of defendants concluding that the EC regime of coexistence between GIs and prior trademarks meets the trademarks exception in TRIPS Article 17.

1. Canada – Pharmaceutical Patents

Assessing WTO rulings on TRIPS exceptions chronologically and somewhat more substantively, the first was issued in March 2000 (*Canada – Pharmaceutical Patents*), an exemplary brief and clear Panel report, chaired by the legendary U. S. trade lawyer and academic Robert Hudec.

The Panel interpreted the term « limited exception », the first prong of TRIPS Article 30›s three-step test, « to connote a narrow exception – one which makes only a small diminution of the rights in question ... focusing on the extent to which legal rights have been curtailed, rather than the size or extent of the economic impact ».[33] On this ground, the Panel found that the « stockpiling exception » was not a « limited exception » but a « substantial curtailment of the exclusionary rights required to be granted to patent owners »[34], in particular because Canada imposed « no limitations at all upon the quantity of production » a generics producer could make and stockpile before expiry of the patent term.[35] The Panel came to this conclusion even though there was a limit in time, namely, only 6 months before expiry of the patent, as well as a limit as to who could invoke the exception, namely, only those relying also on the « regulatory review provision ».

Turning to the « regulatory review provision », in contrast, the Panel found that this exception was a « limited exception » as it was « confined to conduct needed to comply with the requirements of the

33 Panel Report, para. 7.30-1.

34 Panel Report, para. 7.36.

35 Panel Report, para. 7.34.

regulatory approval process » and « no commercial use is made of resulting final products ».[36] The Panel came to this conclusion even though it acknowledged that « the economic impact of the regulatory review exception could be considerable ». In Canada, for example, it takes 3 to 6.5 years for generic drug producers to develop and obtain regulatory approval for their products. This means that if the exception were not provided, patent terms would effectively be extended with 3 to 6.5 years.[37]

Moving to the second prong of Article 30, the Panel concluded that the regulatory review provision did not « unreasonably conflict with a normal exploitation of the patent », agreeing with Canada that « the additional period of de facto market exclusivity created by using patent rights to preclude submissions for regulatory authorization should not be considered ‹ normal › ».[38]

Under the third and final prong, the Panel concluded that the exception did not « unreasonably prejudice the legitimate interests of the patent owner, taking into account the legitimate interests of third parties ». The Panel defined « legitimate interests » as something different from purely « legal » interests, more specifically, « as a normative claim calling for protection of interests that are ‹ justifiable › in the sense that they are *supported by relevant public policies or other social norms.* »[39]

This is an important interpretative move as it allows for consideration of other public or social interests (« legitimate interests of third parties ») to outweigh or at least be balanced against IP interests (« legitimate interests of the patent owner »). In this case, Canada did, however, not raise specific third party or social interests (e. g. the fact that more patients may be able to afford generics). Instead, the only « legitimate interest » considered (and ultimately rejected) by the Panel was one invoked by the EC as held by the *patent holder*, namely : the fact that patent holders of innovative pharmaceutical products must also go through regulatory review, costing them anywhere between 8 and 12 years of their 20 year patent term ; since this means that patent holders effectively lose 8 to 12 years of their exclusivity, without any compensation, the EC argued that no exception should be provided

36 Panel Report, para. 7.45.

37 Panel Report, para. 7.48.

38 Panel Report, para. 7.57.

39 Panel Report, para. 7.69, emphasis added.

either for generics producers when they have to go through regulatory review.[40]

In another interesting move, the Panel refused to recognize this as a « legitimate interest » of the patent holder. For the Panel, the question in this respect is « whether the normative basis of that claim rested on a *widely recognized policy norm* »[41], a criterion that is stricter as compared to the Panel's definition a few paragraphs earlier (claim « supported by relevant public policies or other social norms »): in the latter definition, the Panel seems willing to accept any *domestically*-defined « public policy or other social norm »; in the former definition, however, the Panel limits « legitimate interests » to those that find support in a « widely recognized », apparently *internationally* (or WTO-wide)-supported, policy norm.

In this context, the Panel conceded that the EC's claim had been affirmed by extensions of the patent term in countries like the EC, Switzerland, the United States, Japan, Australia and Israel (the EC and Switzerland doing so without even granting a « regulatory review » exception to generics producers). However, the Panel also noted that other countries had granted a regulatory review exception without extending the patent term and concluded that

> *« [o]n balance ... the interest claimed on behalf of patent owners whose effective period of market exclusivity had been reduced by delays in marketing approval was neither so compelling nor so widely recognized that it could be regarded as a « legitimate interest » within the meaning of Article 30 of the TRIPS Agreement ... The Panel believed that Article 30›s « legitimate interests » concept should not be used to decide, through adjudication, a normative policy issue that is still obviously a matter of unresolved political debate. »*[42]

In doing so, the Panel added an additional threshold for an interest of the patent holder to be « legitimate », namely that it must not only be « widely recognized » but also be « compelling ». This line of reasoning is further discussed below in section 4.

40 Panel Report, para. 7.74-5.

41 Panel Report, para. 7.77, emphasis added.

42 Panel Report, para. 7.82, emphasis added.

On these grounds, the Panel concluded that the « regulatory review provision » was justified under TRIPS Article 30, whereas the « stockpiling exception » was not.[43] Indications that this outcome found broad support and is difficult to qualify as hard-line, pro-IP are (i) the fact that today the « regulatory review » or « Bolar » exception is commonly accepted and implemented around the world (including in the EC itself), and (ii) the fact that Canada's withdrawal of the « stockpiling exception » had a relatively minor impact: stockpiling prior to patent expiry, even if there were no quantity limits, at best saved 6 months; an early start in the regulatory review process, which the Panel did grant, saves up to 6.5 years.

2. *US – Copyright*

Only three months after this (unappealed) report on *Canada – Pharmaceutical Patents*, a second report on TRIPS exceptions was issued, this time squarely addressing copyright exceptions under TRIPS Article 13.

Under the first prong of Article 13, the Panel found that for an exception to be covered under « limitations or exceptions to exclusive rights to certain special cases » the exception « should be narrow in a quantitative as well as a qualitative sense. This suggests a narrow scope as well as an exceptional or distinctive objective ».[44] In sum, the exception « should be clearly defined and should be narrow in its scope and reach ».[45] Importantly, the Panel rejected the idea that under this first prong, « the public policy purpose of an exception is relevant » or that « an exception or limitation must be justified in terms of a legitimate public policy purpose in order to fulfill the first condition of the Article ».[46] At the same time, the Panel did announce that

> *« [o]n a subsidiary basis, we consider whether it is possible to draw inferences about the reach of the business and homestyle exemptions from the stated policy purposes underlying these exemptions according to the statements made during the US legislative process. »*[47]

43 Panel Report, para. 7.84.

44 Panel Report, para. 6.109.

45 Panel Report, para. 6.112.

46 Panel Report, para. 6.111.

47 Panel Report, para. 6.113, emphasis added.

Turning to the « business exemption », the Panel concluded that this exemption does not qualify as a « certain special case » on the ground that « a substantial majority of eating and drinking establishments and close to half of retail establishments are covered by the exemption ».[48] In contrast, the Panel found that the « homestyle exemption » did qualify as a « certain special case », *inter alia*, since « from a quantitative perspective the reach of [the « homestyle exemption »] in respect of potential users is limited to a comparably small percentage of all eating, drinking and retail establishments in the United States ».[49]

Notice that for this Panel, under the first prong (« certain special cases » further defined as « narrow in its scope and reach »), the *economic impact* of the exception seemed to matter a great deal (in particular, the number of establishments covered by the respective exemptions). For the Panel on *Canada – Pharmaceuticals*, in contrast, under the first prong of Article 30 (« limited exceptions » further defined as « focusing on the extent to which legal rights have been curtailed »), « the size or extent of the economic impact »[50] should play *no* role. Indeed, as pointed out earlier, the « regulatory review » exemption that this Panel ultimately accepted had a much greater economic impact than the « stockpiling provision » which was found not to meet the Article 30 exception. In *US – Copyright*, on the other hand, it was the exemption with the *least* economic impact (the « homestyle exemption ») that was ultimately tolerated.

Continuing under the first prong, the *US – Copyright* Panel also found support for a narrow scope of the « homestyle exemption » in the « stated public policy purposes » of the exception. In this respect, the Panel referred, *inter alia*, to the US argument that the « homestyle exemption » aimed at the « protection of small ‹ mom and pop › businesses which ‹ play an important role in the American social fabric › because they ‹ offer economic opportunities for women, minorities, immigrants and welfare recipients for entering the economic and social mainstream › ».[51]

Moving to the second prong of TRIPS Article 13 (« do not conflict with a normal exploitation of the work »), the Panel found that « normal » exploitation « clearly means something less than full use of an

48 Panel Report, para. 6.133.

49 Panel Report, para. 6.143.

50 Panel Report, para. 7.30-1.

51 Panel Report, para. 6.156.

exclusive right »[52] since otherwise no exceptions under this second prong would be allowed. The Panel found both a « quantitative or empirical » and a « normative » (as in « conforming to a type or standard ») connotation to the term « normal exploitation ». Under the first connotation it accepted the US-suggested test of « an economic analysis of the degree of ‹ market displacement › in terms of foregone collection of remuneration by right owners caused by the free use of works due to the exemption at issue ».[53] As to the second connotation, the Panel found that « one way of measuring the normative connotation of normal exploitation is to consider, in addition to those forms of exploitation that currently generate significant or tangible revenue, those forms of exploitation which, with a certain degree of likelihood and plausibility, could acquire considerable economic or practical importance ».[54]

Applying this test, the Panel concluded that the « business exemption » conflicted with « a normal exploitation of the work », whereas the « homestyle exemption » did not.[55]

Turning, finally, to the third prong of Article 13 (« do not unreasonably prejudice the legitimate interests of the right holder »), notice that in contrast to Articles 17 and 30, Article 13 does not explicitly refer to the legitimate interests of « third parties » as interests that could potentially counter-balance or outweigh the interests of the right holder. The Panel found that the term « legitimate » (as in « legitimate interests of the right holder »)

> « *relates to lawfulness from a legal positivist perspective, but it has also the connotation of legitimacy from a more normative perspective, in the context of calling for the protection of interests that are justifiable in the light of the objectives that underlie the protection of exclusive rights.* »[56]

The Panel then limited itself to « the economic value » of the exclusive rights conferred by copyright on their holders, but was quick to add that « [t]hat is not to say that legitimate interests are necessarily limited

52 Panel Report, para. 6.167.

53 Panel Report, para. 6.177.

54 Panel Report, para. 6.180.

55 Panel Report, paras. 6.211 and 6.219.

56 Panel Report, para. 6.224, emphasis added.

to this economic value ».[57] Indeed, even if Article 13 only explicitly mentions the « legitimate interests of the right holder », when considering whether an alleged right holder interest is « legitimate » and / or « unreasonably prejudiced », Panels can and, when asked, would no doubt look at possibly countervailing interests of third parties including broader social or public interests. As quoted above, the Panel itself stated that an interest of the right holder will only be « legitimate » if it is « justifiable in the light of the objectives that underlie the protection of exclusive rights ». It is generally agreed that these « objectives », as stated, for example, in TRIPS Article 7, include not only « the promotion of technological innovation » but also « the transfer and dissemination of technology … in a manner conducive to social and economic welfare ».

Using this test, the Panel found that the « business exemption » unreasonably prejudiced the legitimate interests of the right holder, whereas the « homestyle exemption » did not.[58] Since the « homestyle exemption », therefore, met all three, cumulatively applicable, conditions under Article 13, the Panel concluded no violation. Since, in contrast, the « business exemption » did not meet any of these three conditions, the Panel found it to be in violation of Article 9.

As in *Canada – Pharmaceutical Patents*, the Panel outcome in *US – Copyright* found broad support in the world of IP commentators. Indeed, had the Panel found against the « homestyle exemption », standard exceptions in many copyright regimes (including some within the EC itself) would have been at risk.

3. *EC – Trademarks & GIs*

A third and final Panel that addressed TRIPS exceptions is the Panel on *EC – Trademarks & GIs*. This Panel agreed with complainants that, under TRIPS Article 161, « Members are required to make available to trademark owners a right against certain uses, including uses as a GI ».[59] The Panel then found, however, that the EC regime of coexistence between GIs and prior trademarks is justified under TRIPS Article 17 as (i) a « limited exception »[60] which (ii) « was, in fact, applied to take

57 Panel Report, para. 6.227.

58 Panel Report, paras. 6.266 and 6.272.

59 Panel Report, para. 7.625.

60 Panel Report, para. 7.661.

account *inter alia* of the legitimate interest of the trademark owners to protect the distinctiveness of their respective marks »[61] and (iii) « was, in fact, applied to take account *inter alia* of the legitimate interests of [third parties, namely] consumers », e. g., by refusing GI registration where « registration is liable to mislead the consumer as to the true identity of the product »[62] as well as the interests of « GI users » pursuant to the third prong of TRIPS Article 17.[63]

4. *Have TRIPS exceptions been interpreted too narrowly ?*

The above overview of Panel rulings on TRIPS exceptions shows that both in outcome and analysis WTO Panels to date have not followed a hard-line, uniformly pro-IP direction, but an overall rather nuanced and carefully balanced approach. Indeed, at least two commentators (wrongly) predicted that the WTO would find against *both* exceptions in *US – Copyright*[64] and, as noted earlier, when that Panel found that the « homestyle exemption » was justified under TRIPS Article 13, another commentator wrote a scathing critique on why the Panel had been too lenient.[65]

One forceful critique has been offered against the Panel on *Canada – Pharmaceutical Patents* arguing that « the Panel was only interested in how much the rights holder might lose, not in how much society might gain, from a given exception. It never asked what scope the exception might require to achieve the social purposes at issue ». The author adds that the Panel should have considered « the meaning of the word ‹ limited › [exception] in reference to Article 7 of TRIPS, which evokes the mutual

61 Panel Report, para. 7.668.

62 Panel Report, para. 7.676-7.

63 Panel Report, para. 7.682.

64 See Laurence Helfer, World Music on a U. S. Stage : A Berne / TRIPs and Economic Analysis of the Fairness in Music Licensing Act, 80 Boston University Law Review 93 (Feb. 2000) and Laurence Helfer, World Music on a U. S. Stage : An Analysis of the Section 110(5) WTO Dispute, *in* Hugh C. Hansen (ed), International Intellectual Property Law and Policy, Volume 6, chapter 48 (2001, Huntington, NY, Juris Publishing); as well as Laura McCluggage, Section 110(5) and The Fairness in Music Licensing Act : Will the WTO Decide the United States Must Pay to Play ?, 40 IDEA : The Journal of Law and Technology 1 (2000) at p. 20 concluding : « It is this author's opinion that both the original exemption [homestyle exemption] and the amendment [business exemption] fail the three-part test of Article 13 ».

65 See *supra* note 30.

advantage of producers and users, the notion of a balance of rights and obligations and, moreover, the notion that protection and enforcement of intellectual property rights should be undertaken ‹ in a manner conducive to social and economic welfare ».[66]

As much as the suggested approach may generally be correct[67], the summary above shows, firstly, that Canada never invoked specific third party or social interests. Both parties focused exclusively on the interests of right holders and generic producers. As a result, the Panel was not asked and could not at its own initiative put forward competing social concerns. WTO rulings are, to a great extent, determined by how the parties litigate the case. Neither were broader social concerns at stake in *US – Copyrights*. As one US commentator noted, the « controversy, it bears emphasis, concerned a pork barrel exemption purely for the benefit of certain business consumers of copyrighted works; it did not implicate any of the free speech or scholarship interests that underlie many copyright exceptions ».[68] For guidance on how WTO Panels will resolve tensions between IP rights and the creative interests of other authors or broader public concerns, we need to await another dispute.

Secondly, TRIPS Articles 13, 17 and 30 are, indeed, written differently than standard WTO / GATT exceptions. In contrast to GATT Article XX which permits, for example, certain trade restrictions « necessary to protect human health », the TRIPS exceptions do not explicitly refer to justification under a non-trade or non-IP concern. They focus instead on limiting the scope and nature of the IP right's carve-out as such. The summary above shows, however, that TRIPS exceptions do refer to countervailing « legitimate interests » of « third parties » which Panels have found to include non-economic interests as well as consumer interests and interests of competing right holders. Moreover, even where « third party » interests are not explicitly included in the terms of the TRIPS exception as such (as in TRIPS Article 13), the other qualifiers in these exceptions – i. e., « legitimate » interests of right holders, « normal » exploitation and « unreasonably » conflict or prejudice – are broad enough to allow for a balancing of the interests of IP right holders and other interests including broader social or public interests.[69]

66 Robert Howse, The Canadian Generic Medicines Panel – a Dangerous Precedent in Dangerous Times, Journal of World Intellectual Property, vol. 3, issue 4 (July 2000), at p. 496.

67 See Frederick M. Abbott, *supra* note 24, 733-737 (2003).

68 Jane C. Ginsburg, *supra* note 31, p. 9.

Thirdly, Panel rulings that the first prong under TRIPS exceptions (be it « limited exception » in Articles 17 and 30 or « certain special cases » in Article 13) does not require justification under a legitimate public purpose, but addresses the scope of curtailment of the legal right, works both ways. It *broadens* the exception since even restrictions that do not serve a legitimate public purpose can still be justified.[70] At the same time, it may also *narrow* the exception as it may preclude exemptions that are fully justified under a public policy purpose simply because the scope of the exception is too broad. Under GATT Article XX, in contrast, a full or 100 per cent trade ban on, for example, Indian shrimp or EC retreaded tires has been justified even if it means that the non-trade objective will need to weigh in more heavily.[71] To align both types of exceptions, one would then need to either flexibly interpret the notion of « narrow scope and reach » (to include, for example, the full curtailment of an IP right for as long as it is limited in time and / or subject to relatively narrow conditions) or, as the critique above suggested, allow for reference to broader social concerns not only under the second and, especially, third prong of the exceptions but also under the first. The Panel on *US – Copyright* moved into the latter direction when, under the first prong of Article 13, it drew « inferences about the *reach* of the business and homestyle exemptions from the stated policy *purposes* underlying these exemptions ».[72]

69 See, for example, GINSBURG, *supra* note 31, at p. 15, arguing that if there would be « a non economic motivation for the exception ... it would be appropriate to develop the neglected normative dimension of ‹ normal › exploitation » and at p. 16, « the third step may reduce to a balancing of the legitimacy of the interests of the rights holders and of the beneficiaries of the exception ... the reasonableness (if not also the legitimacy) criterion of step three by its own terms requires some weighing of conflicting interests ».

70 Prof. GINSBURG, for example, is of the view that « the Panel decision [on *US – Copyright*] correctly eschewed inquiry into the motivation for a particular exception », but she did so to *broaden* the exception (not to narrow it) so that it does not « preclude pork barrel-type exceptions (if they are sufficiently discrete) » since, in her view, « the WTO may be ill-suited to condemn local giveaways of this kind » (GINSBURG, *supra* note 31 at 12).

71 See AB Report on *Brazil – Tyres (DS332).*

72 Panel Report, para. 6.113, emphasis added. The leading authority on the Berne Convention is, indeed, of the view that an exception must be justified by some « clear reason of public policy or some other exceptional circumstance » (SAM RICKETSON, The Berne Convention for the protection of literary and artistic works : 1886-1986, London, 1987, at 482).

Indeed, if one thing may be somewhat worrying about the Panel on *Canada – Pharmaceuticals* it is that it defined « legitimate » interests of *right holders too narrowly*, not only requiring that they be «›justifiable› in the sense of being supported by « relevant public policies or other social norms »[73] but adding later that they must, moreover, rest « on a widely recognized policy norm » in the sense of having a high degree of international recognition and be « compelling ». Even if this approach may be convincing when it comes to interests of IP right holders – whose « legitimate interests » originate, in the first place, from internationally negotiated TRIPS provisions which ought not too readily be expanded (the Panel's main concern) – the qualifiers of « widely recognized » and « compelling » would seem too restrictive when applied to « legitimate » third party or social interests competing with the interests of IP right holders. The same way WTO members have the sovereign right to decide on their own level of health or environmental protection under GATT Article XX exceptions, it should be for WTO members themselves to decide on the nature and extent of these countervailing interests (confirmed, *inter alia*, in TRIPS Articles 7 and 8), even if it may then ultimately be up to a WTO Panel to balance these interests against the interests of IP right holders under TRIPS exceptions.

Finally, and most importantly, in contrast to GATT Article XX, TRIPS Articles 13, 17 and 30 are by far not the only exceptions, or opportunity to refer to countervailing interests, provided for in the TRIPS Agreement. TRIPS Articles 13, 17 and 30 allow for certain *limitations* to copyright, trademarks and patents that have been conferred. In addition, other exceptions allow for situations where no IP *rights* must be granted in the first place (such as in respect of « inventions, the prevention ... of which is necessary to protect *ordre public* or morality, including to protect human, animal or plant life or health or to avoid serious prejudice to the environment », pursuant to TRIPS Article 27.2[74]). In addition,

73 Panel Report, para. 7.69.

74 See also TRIPS Article 27.3 in respect of « diagnostic, therapeutic and surgical methods for the treatment of humans or animals », certain « plants and animals » and certain « biological processes ». For copyright, for example, there are Articles *2bis* and 10 and *10bis* of the Berne Convention (incorporated into TRIPS through TRIPS Article 9) which permit limitations for certain speeches, lectures and addresses and certain free uses of work as well as the Appendix to the Berne Convention with special provisions for developing countries. For trademarks, there is, for example, Article *6ter* of the Paris Convention (incorporated into TRIPS through TRIPS Article 2.1) in respect of State emblems.

whereas under GATT trading opportunities are automatically granted in respect of any product, TRIPS provisions, as the outcome of a balancing process, limit the eligibility for IP rights and, even where IP rights are granted, limit their scope and term. Finally, there are provisions allowing for compulsory licenses without authorization of the right holder, for patents (in TRIPS Article 31 and Article 5 of the Paris Convention) as well as for certain copyrights or related rights (see, for example, Articles 11*bis* and 13 of the Berne Convention); TRIPS Article 6 explicitly states that the agreement leaves the question of « exhaustion » of IP rights untouched thereby allowing countries to engage in so-called « parallel importation », that is import, for example, cheaper medicines licensed and sold by the patent holder in a foreign country at a lower price; and TRIPS Article 40 points at the limits of IP protection when such leads to anti-competitive practices. TRIPS Articles 7 and 8, which admittedly cannot overrule other TRIPS obligations, state the « objectives » and « principles » of the TRIPS agreement and underline and potentially broaden all of these flexibilities with references to, *inter alia*, « social and economic welfare » and « measures necessary to protect public health » or « to prevent the abuse of intellectual property rights ».[75]

C. Crucial rulings on IP enforcement

A final way in which WTO jurisprudence to date may have shattered the hopes of IP enthusiasts – but alleviated the fear of critics especially in developing countries – is in rulings on the extent of TRIPS obligations in the field of IP enforcement. In both *US – Havana Club* and *China – IP Rights*, Panels highlighted that TRIPS obligations in respect of domestic IP enforcement are generally limited to having certain rules and procedures in place or providing « access » or « authority » to do things at the request of right holders; not substantive obligations of result or active « policing » on behalf of the government itself.

In *US – Havana Club*, the US law at issue prevented US courts from recognizing, enforcing or otherwise validating certain assertions of IP rights. The Panel found this to be contrary to TRIPS Article 42 which obliges WTO members to « make available to right holders civil

75 Note, however, that measures referred to in TRIPS Article 8 must be « consistent with the provisions of » the TRIPS Agreement and cannot therefore justify violations found under other TRIPS articles.

judicial procedures concerning the enforcement of any intellectual property right covered » by TRIPS and to ensure that « [a]ll parties to such procedure [are] duly entitled to substantiate their claims and to present all relevant evidence ». The Panel did not « see how a right holder would be able effectively to assert its rights under these circumstances » or be « entitled to effective procedures as the court is *ab initio* not permitted to recognize its assertion of rights ».[76] The Appellate Body reversed this conclusion. It agreed with the Panel that right holders must « have *access* to civil judicial procedures that are effective in bringing about the enforcement of their rights covered by » TRIPS.[77] However, it found that « the rights which Article 42 obliges Members to make available to right holders are *procedural* in nature ».[78] On that ground, the Appellate Body concluded that the US law in question

> *« does not prohibit courts from giving right holders access to fair and equitable civil judicial procedures and the opportunity to substantiate their claims and to present all relevant evidence. Rather, [it] only requires the United States courts not to recognize, enforce or otherwise validate any assertion of rights by [certain persons] who have been determined, after applying [relevant US rules of civil procedure], not to own the trademarks referred to … [the US law in question] deals with the substance of ownership. Therefore, we do not believe that [it] denies the procedural rights that are guaranteed by Article 42. »*[79]

In *China – IP Rights*, the United States argued that China's procedures for the disposal or destruction of IP infringing goods confiscated by Chinese customs violate TRIPS Article 59. Article 59 provides, in relevant part, that WTO members « shall have *the authority* to order the *destruction or disposal* of infringing goods in accordance with the principles set out in Article 46 ». Article 46, in turn, provides, in relevant part, that « the judicial authorities shall have the authority to order that goods that they have found to be infringing be … disposed of outside the channels of commerce in such a manner as to avoid any harm to the right holder or … destroyed. »

76 Panel Report, para. 8.102.

77 AB Report, para. 215.

78 Ibid., para. 221.

79 Ibid., para. 227, emphasis added.

In a first, crucial ruling the Panel found that TRIPS Article 59 only applies to imported goods and not to goods destined for exportation. In the case of China, a major exporter, infringing *imports* represent only 0.15 percent by value of the goods disposed of or destroyed, with the rest being goods destined for export.[80] Put differently, whatever Article 59 prescribes in terms of combating IP infringement, China only needs to worry about it in respect of imports from other countries; not in respect of goods produced within China itself destined either for exportation or domestic consumption.

Secondly, in respect of China's procedures for IP infringing *imports* – which provide for, in this order: first, donation to social welfare bodies, second, sale to the right holder and, third, auction – the Panel found that the United States had failed to establish that any of these steps or options *precluded* or *took away* China's « authority » to dispose of the goods without harm to the right holder in line with Article 46, first sentence.[81] Put differently, the United States was put in the rather difficult situation of having to prove a negative, namely: that any of China's options provided for *precluded* appropriate « disposal », thereby taking away China's « authority » to appropriately « dispose » of or « destroy » infringing goods.

In one respect, however, the Panel did find a violation of Article 59 on the ground that Chinese law stipulates that, under certain conditions, China's customs authorities « can, *after eradicating the infringing features*, auction [the infringing goods] off according to law ». The Panel found that this is contrary to TRIPS Article 46, fourth sentence, and consequently a violation of Article 59. Article 46, fourth sentence, provides that « [i]n regard to counterfeit trademark goods, the *simple removal of the trademark* unlawfully affixed shall not be sufficient, other than in exceptional circumstances, to permit release of the goods into the channels of commerce ».[82]

Finally, the United States also lost on what was no doubt its most important claim in this dispute, namely, that Chinese volume and value « thresholds » (e. g. minimum 500 pirated CDs or DVDs) before criminal procedures and penalties are triggered violate TRIPS Article 61. Article 61 states: « Members shall provide for criminal procedures and pen-

80 AB Report, para. 233.

81 Ibid., para. 7.355.

82 Ibid., para. 7.394, emphasis added.

alties to be applied at least in cases of wilful trademark counterfeiting or copyright piracy on a commercial scale ». The US claim failed under the last prong of « commercial scale ». For the Panel, a « commercial scale » is « the magnitude or extent of typical or usual commercial activity » and « counterfeiting or piracy ‹ on a commercial scale › refers to counterfeiting or piracy carried on at the magnitude or extent of *typical or usual commercial activity with respect to a given product in a given market* ».[83] The Panel then reviewed China's thresholds and agreed that « on their face, they do exclude certain commercial activity from criminal procedures and penalties » (think of a shop displaying 499 DVDs, that is, just one DVD below the threshold for criminal prosecution). However, the Panel said, « based solely on the measures on their face, the Panel cannot distinguish between acts that, in China's marketplace, are on a commercial *scale*, and those that are not ».[84] Ultimately the US claim was rejected for lack of evidence specific to China's market. This puts a rather heavy evidentiary burden on complainants especially when dealing with opaque markets such as the Chinese market where obtaining reliable information, or even convincing people to submit it (without fear of some form of governmental retaliation) may be difficult.

In conclusion, as one commentary pointed out well before *China – IP Rights*, « [i]t is important to note ... that the TRIPS Agreement generally establishes a regime under which private IPRs holders are responsible for taking steps to enforce their rights. With limited exception, Members are not obligated to ‹ police › the private interests of IPRs holders ».[85] The « limited exception » referred to was TRIPS Article 61. The *China – IP Rights* findings above, in combination with the Appellate Body's reversal under TRIPS Article 42 in *US – Havana Club*, put a further question mark behind TRIPS as a forceful tool to achieve IP enforcement within WTO member countries. At the very least, this jurisprudence cannot be called biased, pro-IP activism.

83 Ibid., para. 7.577-8, emphasis added.

84 Ibid., para. 7.,607-9.

85 Frederick M. Abbott, Thomas Cottier & Francis Gurry, International Intellectual Property in an Integrated World Economy, Aspen (2007), at p. 608.

V. Reality Check 4: Institutional Approach of WTO Panels and the Appellate Body

Contrary to what some observers expected in the mid 1990s, no major turf wars or inconsistencies emerged between the WTO and WIPO. On the contrary, at each juncture, WTO Panels made institutional decisions that favored and enhanced WTO-WIPO cooperation.

First, in each dispute where the Paris or Berne Convention was substantively at issue, WTO Panels sought the input of WIPO (that is, in 4 of the 9 Panels issued so far).[86] These requests concerned information on negotiating history and subsequent developments. They were responded to in the form of a note by WIPO's Director-General. Even if WTO Panels could have done most of this research themselves, the fact that they opted for such formal route illustrates good WTO-WIPO relations. That WIPO each time cooperated and submitted the information in what were often strict timeframes is equally positive. The cooperation between WIPO and the WTO finds support in the Preamble of TRIPS (« *Desiring* to establish a mutually supportive relationship between the WTO and [WIPO] ») as well as in a general 1995 WTO-WIPO Cooperation Agreement focused on exchange of information and technical cooperation.

Second, Panels were careful to interpret TRIPS in line with WIPO conventions, including the negotiating history of the Berne and Paris Conventions as well as subsequent developments. Most tellingly, the Panel on *US – Copyright* went through great pains to read the so-called « minor exceptions » doctrine under the Berne Convention (a doctrine which is not explicitly written into the Berne Convention) to be, what it referred to as, Berne *acquis* which had, in turn, also been incorporated into TRIPS. Moreover, to avoid contradicting TRIPS Article 2.2 (which states that nothing in TRIPS Articles 1 to 62 « shall derogate from existing obligations that [WTO] Members may have to each other » under, *inter alia*, the Berne Convention), the Panel found that the copyright exceptions in TRIPS Article 13 inform and apparently occupy the same space as these « minor exceptions ». Indeed, if Article 13 were seen as

86 In reverse chronological order: *China – IP Rights*, *US – Havana Club*, *EC – Trademarks & GIs* and *US – Copyright*. The only case where the Panel might have sought WIPO input but did not was *Canada – Pharmaceutical Patents*. Yet, even that panel referred to the negotiating history of the Paris and Berne Conventions as relevant also to interpret TRIPS.

providing for broader exceptions than those in the Berne Convention, such interpretation could « derogate from existing obligations » under Berne and contradict TRIPS Article 2.2.

In the earlier *US – Havana Club* dispute as well, the Appellate Body reversed a Panel finding that TRIPS does not cover trade names invoking, in particular, a desire to give sense to TRIPS› incorporation of Article 8 of the Paris Convention (which covers trade names). This confirmation that TRIPS does apply to trade names substantively aligns TRIPS with the Paris Convention.

In sum, both institutionally and substantively, WTO dispute settlement has not approached incorporated-WIPO provisions as leading a « life of their own » within a TRIPS agreement which, as of 1994, would somehow be cut-off from the WIPO mother-ship. On the contrary, the umbilical cord between WIPO and the WTO remained and, if anything, was strengthened through WTO dispute settlement.

VI. Reality Check 5: Implementation of Adverse WTO Rulings

Of the 9 TRIPS disputes decided, 8 found violations. The exception is *Indonesia – Autos* where the Panel found GATT, TRIMS and SCM violations, but no TRIPS violations. Losing countries normally ask for and obtain a so-called « reasonable period of time » to implement the adverse ruling. This period can be mutually agreed or be decided by arbitration and is reflected in the table below for each of the 8 cases (*India – Patent*, where there were 2 reports on the same matter, is listed as one case). The third column gives information about the current status of implementation. Of the 8 cases, 5 have been implemented. For one case (*China – IP Rights*) the implementation period has, at the time of writing, just ended and although China announced amendments to its copyright law, those are still being examined by the United States.[87] The two remaining cases have been more problematic and are the 2 reports decided against the United States.

87 See discussions at the DSB of 19 March, 2010, at http://www.wto.org/english/news_e/news10_e/dsb_19mar10_e.htm.

IMPLEMENTATION OF FINDINGS OF TRIPS VIOLATION

Case	Reasonable period of time to implement	Current Status
India – Patents (EC and US complaints)	15 months (agreed)	Implemented
Canada-Pharmaceutical Patents	6 months (arbitration)	Implemented
US – Copyrights	12 months (arbitration)	3.3 million US$ compensation
Canada-Patent Term	10 months (arbitration)	Implemented
US – Havana Club	12 months (agreed)	Pending
EC – Trademarks & GIS	11.5 months (agreed)	Implemented
China – IP Rights	12 months (agreed)	Amendments made

In *US – Copyright,* the parties resorted to special arbitration (pursuant to DSU Article 25) to obtain a decision on the annual « nullification or impairment » caused by the US TRIPS violation (i. e., the United States maintaining the « business style exemption »). The arbitration Panel calculated the amount of lost royalties and, in an important interpretative move, decided that (i) it would only count royalty income that EC right holders « could reasonably expect » to receive without the « business exemption », more specifically, licensing revenue from the numbers of users that *would* be licensed (and not from each and every use, or royalty income which EC right holders forego by not exercising or enforcing their exclusive rights), based on past, historical data extrapolated to the present; and (ii) it would only count the royalties that US collecting agencies would have paid out to EC right holders, after deduction of collection and administration costs (that is, royalties distributed, not royalties collected). On that basis, the annual nullification amount was set at 1,219,900 euro.

For the 3 year period between 2002 and 2004, the United States paid the EC compensation of 3.3 million US$. This was the first and so far only time where a losing party in WTO dispute settlement paid off non-compliance in cash. In other cases, continued non-compliance resulted rather in trade retaliation (that is, the winning state blocking an amount of trade equivalent to that kept out by the original violation) or, less often, trade compensation (that is, the losing state compensating not in cash but by opening its market in some other field or product).

Since 2004, however, the United States has not paid for, nor withdrawn the violation in *US – Copyright*. Since then, at each and every DSB meeting in Geneva (normally convened at least once a month), the EC puts the dispute on the agenda and each time the United States claims to be working on implementation. The same is true for *US – Havana Club*, also discussed at every DSB meeting, which the United States has still not implemented and for which the EC, in contrast to *US – Copyright*, did not obtain any compensation. Indeed, given the US embargo on imports from Cuba, the US violations in *US – Havana Club* have no actual trade impact. Since WTO remedies have normally been limited to actual losses (see *US – 1916 Act*), this means that EC compensation or retaliation rights in *US – Havana Club* would most likely be zero. After all, this case and the broader battle between Pernod-Ricard and Bacardi did not focus on immediate commercial interests but rather on market shares that would arise when the United States eventually restores trade relations with Cuba in the future.

Finally, notwithstanding the much touted novelty of linking trade sanctions to the enforcement of IP rights – whereby *developed* countries would be able to enforce IP protection in *developing* countries with the use of trade restrictions – in not a single TRIPS case so far have trade sanctions been used. Indeed, all 3 TRIPS disputes where continued non-compliance was an issue were disputes between the United States and the EC (*US – Copyright*; *US – Havana Club*; *EC –Trademarks & GIs*) and in none of these cases were trade sanctions imposed.

In contrast, three WTO disputes where WTO agreements other than TRIPS were at issue, led to authorizations to cross-retaliate in the field of TRIPS (*EC – Bananas*, *US – Gambling* and *US – Cotton*). In none of these three disputes, however, have TRIPS sanctions actually been implemented, although at the time of writing, Brazil is getting very close to suspending U. S. IP rights in response to *US – Cotton*.[88] Ironically, therefore, the link between IP and trade has so far played out in exactly the opposite way: Rather than developed countries imposing trade sanctions against developing countries violating TRIPS, it is developing countries (Ecuador in *Bananas*, Antigua in *Gambling* and Brazil

88 See Raymond Colitt & Stuart Grudgings, Brazil delays trade retaliation against U. S., Reuters, 5 April 2010, available at http://www.reuters.com/article/idUSTRE63500R20100406.

in *Cotton*) that have sought to suspend IP protection in response to trade violations by the EC or the United States.

The arbitration report on retaliation in *EC – Bananas* (at the request of Ecuador) elaborated on how a WTO member should proceed when suspending TRIPS obligations. First, the arbitrator stressed that Ecuador could only suspend IP rights held by EC nationals in a way that does not adversely affect other right holders. This raises the problem of making sure that when, for example, Ecuador copies CDs or DVDs, the related IP rights are exclusively held by EC nationals. Many CDs and DVDs, of course, include IP rights of many different nationalities.

Second, the arbitrator found that TRIPS permits the suspension of obligations incorporated from WIPO conventions, but left the question open of whether such suspension would be consistent with WIPO conventions themselves (or, for that matter, other international agreements such as bilateral investment treaties which protect IP as an « investment »). In this context, the arbitrator added that, contrary to GATT or GATS suspensions, « the interference with private property rights of individuals or companies may be perceived as more far reaching under the TRIPS Agreement » and « may give rise to legal difficulties or conflicts within the domestic legal system of the Member so authorized (and perhaps even of the Member(s) affected by such suspension) ».[89] The arbitrator in *US – Gambling* echoed this sentiment when finding that TRIPS suspension « may involve more complex means of implementation than, for example, the imposition of higher import duties on goods, and that the exact assessment of the value of the rights affected by the suspension is also likely to be more complex ».[90] These uncertainties at least partially explain why so far not a single WTO member has actually implemented a WTO authorization to suspend TRIPS obligations.

Finally, and most importantly, the arbitrator in *EC – Bananas* found that Ecuador's suspension of IP rights held by EC nationals was authorized « only for the purposes of supply destined for the domestic market ».[91] In other words, Ecuador could start copying EC music CDs but could only sell those CDs within Ecuador and not, for example, export them for profit or otherwise to Brazil or the United States. This, of

89 Arbitration report, paras. 157-8.

90 Arbitration report, para. 5.10.

91 Arbitration report, para. 156. A finding confirmed also in the arbitrations in *US – Gambling* and *US – Cotton*.

course, imposes a serious practical limit on TRIPS suspension, especially in countries where IP rights are not broadly respected on the domestic market in the first place (in those cases, what added-value does it offer to have the right to copy CDs if the domestic market is already rife with piracy ?). In contrast, if Ecuador had been given the right to legally export « pirated » goods to, for example, the United States, the possible impact of TRIPS retaliation would have been significantly higher, both commercially and symbolically (e. g. as to the stability and respectability of copyright protection worldwide). The arbitrator came to this conclusion on the (not uncontestable) ground that, in the hypothetical case above, an authorization for Ecuador to suspend IP rights does not relieve the United States from its obligation under, *inter alia*, TRIPS Article 51 to block the importation of pirated copyright goods, defined in footnote 13 as copies « made without the consent of the right holder ».[92] Thus, even if Ecuador could make and export « pirated » copies pursuant to a WTO authorization to suspend TRIPS, the United States would still have to block these copies when they reach US customs.

In sum, the implementation record in TRIPS disputes stands at 5 out of 7 (counting the *India – Patent* cases as one; and not yet including *China – IP Rights*). At around 70 per cent, this is slightly lower than the overall implementation rate of about 80 per cent in WTO dispute settlement.[93] That the two TRIPS cases with long-term non-compliance (*US – Copyright* and *US – Havana Club*) are against the United States is, however, not exceptional. So far, the most recalcitrant defendants in WTO dispute settlement have been the United States and the EC. Indeed, the five most notorious and long-standing cases of non-compliance have been, on the one hand, the *EC – Bananas*, *EC – Hormones* and *EC – Biotech* cases and, on the other hand, *US – Havana Club* and *US – Copyright*. What is more surprising is that, whereas the first three cases against the EC involve long-standing and extremely sensitive questions of public health or former colonial preferences, the two TRIPS cases against the United States require relatively minor changes in US IP law (eliminate discrimination in *US – Havana Club* without having to recognize confiscated Cuban trademarks; drop the « business style

92 Ibid., paras. 153-6.

93 William Davey, Compliance Problems in WTO Dispute Settlement, 42 Cornell Journal of International Law (2009) 119, at 119 (« A recent examination of the implementation record of WTO decisions for the first ten years of WTO dispute settlement found a compliance rate of 83 % »).

exemption » in *US – Copyright*). Indeed, *EC – Bananas, EC – Hormones* and *EC – Biotech* have, after many years, recently been settled. There is no immediate resolution in sight of the two TRIPS cases against the United States. The relatively minor nullification award in *US – Copyright* (less than 1.3 million euro per year) and the absence so far of any actual trade or other damage in *US – Havana Club* may have something to do with this.

VII. Explaining Factors

A. Core features of WTO dispute settlement

Many of the results described in this article can, at least partially, be explained by the broader features of WTO dispute settlement. Firstly, the fact that only states have standing to file a complaint (not, say, Novartis or Microsoft itself) and that only state laws or conduct (not, for example, IP infringement by private operators) is subject to challenge, goes a long way in explaining the relatively low number of TRIPS complaints (27 out of 402 WTO complaints; 3 per cent of all claims under WTO agreements; only 9 Panels and 3 Appellate Body reports).

Secondly, given this purely state-to-state nature of WTO dispute settlement and the general rules TRIPS imposes on member countries, it should come as no big surprise either that almost all TRIPS disputes involved laws or legislation (not specific commercial incidents) and are systemic in nature, aimed at « signaling » the WTO membership as a whole as much as attacking specific rules in a particular country.

Thirdly, both the low numbers and the systemic type of TRIPS disputes are further explained by the limited remedies the WTO offers to winning complainants. The remedies in WTO dispute settlement are purely prospective, namely, implementation or cessation of the violation by the end of a « reasonable » implementation period and, in the absence of that, mutually agreed, prospective trade compensation or WTO-authorized retaliation until rulings are implemented. Private IP right holders, albeit through their national government, do not obtain reparation for past harm nor do they get compensation for continued violation subsequent to a WTO ruling. At best, they see prospective changes in legislation or other general rules. If not, the government representing them may impose trade restrictions or suspend the IP rights of other people (retaliation) or obtain market access for goods or services abroad (compensation). Yet, neither retaliation nor trade compensation is of any direct help to these right holders (which may explain why the EC is not pushing these options in *US – Copyright*). Moreover, both compensation and retaliation are subject to the original TRIPS violation actually causing harm (which clarifies why the EC is not seeking these options in *US – Havana Club* where US violations are not having a commercial impact for as long as the United States maintains its embargo on Cuba). For right holders, the only alternative to implementation may be monetary compensation (that is probably why in *US – Copyright* a cash arrangement was agreed, at least for 3 years).

Given this remedy structure, private right holders, even if they have sufficient clout to convince a government to bring their case, have no incentive to push short-time, commercial disputes all the way to the WTO. Only politically sensitive cases (think of *US – Havana Club* or *EC – Trademarks & GIs*) or matters with a systemic, long-term impact (such as the TRIPS phase-in disputes or *Canada – Pharmaceutical Patents* and *China – IP Rights* cases) will be filed. As one comment put it, « [t]he TRIPS Agreement was presumably designed to address systemic IP enforcement issues, and not to serve as a court of appeals on individual cases or controversies ».[94]

B. Core features of the TRIPS agreement

Trade agreements are traditionally about enhancing and securing reciprocal market access and opportunities (not rights) to trade in goods and services. They focus on so-called « negative integration » where member countries agree and are told what not to do (e. g. not to impose tariffs above a certain ceiling or not to discriminate). TRIPS, in contrast, is about the protection of private rights.[95] It is the first WTO agreement centered on « positive integration » where member countries agreed and are told to take positive steps toward harmonization, more particularly, to set up an often costly system of IP registration and enforcement that meets agreed minimum standards. To put it bluntly, a « failed state » or country without a government would not have a hard time complying with GATT and GATS (as these agreements focus on not doing certain

94 Abbott & Cottier, *supra* note 18, p. 443.

95 See TRIPS Preamble.

things); it would be much more difficult to comply with TRIPS (which requires positive steps and enforcement).

The novelty and uniqueness of TRIPS as compared to other WTO agreements may partly explain why, at least in these first 15 years, the type of TRIPS claims decided continues to focus on more traditional trade matters such as non-discrimination (as in *Indonesia – Autos*, *US – Havana Club* and *EC – Trademarks & GIs*). Discrimination or preventing certain action is what negotiators, litigators and the system as a whole is used to and good at.

It may also explain the low appeals rate of TRIPS Panels and the fact that so far none of the three genuine, substantive IP disputes described above were appealed: Not only were TRIPS Panels to date carefully balanced giving something to each side which neither side was willing to risk on appeal; parties may also be apprehensive of involving the Appellate Body whose rulings on new and rather different TRIPS provisions carry more weight and set a deeper precedent than Panels. A further contributing factor may be that Panels are appointed *ad hoc* and can be composed of IP specialists, whereas the Appellate Body, in its 15 years of existence, has only had one member who is an IP specialist.[96]

More importantly, the positive and often complex and costly steps that TRIPS requires countries to take, may explain why complainants have focused on consultations and cooperative strategies rather than confrontation and litigation. This may have kept the number of TRIPS disputes low, including and especially against developing countries.[97] Losing a traditional trade dispute requires a country to get rid of a tariff or protectionist rule. Losing a substantive IP dispute often forces a country to set up an institution, mechanism or procedure. If a country needs time to do so, for example, because it has limited resources, other urgent priorities or political difficulties to get laws through parliament,

96 Mr. A.V. Ganesan, former TRIPS negotiator for India.

97 As predicted and recommended by Reichman, *supra* note 11, at 124-6: « hard-nosed confrontational strategies for implementing the TRIPs standards risk backfiring by revealing the full extent of the residual disagreement … Undue pressure may also convince governments in the developing countries to resist further harmonization at all costs … putting too much pressure too soon on the developing countries will induce them to push back by invoking safeguards codified in [TRIPS] Articles 7 and 8 … Besides exploiting the ‹ wiggle room › that pervades existing international minimum standards of [IP] protection, the developing countries retain broad powers to tax and otherwise regulate [IP] owners in ways that could significantly undermine their commercial expectations ».

for another country to drag it to court or a WTO Panel may backfire. It may do more harm than good. In such cases, what is often more needed and effective is technical or financial support or a subtle political or diplomatic push to tip the political balance in favor of enacting the required IP law changes.

This, in turn, may explain the high settlement rate for TRIPS complaints: Given the relative clarity of at least the core TRIPS rules, both parties often realize that the defending country is in violation and needs to pass a particular amendment.[98] With the extra push and pressure of a formal request for WTO consultations, the deal may be struck, without the need for a Panel to be established. Indeed, some defendants may welcome this (limited amount of) pressure as it may lend them a hand with pushing through IP reforms domestically, and offer them the TRIPS agreement as a scapegoat to deflect criticism by their own constituencies.

It is no coincidence that the TRIPS provisions on dispute settlement (Part V) are entitled « Dispute *Prevention* and Settlement » whereas most other WTO agreements simply refer to « Consultations and Dispute Settlement ». On the prevention side, TRIPS set up the TRIPS Council to which members must notify their IP laws and regulations for review by the entire membership. Unlike many other WTO notification requirements (such as those in respect of subsidies), the TRIPS requirement has been closely respected: The WTO Secretariat has received notifications from all WTO members (except one: St Kits & Nevis). TRIPS Council meetings are used also to diffuse and settle IP disputes. Its activity and level of success may further explain the low number of formal WTO complaints filed as well as the high settlement rate of TRIPS complaints that have been filed.[99]

Conversely, where a Panel does get established and finds TRIPS violations, the unique nature of TRIPS may make implementation more difficult and traditional WTO remedies inappropriate. As noted earlier, most TRIPS violations found so far require legislative changes which by definition, and especially in the US Congress, are more difficult to

98 In support, ABBOTT & COTTIER, *supra* note 18, p. 431. Note, indeed, that almost all TRIPS complaints that were settled were settled largely in favor of the complainant, that is, with the defending country implementing changes. There are only two partial exceptions, namely: the US v. Argentina and US v. Brazil cases which were settled in the context of the Doha Declaration and access to medicines debate largely in favor of defendants.

99 See ANDREW LANG & JOANNE SCOTT, The Hidden World of WTO Governance, European Journal of International Law, vol. 20, issue 3, 2009, p. 575.

push through. This makes implementation longer and more difficult (and goes some way in explaining why the United States has still not implemented in *US – Havana Club* and *US – Copyright*). In addition, if non-compliance is due to a lack of financial or technical resources or domestic political deadlock, external pressure from the WTO may hurt rather than help.

In the IP context, the standard WTO remedy of tit-for-tat retaliation is hard to put to work: few IP industries will support the suspension of foreign IP rights as a means to convince a foreign country to respect their IP rights. More than trade, IP protection is a culture or carefully nurtured custom which needs stimulation (not suspension) both abroad and at home. As noted by WTO arbitrators on retaliation, TRIPS suspension may not only dilute overall respect for IP, as it relates to private property rights it may also run into trouble under domestic constitutional law or other international treaties that protect property (be it WIPO, investment or human rights treaties).

Cross-retaliation may be more effective, in that trade restrictions may activate the export lobby within the violating country itself for that lobby to support the required IP changes if only to get rid of the trade sanctions. Yet, ultimately, cross-retaliation does not offer any direct help to the original victims: for the EC to block importation of, for example, US soybeans does not help Irish songwriters who won the case on *US – Copyright*. This problem is present also in standard trade disputes, but stands out even more so in a regime such as TRIPS which is supposed to protect private rights. All of this makes forced implementation of TRIPS rulings more difficult which, in turn, provides an incentive for early settlement and a disincentive to file complaints in the first place.

Other, more subtle features of TRIPS illustrate the at times uneasy marriage of protecting private IP rights in a state-oriented trade organization: first, the finding by the Panel on *China – IP Rights* that TRIPS enforcement obligations are limited to counterfeit and pirated *imports* and leave domestic production untouched; second, the fact that arbitrators on TRIPS retaliation limited the suspension of IP rights to copies for sale only on the *domestic* market and precluded victims to exploit the bigger impact that free copying for export would have.

C. The win-win situation of WTO-WIPO cooperation

Unlike some predictions, TRIPS did not mean the end of WIPO. Closer cooperation rather than turf battles and inconsistencies emerged. WTO rulings on IP have found broad support amongst IP experts. They have not been derided as amateur opinions written by trade (not IP) experts. Many of these developments can be explained by a rather obvious win-win deal between the WTO and WIPO. On the WTO's side, it was clear from the beginning that the WTO secretariat (which to date still has less than 10 IP specialists on its staff) could not offer the type of technical cooperation and advice that WIPO, with its army of IP specialists, offers. The WTO budget would, for that matter, also fall short, especially as compared to the generous budget of WIPO largely composed of IP filing fees from the private sector. Hence, the WTO (including WTO Panels) gladly deferred to WIPO to get IP advice, and to offer its members technical cooperation on IP matters.

Similarly, on WIPO's side, it soon emerged that with TRIPS ratified more countries especially developing countries also ratified WIPO conventions. For one thing, if a country is already bound to most of what is in the Paris and Berne Conventions through TRIPS and WTO membership, why not become a party also to these WIPO conventions directly and, in the process, benefit from the technical assistance and financial flows offered by WIPO ? Put differently, TRIPS, rather than casting a shadow over WIPO, reinvigorated the organization both in membership and political debate and rule-making activity.

This symbiotic relationship surely made it easier for WIPO to tolerate and support its smaller, but in some respects stronger IP brother (think of dispute settlement). It also led WTO parties to appoint individuals on TRIPS Panels with IP expertise (often at least partly gained at WIPO) and Panels, in turn, to carefully consult with WIPO and a small but strong group of IP specialists on the WTO Secretariat staff. This and other factors enabled WTO Panels to overcome the critique that the WTO would not be « up to the task » of deciding complex IP cases.

D. Barking dogs that woke a giant : Big Pharma and the Access to HIV / AIDS medicines debate

One of the most important factors influencing TRIPS dispute settlement activity – or the lack thereof, especially against *developing* countries even after 2000 – happened out-of-court. It had little to do with TRIPS or WTO rules as such but rather with the perception of these rules as « spinned », first, by IP industries and then by NGOs and developing countries.

The story goes something like this. Upon conclusion of TRIPS, IP industries touted the agreement as a big victory that would widen and deepen worldwide IP protection with little or no flexibility including for developing countries once TRIPS entered into force for those countries on 1 January 2000. Whether the IP lobby did so as a strategy knowing too well that TRIPS had plenty of flexibility, misread the text of TRIPS or were in denial of the deal that was actually struck is everyone's guess. What we do know is that this position seriously backfired and led to an escalating cycle of IP skepticism. In the early 1990 s, the then GATT had already been the subject of public outrage especially by environmental groups after GATT rulings prohibiting the United States to ban tuna because it had killed dolphin when caught in Mexico. With the inclusion of IP in the new WTO package, anti-globalization protesters saw a new and, in their eyes, even more obvious cause for outrage, especially if IP industries and their hard-line TRIPS position were to be believed: Since most IP rights are held by rich country nationals, the protesters argued, TRIPS is a pure *win-loss* situation, a wealth transfer, in the form of royalties, from the poor to the rich.

Protests culminated in the 1999 « Battle for Seattle », the WTO's ministerial conference where street protests blocked the start of a new trade negotiations round. In the meantime, IP industries, especially « big pharma », continued their push, suing governments and generics producers of HIV / AIDS medicines in Brazilian and South African courts. This, of course, was oil on the fire of TRIPS protests and a rallying call for a new, powerful anti-TRIPS coalition of NGOs (such as *Médecins Sans Frontières*) and developing countries (such as Brazil, India and South Africa). In 2001, when a new trade round was started, it led to a stunning victory for IP skeptics in the form of the Doha Declaration on TRIPS and Public Health. This Doha Declaration was stunning, not so much for its content, but for the fact that WTO members were able to reach consensus on such a very sensitive issue in the first place (some commentators have argued that both the kick-off of the Doha Round and the Doha Declaration on Public Health were enabled by a sense of global solidarity following the September 2001 terrorist attacks).

That this cycle of events had more to do with spin and perception is confirmed by what the Doha Declaration actually states: It simply explains and reiterates the many exceptions and flexibilities that TRIPS includes and which allow developing countries to weaken patent protection in their fight for access to essential medicines. That such explicit confirmation was needed shows the extent to which IP industries had managed to convince public opinion as well as seasoned experts of the imagined or hoped-for strictness of TRIPS. Indeed, it took the 2001 Doha Declaration to end the denial of hard-line IP proponents as to what the 1994 TRIPS bargain actually provides. To this date many still (wrongly) believe that it is because of Doha (not the original TRIPS itself) that there is TRIPS flexibility. That said, the Doha Declaration also paved the way for one additional element of TRIPS flexibility in the form of a TRIPS amendment – a first in the WTO's history – allowing the production of essential medicines under compulsory license not only « predominantly for the supply of the domestic market » (as TRIPS Article 31(f) obliges) but also for export to developing countries that do not have manufacturing capability.

Whether any of this actually provided better access to HIV / AIDS medicines in the field remains unclear. What is clear, however, is that NGOs and developing countries called big pharma's bluff and partly silenced them in the court of public opinion and the political negotiations in Doha. This, in turn, created a much broader wave of IP skepticism that still reverberates at the WTO and found an ear also in other fora such as the WHO, FAO, UNCTAD and, most recently, WIPO itself where in 2007 the so-called « Development Agenda » was adopted, underlining and calling for further flexibility in IP protection to stimulate development. What is more, big pharma's push also unearthed and further exacerbated fissures and differences of opinion amongst the concentration of global businesses and developed country governments that had, as one front, enabled the conclusion of TRIPS.[100] This fragmentation further contributed to the snowball effect of IP skepticism. Big pharma and the essential medicines debate is, in sum, a story of barking dogs waking a giant, the giant of public opinion and broader IP skepticism.

100 On fragmentation of the IP lobby post-TRIPS: Duncan Matthews, Globalising Intellectual Property Rights: The TRIPs Agreement, London, Routledge, 2003.

The consequences for TRIPS dispute settlement were twofold. First, in the sensitive political climate immediately before and after Doha, it would have been risky and most likely counterproductive to file major TRIPS cases against developing countries, even if in 2000 their phase-in period ended. Doha also confirmed and further expanded TRIPS flexibilities, further reducing the industries› appetite for a major offensive. The two WTO disputes filed on the question of patents and access to essential medicines, respectively, in 1999 (expanded in 2000) against Argentina and in 2000 against Brazil, were, indeed, settled with little gained by the complainant (the United States). The essential medicines story may, therefore, go quite some way in explaining the low number of TRIPS disputes filed, especially against developing countries including post-2000. Indeed, the political victory of IP skeptics at Doha led many IP proponents to shift attention, tail-between-legs, away from the WTO and toward unilateral enforcement (in the United States, under « Special 301 ») and, especially, preferential trade agreements where so-called TRIPS-plus commitments were sought and obtained.[101] Importantly, this move, in turn, meant that one of the core objectives of TRIPS was jeopardized, that is, as noted earlier, to have multilateral rules and dispute settlement at the WTO, not unilateral or bilateral deals where weaker countries are at a disadvantage.[102]

Second, and more difficult to prove, the public outrage against TRIPS and emerging consensus that TRIPS had to offer flexibility to deal with public health emergencies, partly triggered by IP industries themselves, may have played a role as context in which the handful of TRIPS Panels that were established did their work. This is not to say that these Panels were unduly influenced not to find TRIPS violations. Only to say that the general climate made it less likely for these Panels

101 See LAURENCE HELFER, *supra* note 9, at 41 : « With negotiations in the WTO effectively stalled, both proponents and opponents of stronger intellectual property rules groups of states sought out greener pastures in other international regimes. Developing countries decamped to the WHO, FAO, and CBD ... The United States and the European Communities, by contrast, shifted their efforts from the WTO and WIPO to bilateral and regional trade and investment treaties, incorporating IP protection rules into these agreements ».

102 But note the Panel on *US – Section 301* which found that Section 301 gave the US administration *discretion* to unilaterally enforce WTO rules in violation of the DSU but refrained from finding against the United States on the ground that the United States had committed not to exercise this discretion and to abide by the multilateral rules in the DSU.

to take a hard-line, pro-IP approach. They certainly realized that the world was watching them. If correct, this may partly explain why both rulings on TRIPS exceptions and IP enforcement were carefully balanced (if not liberal) or at least difficult to qualify as overly strict or biased in favor of IP protection

VIII. Conclusion

15 years on, TRIPS and, in particular, dispute settlement under TRIPS, is the dog that barked but did not bite. As early as 1998, when the euphoria of a new and thickening worldwide IP system based on the rule of law was still prevailing, Reichman and Lange stressed the gaps and flexibilities in the TRIPS regime and the importance of « cooperative – rather than coercive – forms of implementation » of TRIPS :

> *« we predict that the level of enforcement under the TRIPS Agreement will greatly disappoint rightsholders in the developed countries, and that recourse to coercive measures will not appreciably improve the situation in the short and medium terms … we believe that the relevant interest groups in both developed and developing countries should consider treating the TRIPS Agreement as a set of default rules to be bargained around within a cooperative framework. »*[103]

This is exactly what we are seeing now.

The goal of this article was not to argue that TRIPS as such, or as interpreted in WTO dispute settlement or the Doha Declaration on TRIPS and Public Health, is either too strict, not strict enough or about right. Rather, the point was (i) to check and dispel common hopes and fears expressed in the context of TRIPS, which persist to this very day, and (ii) to explain this reality 15 years on, with reference to core features of WTO dispute settlement and the nature of the TRIPS Agreement itself, as well as a rather obvious win-win case for WTO-WIPO cooperation and, crucially, the access to essential medicines debate.

The TRIPS agreement inspired both exaggerated hopes in the minds of the IP lobby, and overblown fears in the hearts of NGOs and developing countries. This is confirmed in the number and types of

103 JEROME REICHMAN & DAVID LANGE, *supra* note 4, at 38-39.

disputes filed before the WTO dispute settlement system as well as the decisions reached by WTO Panels and the Appellate Body and their subsequent implementation record. Relatively few substantive IP disputes have been filed. Rather than developing countries, the main target so far has been the EC. Moreover, the two non-implemented TRIPS rulings to date are not against India or China, but the United States, the main *demandeur* of TRIPS. Not once did the WTO authorize trade sanctions to back-up TRIPS enforcement, a novelty that was nonetheless much advertised when TRIPS was concluded. On the contrary, and quite ironically, it is developing countries that cross-retaliated in TRIPS to enforce GATT and GATS rulings against the EC and the United States. Contrary to some expectations, WTO Panels and the Appellate Body have demonstrated that they can deal with complex IP disputes and gained the general trust and respect of the IP community in no small part by working very closely with WIPO. Substantive Panel and Appellate Body findings, in turn, illustrate that TRIPS does, indeed, only impose minimum standards, that TRIPS› exceptions provide for ample « wiggle room » and that TRIPS disciplines on domestic IP enforcement are largely procedural focused on imports (not domestic production) rather than obligations of result. The Doha Declaration on TRIPS and Public Health drove TRIPS flexibility home and triggered a broader cycle of IP skepticism which, rather than drowning, reinvigorated WIPO and IP activity in other fora.

TRIPS, therefore, was not the beginning of a unidirectional strengthening of worldwide IP protection. On the contrary, it turned out to be the beginning of a global wave of IP skepticism. What, indeed, if, contrary to conventional wisdom, developing countries were not simply forced or lured into signing TRIPS with the threat of US, unilateral trade sanctions or in exchange for uncertain market access benefits in agriculture and textiles ? What if, instead, developing countries considered that TRIPS, in and of itself, was actually not such a bad deal: First, because of the many TRIPS flexibilities and loopholes they were able to negotiate; Second, since, in any event, many developing countries were planning to beef up IP protection in their economies› own interest anyhow and could use the helping hand of TRIPS as a scapegoat to push through unpopular reforms at home ?

What lies ahead for TRIPS dispute settlement is difficult to predict. Business as usual with around one, systemic TRIPS case per year ? Even less cases given disappointment in earlier disputes ? Or, at some point, a renewed increase in TRIPS disputes? Though not likely given the systemic features of TRIPS and WTO dispute settlement pointed out earlier, the last possibility could materialize under different scenarios such as entry into force of TRIPS for least-developed countries (partly in 2013, fully in 2016); discrimination complaints before the WTO against favorable IP treatment granted in preferential trade agreements (unlike GATT Article XXIV, TRIPS does not have an exception for preferential arrangements) or South-South cases where larger developing countries with an increasing interest in IP protection start to sue smaller developing countries.

The most recent TRIPS dispute is, in any event, telling. It does not concern a developed country suing a developing country for lack of IP protection or weak IP enforcement. It is a complaint by India and Brazil against the EC, arguing that the EC violates GATT and TRIPS by enforcing IP rights too strictly, in particular, as against generic drugs in transit, patented within the EC, but on their way from India to Brazil where they are not patent-protected.[104] This is not a case brought by big pharma or the IP lobby. It is a case filed on behalf of the generic drug industry against IP protection beyond minimum standards, a revenge of the IP skeptics. Man bites dog.

104 *European Union and A Member State – Seizure of Generic Drugs in Transit* (DS408 and DS409).

Le contentieux de la propriété industrielle en Europe : état des lieux, stratégies et perspectives

*Pierre Véron**

C'est une situation complexe que je vais vous présenter, en vous parlant tout d'abord du système judiciaire communautaire et de la façon dont il est appliqué à la propriété industrielle (ci-dessous I): je vous dirai, ensuite, comment nous vivons en pratique avec ce système complexe (ci-dessous II) et quelles perspectives s'ouvrent à nous, plus particulièrement dans le domaine du contentieux des brevets d'invention qui est celui que je pratique.

I. Le système judiciaire communautaire

Il faut toujours garder présent à l'esprit que le juge de droit commun, le juge ordinaire du droit communautaire, n'est pas la Cour de justice de l'Union européenne, c'est comme nous aimons le dire dans l'Union, le juge du coin de la rue.

Le juge national est le juge de droit commun et la Cour de justice au sens large (la Cour et le Tribunal) sont quant à eux, des juges d'exception.

Leur compétence d'attribution est strictement celle qui leur est dévolue par les traités.

Selon le traité de Lisbonne[1], la compétence de la Cour de justice de l'Union européenne (vous noterez le changement d'étiquette, la Cour de justice des communautés est passée aux oubliettes) est limitée :

* Avocat à la cour de Paris, Président d'honneur de l'AAPI (Association des avocats de propriété industrielle) et de l'EPLAW (European Patent Lawyers Association).

1 Article 19 du traité de Lisbonne modifiant le traité sur l'Union européenne et le traité instituant la Communauté européenne, signé à Lisbonne le 13 décembre 2007, entré en vigueur le 1er décembre 2009.

« 3. La Cour de justice de l'Union européenne statue conformément aux traités :

a) sur les recours formés par un État membre, une institution ou des personnes physiques ou morales ;
b) à titre préjudiciel, à la demande des juridictions nationales, sur l'interprétation du droit de l'Union ou sur la validité d'actes adoptés par les institutions ;
c) dans les autres cas prévus par les traités. »

Lorsqu'il s'agit de recours contre les actes communautaires, la compétence de la Cour de justice de l'Union européenne s'exerce comme celle – comme nous dirions en France – d'une juridiction administrative ; un tel recours contre la décision faisant grief va aboutir devant la Cour de justice de l'Union européenne :

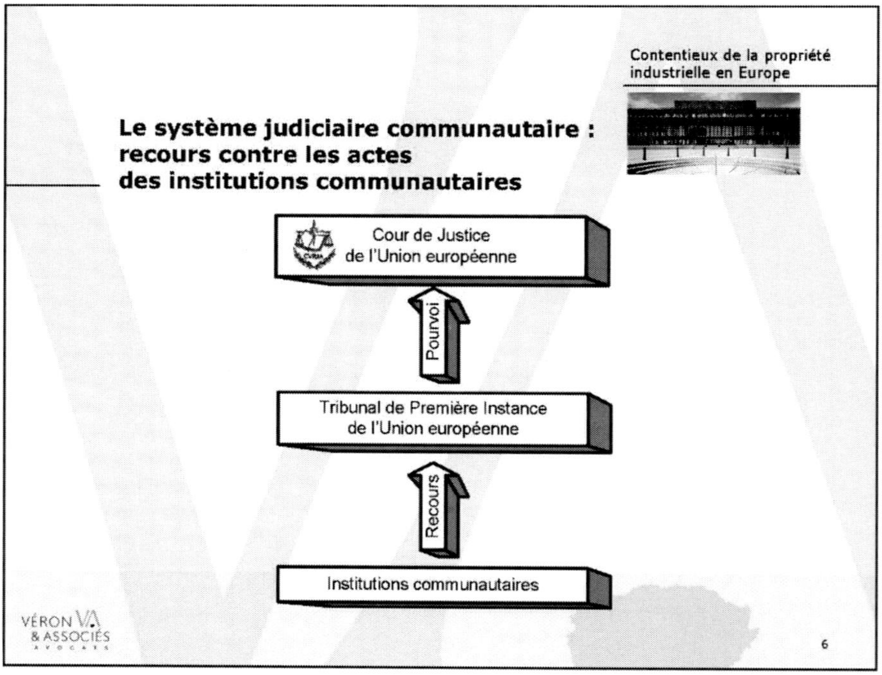

Dans les litiges entre parties, la Cour de justice européenne a un rôle particulier : ces litiges sont soumis aux juridictions étatiques de droit commun, en première instance, en appel et au niveau suprême :

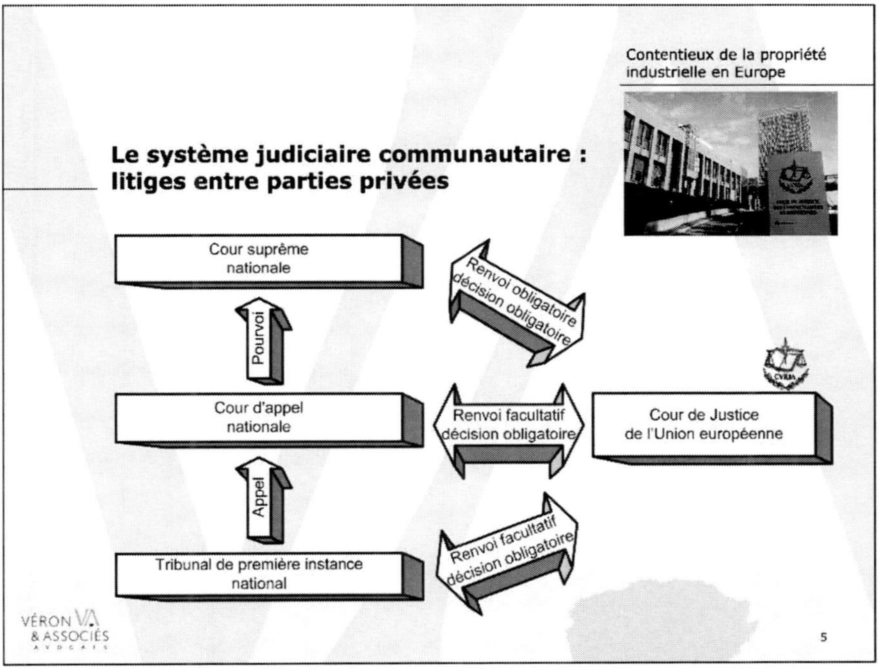

Mais, s'il advient une question de droit communautaire dans l'examen de l'affaire, la juridiction nationale a le droit et, dans certains cas, le devoir, de soumettre cette question préjudicielle à la Cour de justice de l'Union européenne.

C'est donc un système de coopération entre le juge national et la Cour de justice.

Ceci constitue le cadre des institutions juridiques qui sont en place.

Comment l'applique-t-on aux titres de propriété industrielle communautaires, ceux qui existent aujourd'hui et ceux qui n'existent pas encore ?

II. Le système juridictionnel des titres de propriété industrielle européens et communautaires

Nous parlerons de la marque communautaire et des dessins et modèles communautaires (ci-dessous A), puis de la protection communautaire des obtentions végétales (ci-dessous B), avant d'aborder le brevet européen et le futur brevet communautaires (ci-dessous C).

A. La marque et le modèle communautaire

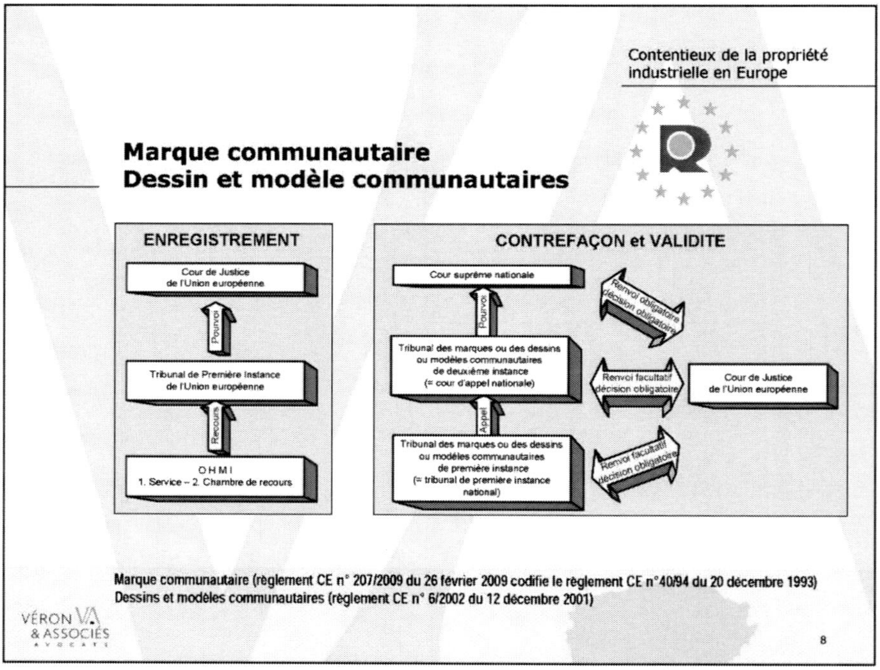

L'organisation du contentieux des marques et des dessins et modèles communautaires est complexe :

- l'enregistrement est confié à une institution communautaire qui est, en première instance, l'OHMI (Office de l'harmonisation dans le marché intérieur);
- en cas de refus d'enregistrement, le recours est porté devant la chambre de recours de l'Office ;

- un recours étant ouvert contre les décisions de l'Office devant le Tribunal de première instance puis devant la Cour de justice (cf. à gauche sur le schéma ci-dessus).

On peut voir là un contentieux à caractère administratif qui remonte sur quatre étages, en partant de l'Office pour aboutir, le cas échéant, à la Cour de justice.

Ce contentieux est devenu important; le nombre d'affaires soumises au Tribunal de première instance de l'Union européenne est désormais d'environ 200, chaque année, ce qui embouteille le Tribunal.

Certains observateurs estiment qu'il n'est peut-être pas nécessaire de mobiliser les juristes les plus éminents de l'Union européenne, pour statuer sur la distinctivité d'une forme de pastille de lessive ou de bouteille de soda et qu'il serait peut-être plus efficace de confier ce contentieux à une juridiction spécialisée.

Mais les droits de propriété industrielle sont quelquefois violés et contrefaits. Dans ce cas, les juridictions compétentes sont les juridictions, j'allais dire – mais c'est un lapsus révélateur – nationales.

Car ce ne sont pas les juridictions « nationales », puisque, par une sorte d'hypocrisie juridique, nous avons dû, dans l'Union européenne, étiqueter « juridictions communautaires » nos tribunaux nationaux pour pouvoir leur confier le contentieux de la validité des titres de propriété industrielle communautaire.

C'est la conséquence de la jurisprudence *Foto-Frost*[2] de la Cour de justice européenne selon laquelle seule la juridiction communautaire, à l'exclusion des juridictions nationales, peut se prononcer sur la validité d'un titre communautaire.

Par conséquent, nous avons baptisé nos juridictions nationales « tribunal des marques ou tribunal des dessins ou modèles communautaires de première instance et deuxième instance »: avec cette étiquette, elles ont la possibilité de statuer sur ce contentieux.

2 Cour de justice des Communautés européennes (CJCE, Cour de justice de l'Union européenne (CJUE) depuis le 1er décembre 2009), 22 octobre 1987, Foto-Frost contre Hauptzollamt Lübeck-Ost, affaire 314 / 85, Recueil de la jurisprudence de la Cour, 1987, p. 4199.

B. La protection communautaire des obtentions végétales

Le système est très similaire pour les obtentions végétales, ces sortes de brevets sur les plantes, dans lequel l'enregistrement se passe par les soins de l'Office communautaire des variétés végétales, avec une possibilité de recours.

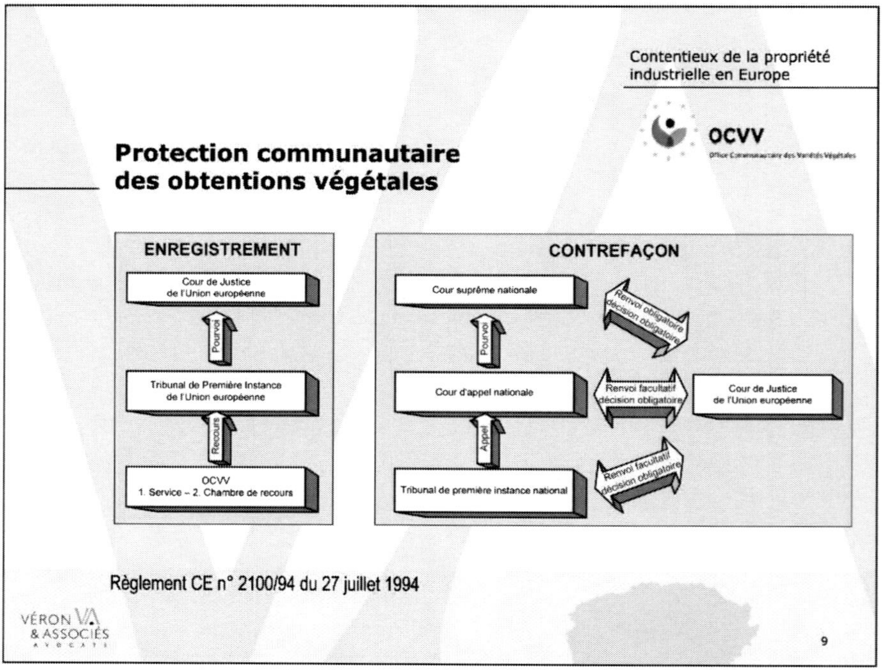

Bien que nous n'en soyons qu'à la deuxième famille de droit de propriété industrielle communautaire, nous constatons déjà une différence.

Car, si les juridictions nationales sont compétentes pour la contrefaçon, elles n'ont pas été étiquetées, cette fois-ci, « juridictions communautaires », ce qui n'est pas sans conséquence.

En effet, en pure logique, ces juridictions n'ont pas le droit de statuer sur la validité de l'enregistrement d'un certificat d'obtention végétale communautaire.

Mais cette situation présente des graves inconvénients, car l'action en nullité d'une protection d'une obtention végétale qui aurait été indûment délivrée, n'est pas prévue par les textes et la pratique est en train d'essayer de l'inventer.

Tel est l'état de l'existant pour les titres de propriété industrielle communautaire qui existent.

C. Le brevet européen et le futur brevet communautaire

Comme vous le savez, l'Europe est à géographie variable.

Car il existe au moins trois Europes juridiques, celle, politique, de Bruxelles, celle, des droits de l'homme, de Strasbourg et celle, des brevets d'invention, de Munich.

Or la Suisse est un acteur important de l'Europe du brevet européen, l'Europe de Munich.

Mais elle n'est pas membre de l'Union européenne, l'Europe communautaire qui, jusqu'à ce jour, n'a pas été capable de mettre en œuvre un système de véritable brevet communautaire.

L'état des lieux est donc complexe.

Je vais vous le rappeler (ci-dessous 1), puis vous présenter ses conséquences (ci-dessous 2), et les vœux des entreprises (ci-dessous 3) avant de passer très brièvement en revue 37 années d'effort (ci-dessous 4).

1. L'état des lieux

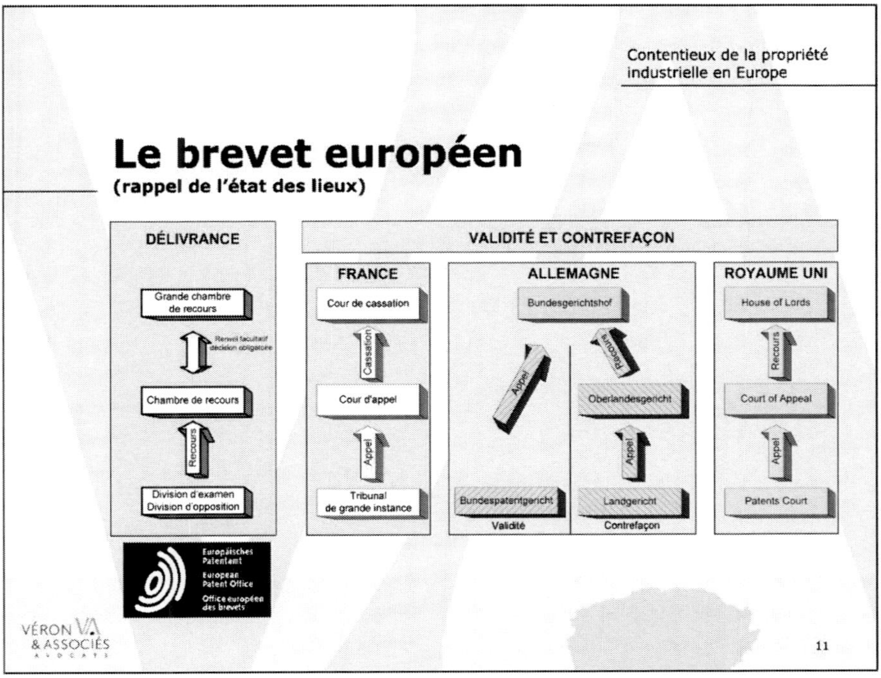

L'état des lieux aujourd'hui, vous le connaissez :

- l'Office européen des brevets examine les demandes de brevet qui lui sont soumises ;
- lorsque les conditions de brevetabilité lui paraissent réunies, il délivre le brevet ;
- si un tiers n'est pas satisfait ou si l'Office a refusé de délivrer le brevet, une opposition est possible ;
- et un recours est ouvert devant les chambres de recours de l'Office.

Cette procédure aboutit à une décision de délivrance d'un brevet européen, qui éclate, selon la formule consacrée, en un « faisceau de brevet nationaux ».

Une fois cette procédure de délivrance terminée, le dossier est fermé à Munich et les dossiers contentieux peuvent s'ouvrir, de façon parallèle et totalement indépendante, dans chacun des pays où le brevet européen produit ses effets.

Donc, s'il survient une contrefaçon multinationale, par exemple en France, en Allemagne et au Royaume-Uni, chacun des trois ordres juridictionnels pourra en être saisi séparément et en connaître de bas en haut, avec des différences selon les pays (par exemple en Allemagne, qui connaît le système de la bifurcation du contentieux de la validité de la contrefaçon).

Et chacun de ces trois ordres étatiques va pouvoir rendre des décisions indépendantes et, nous le verrons, quelquefois, contradictoires.

2. *Conséquences de l'état des lieux : forum shopping et décisions contradictoires*

Cet état des lieux génère deux phénomènes : le *forum shopping* (ci-dessous a) et les décisions contradictoires des tribunaux d'États différents (ci-dessous b).

a) Le forum shopping

La pratique a appris à vivre avec cette situation et à se livrer à ce que l'on appelle, dans les milieux qui tolèrent les anglicismes, le *forum shopping*, que nos amis canadiens appellent le *tourisme judiciaire*, c'est-à-dire à chercher à saisir le système juridictionnel que l'on présume le plus favorable.

En d'autres termes, quand un praticien est confronté à une situation de contrefaçon qui se produit dans plusieurs États, il se demande où poursuivre, et il choisit le tribunal qu'il va saisir en fonction d'un certain nombre de critères.

Je passerai rapidement en revue les principaux pays de contentieux des brevets d'invention (par le nombre d'affaire dont ils connaissent) qui sont le Royaume-Uni, l'Allemagne, les Pays-Bas et la France.

Le Royaume-Uni offre une procédure de révélation des documents pertinents (*disclosure*) et une procédure d'interrogation croisée des témoins et des experts (*cross examination*) qui est favorable à la manifestation de la vérité, plus peut-être que les procédures de type continental.

Les juges anglais sont très spécialisés, parce qu'il s'agit pour la plupart du temps d'anciens avocats spécialisés dans ce type de contentieux.

Leurs décisions sont longuement motivées, ils y expliquent leurs états d'âme et les détours de leur pensée.

Un avantage, pour certains du moins, est l'usage de la langue anglaise.

Les inconvénients, c'est, d'abord, un coût qui est analogue à celui des belles voitures anglaises de jadis.

C'est aussi, souvent, une jurisprudence peu favorable au breveté (on a souvent comparé l'Angleterre à un cimetière des brevets d'invention) avec des taux d'annulation qui, certaines années, ont atteint 100 %.

Enfin un inconvénient pour certains – mais ce qui est inconvénient pour certains est avantage pour les autres – est la langue anglaise.

L'Allemagne offre un système juridictionnel structurellement favorable au breveté, avec la division du contentieux de la validité et de la contrefaçon, puisque un peu comme avec le Trésor public français, on paye d'abord et on discute ensuite.

Car le tribunal judiciaire considère le brevet comme valable et ne se penche que sur la question de la contrefaçon.

C'est seulement en cas de doutes très sérieux, et si un recours en nullité paraissant avoir de grandes chances de succès est formé, qu'il surseoira à statuer.

Mais les décisions de sursis à statuer sont rares et, par conséquent, le système est globalement favorable aux brevetés.

Les tribunaux allemands vont vite, leurs juges sont très spécialisés et ils rendent des décisions très savamment motivées – si savamment motivées que parfois elles défient l'interprète.

L'avantage, pour ceux qui pratiquent cette langue, est l'usage de l'allemand, ce qui, en miroir, pour ceux qui ne la pratiquent pas, est un inconvénient.

L'obtention des preuves y était jusqu'ici assez difficile, mais l'entrée en vigueur de la directive 2004/48/CE du Parlement européen et du Conseil du 29 avril 2004 relative au respect des droits de propriété intellectuelle a fait évoluer les choses.

Pour ceux qui sont accusés de contrefaçon, la division du contentieux de la validité et de la contrefaçon est un inconvénient, car il ne permet pas de donner une vision aussi précise de la portée d'un brevet ; en d'autres termes, on cerne la portée d'un brevet et la contrefaçon beaucoup mieux quand on a examiné sa validité, que quand on examine abstraitement cette portée.

Les Pays-Bas ont des juges spécialisés et audacieux : n'oublions pas que ce sont eux qui ont inventé les *kort geding*, ces procédures de référé extrêmement rapides, qui permettent de mettre fin, de façon internationale à la contrefaçon.

Ils statuent rapidement et rendent des décisions bien motivées.

Le coût est continental, c'est-à-dire raisonnable.

L'obtention des preuves de la contrefaçon reste, toutefois, difficile.

Le principal inconvénient, pour beaucoup, est la pratique du néerlandais.

La France, pour terminer ce tour d'Europe judiciaire, a pour principal avantage la facilité de l'obtention des preuves : elle a inventé la saisie-contrefaçon il y a deux siècles et cet outil est toujours utile.

Nous avons désormais toujours des juges spécialisés.

En effet, depuis le mois de novembre 2009, le tribunal de grande instance de Paris a compétence exclusive pour l'ensemble du contentieux des brevets d'invention en France.

Et le contentieux des autres droits de propriété intellectuelle a été confié, depuis cette date, à un nombre réduit de tribunaux à compétence régionale.

Les décisions de ces juges sont généralement bien motivées.

Et le coût est raisonnable en comparaison des coûts insulaires.

Les inconvénients c'est, quelquefois, la brièveté de la rédaction de décisions (pour comprendre une décision de la Cour de cassation française, il faut avoir une grande pratique du style des conseillers de la cour suprême), une certaine circonspection des juges français qui ne délivrent pas facilement des décisions d'interdiction provisoire, et, dans le passé, une certaine lenteur.

Voila le catalogue des pratiques dans les différents pays d'Europe.

Quelles stratégies découlent de ce constat, pour nous les praticiens ?

En pratique, nous regardons d'abord si nous agissons pour le breveté ou pour le défendeur : si nous agissons pour un « génériqueur » qui veut faire tomber un brevet d'invention, nous envisagerons de porter le combat au Royaume-Uni, où le taux d'annulation des brevets est important.

Le siège de la partie adverse est souvent à considérer : si nous devons agir contre une fabrique d'automobiles implantée en Allemagne, nous aurons tendance à aller la poursuivre en Allemagne pour arrêter la contrefaçon à sa source.

Mais nous pouvons aussi privilégier la logistique de la contrefaçon : si les produits contrefaisants transitent nécessairement par le port d'Amsterdam, il pourra être astucieux d'attaquer aux Pays-Bas.

On peut également attaquer dans les principaux marchés ; par exemple, on sait que, dans le domaine automobile, si on gagne un procès en contrefaçon en Allemagne et en France, la question est réglée car il n'est plus possible pour une entreprise automobile de diffuser ses véhicules en Europe car la taille des marchés restants est insuffisante.

b) Les décisions contradictoires

Une des conséquences de l'éclatement du brevet européen en un faisceau de brevets nationaux est la possibilité de décisions contradictoires : chaque tribunal peut ignorer ce que les autres tribunaux européens ont jugé sur le même brevet.

Une affaire *Muller / Hilti*, célèbre dans le monde des brevets d'invention, concerne le dispositif visible en haut à droite de l'image ci-dessous, soit un collier de serrage pour les tuyaux qui économise le temps des ouvriers chargés de l'installation de ces dispositifs.

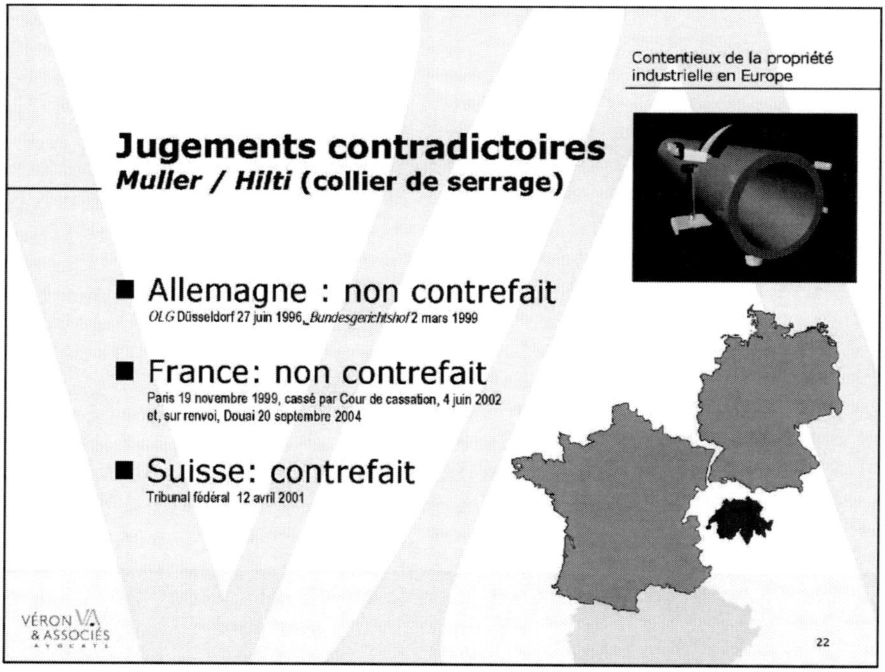

Ce brevet d'invention a donné lieu à des décisions divergentes :

- les tribunaux allemands ont estimé que la contrefaçon n'était pas constituée ;
- les tribunaux français ont été partagés, puisque la cour d'appel de Paris avait estimé que le brevet était contrefait, mais que la Cour de cassation a cassé cette décision et que, sur renvoi, la cour d'appel de Douai a estimé, en définitive, qu'il n'y avait pas de contrefaçon ;
- le brevet a été jugé valable et la contrefaçon constituée seulement en Suisse qui s'est ainsi démarquée des autres pays.

L'affaire *Documents Security System* est célèbre, également pour les décisions divergentes auxquelles elle a donné lieu : au Royaume-Uni, en France et en Autriche, le brevet a été déclaré nul, mais, en Allemagne et aux Pays-Bas, le brevet a été déclaré valable, ce qui risque de poser problème pour la circulation de la monnaie européenne si ces dernières décisions deviennent définitives :

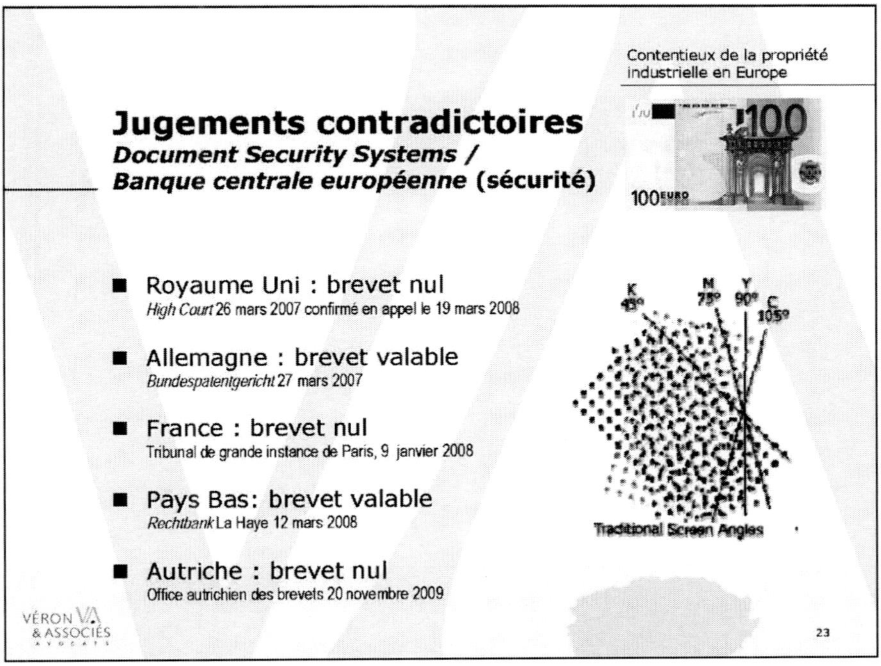

Même scénario et même paysage contradictoire pour un brevet concernant les lentilles de contact appartenant à Novartis, mis en œuvre par Ciba Vision, et opposé au groupe Johnson & Johnson : les Pays-Bas et la France, d'un côté, ont reconnu, en première instance pour l'instant, la validité du brevet et ont ordonné la cessation de la contrefaçon ; mais, d'un autre côté, le Royaume-Uni et l'Allemagne, en première instance également pour l'instant, ont rejeté les demandes, le juge anglais ayant estimé le brevet nul pour insuffisance de description bien qu'il soit jugé nouveau et témoignant d'activité inventive, tandis que le *Bundespatentgericht* a estimé que le brevet était nul pour défaut de nouveauté, bien que l'invention y soit suffisamment décrite :

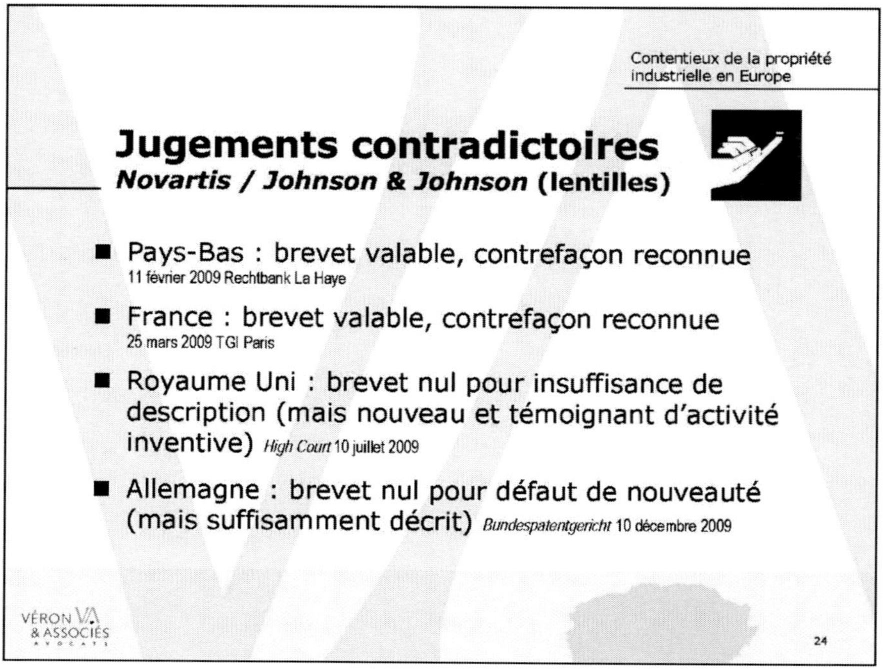

Nous avons donc ici, deux issues différentes, avec au moins trois opinions divergentes.

Mais que veulent les entreprises pour sortir de telles difficultés ?

3. *Les vœux des entreprises*

Un certain nombre d'entreprises voudraient une unité de jurisprudence et éviter d'être confrontée à une situation où leur brevet est valable dans un pays mais n'est pas valable dans un autre pays.

Elles voudraient, bien entendu, une justice de qualité, parce que l'unité sans la qualité, n'est pas un objectif souhaitable.

Elles voudraient, enfin, une praticabilité, si j'ose ce néologisme, c'est-à-dire une proximité de leurs juges et une accessibilité.

4. *37 ans de projets*

Depuis maintenant 37 ans, nous essayons de trouver un système pour sortir du scénario que je vous ai présenté.

En 1975, les plus vénérables d'entre nous s'en souviennent, a été signée la Convention de Luxembourg de 1975 sur le brevet communautaire, mais cette convention internationale signée n'a jamais été ratifiée.

Le temps passant, je ne présenterai pas ces projets : je vous décrirai seulement l'état actuel des travaux.

III. Perspectives

Aujourd'hui, est sur la table un projet d'accord (7928/09), présenté par le Conseil de l'Union européenne sur proposition de la Commission et qui est actuellement soumis à la Cour de justice pour qu'elle exprime un avis sur la compatibilité du système proposé avec le droit communautaire :

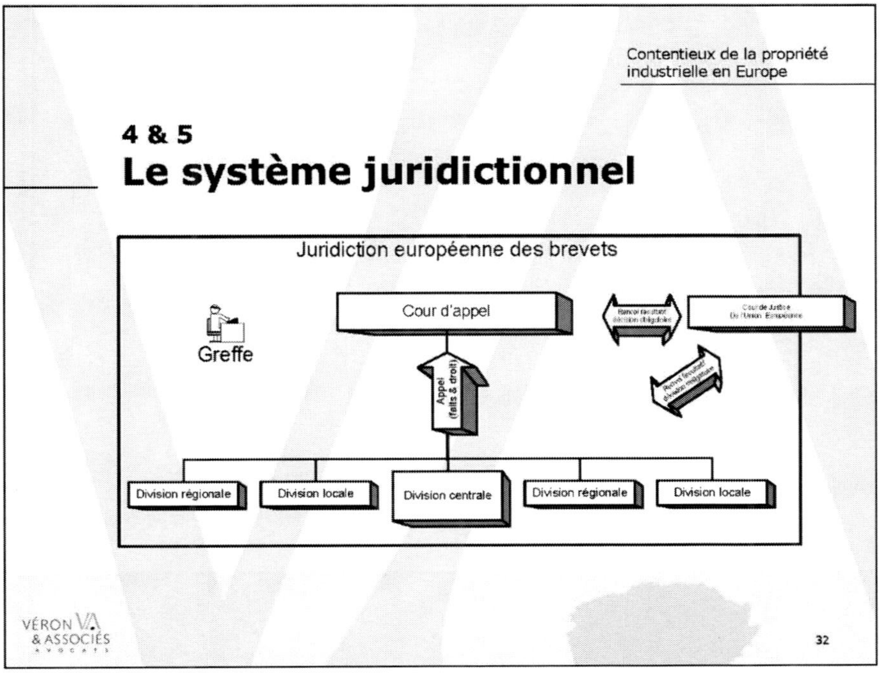

L'architecture générale comporte, au premier niveau, une division centrale et des divisions locales ou régionales (locale signifiant d'un seul État, régionale signifiant de plusieurs États ; les États constituant le Benelux, par exemple, pourront désirer constituer une division régionale).

En appel, toutes les décisions iront devant une juridiction d'appel unique.

Ce sera un appel sur les faits et sur le droit.

Ces juridictions auront le droit, et dans certain cas l'obligation, de questionner la Cour de justice de l'Union européenne sur les problèmes de droit communautaire qui se poseraient.

Une organisation différente a été envisagée, dans laquelle tout remontait à la Cour de justice, mais les praticiens et les entreprises, en particulier, ont très fermement rejeté ce système en indiquant que, comme l'expérience du contentieux des marques communautaires l'avait montré, il n'était peut-être pas souhaitable de confier à des juges, aussi savants soient-ils, un contentieux dans lequel il n'avait aucune expérience pratique, alors même que la pratique a besoin de réponses affirmées et confirmées.

L'instrument de cet accord sera nécessairement une convention internationale : il ne pourra s'agir d'un règlement communautaire puisqu'il faudra couvrir non seulement l'Union européenne, mais aussi l'Europe de l'Organisation européenne des brevets et en particulier ces deux pays importants qui diffèrent, entre autres, par le nombre de minarets, que sont la Suisse et la Turquie.

À cette convention internationale seront parties tous les États membres de l'Union européenne qui devront faire abandon de leur souveraineté nationale, qu'ils détiennent à l'heure actuelle, sur la validité et la contrefaçon des brevets européens.

Les autres pays membres de l'Organisation européenne des brevets, la Suisse notamment, devront, eux aussi, en entrant dans ce système faire abandon de leur souveraineté nationale pour statuer sur la validité et la contrefaçon des brevets européens pour la transférer à la future juridiction européenne.

Le champ d'application concernera le brevet communautaire, lorsqu'il existera, le certificat complémentaire de protection pour le brevet communautaire, le brevet européen et la demande de brevet européen.

Je vous ai déjà présenté, rapidement le système à deux étages, d'une première instance et d'une juridiction d'appel.

Quelques mots plus techniques sur la composition.

Les divisions locales seront nécessairement multinationales : elles devront comporter au moins un juge d'un autre État que celui de la division locale (en France, nous appellerons probablement un juge belge, et nos amis d'outre-quiévrain nous demanderont certainement la pareille).

Il est prévu que la division locale puisse demander le concours d'un juge technicien : *a priori*, nous allons le voir, les juges nationaux sont des juristes, mais on a pensé que, dans certains États où la pratique du contentieux des brevets d'invention est peu développée, il pourrait être souhaitable de faire venir un technicien.

Au niveau de la division centrale, qui a certaines compétences particulières, siègeront deux juges juristes et un juge technicien (« techniquement qualifié», selon la formule consacrée).

En appel, trois juges juristes et deux juges techniciens trancheront les litiges.

Le projet de convention comporte des règles de droit matériel, définit la portée d'un brevet, la contrefaçon et ses sanctions, notamment ; il comporte aussi quelques règles de conflit de lois, mais à mon sens extrêmement insuffisantes – j'espère bien que les professeurs de droit international vont rappeler à la Commission que les conflits de lois sont un sujet important.

Comment sont réglées les questions de compétence ?

- Compétence d'attribution : la future juridiction aura compétence exclusive pour les actions en contrefaçon, en déclaration de non-contrefaçon, en nullité des brevets d'invention et quelques autres actions connexes.
- Compétence territoriale : on retrouve une règle classique en matière de délits, puisque le lieu de la contrefaçon sera un forum possible pour le demandeur, un deuxième forum étant le domicile du défendeur, les défendeurs préférant être assignés à leur siège, jouer à domicile comme disent les footballeurs.

Enfin, les parties pourront choisir, d'un commun accord, un tribunal européen plutôt qu'un autre et décider que leur litige sera traité par la division centrale ou par la division anglaise, plutôt que par une division n'ayant aucune expérience.

Voyons rapidement le concours des actions.

Le cas d'une action en contrefaçon suivie d'une demande en nullité, d'abord :

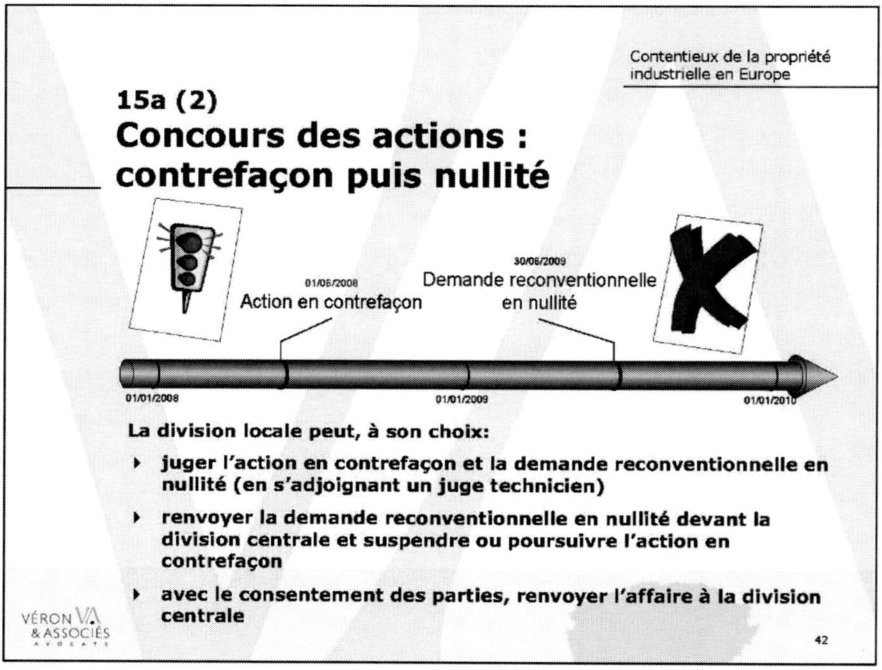

Si, sur une action en contrefaçon, se greffe une demande reconventionnelle en nullité, ce qui est un cas de figure extrêmement fréquent, la division locale pourra, à son choix :

- soit garder les deux affaires (ce qui correspond à la situation actuelle en France et au Royaume-Uni);
- soit renvoyer la demande en nullité à la division centrale et suspendre ou poursuivre l'action (ce qui correspond à la situation actuelle en Allemagne);
- soit renvoyer toute l'affaire à la division centrale.

Le cas d'une action en nullité suivie d'une demande en contrefaçon, maintenant :

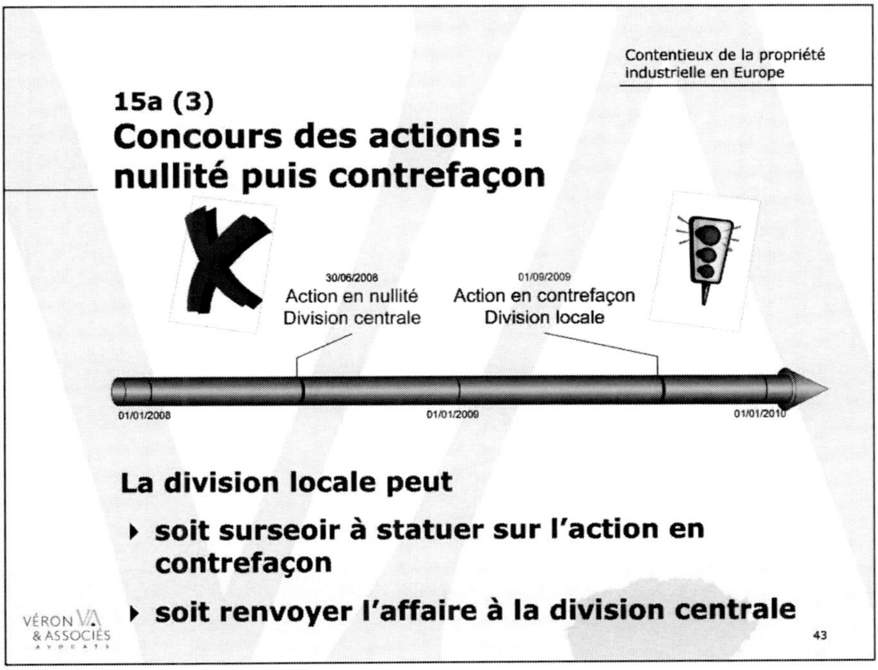

Lorsque, à l'inverse, une action en nullité est d'abord intentée devant la division centrale (une sorte de *preemptive strike*) et lorsque le titulaire du brevet réplique par une action en contrefaçon devant la division locale normalement compétente, la division locale pourra soit attendre la décision de la division centrale sur la validité, soit lui renvoyer l'ensemble de l'affaire.

Enfin, si le défendeur potentiel a pris l'initiative d'une action en non-contrefaçon, qui relève de la compétence de la division centrale, et s'il est ensuite poursuivi en contrefaçon, l'action en contrefaçon entraînera l'extinction de l'action en déclaration de non-contrefaçon, l'ensemble allant donc à la division saisie de la demande en contrefaçon.

Les effets territoriaux de la décision, s'étendront – et c'est ici la principale différence avec le système actuel – à tous les pays où le brevet européen a pris effet et, pour le brevet communautaire, à tous les pays de l'Union européenne.

Les demandeurs pourront être le breveté ou le licencié exclusif, mais pas le licencié non-exclusif, qui ne pourra qu'intervenir.

Enfin un sujet toujours délicat en Europe, celui de la langue :

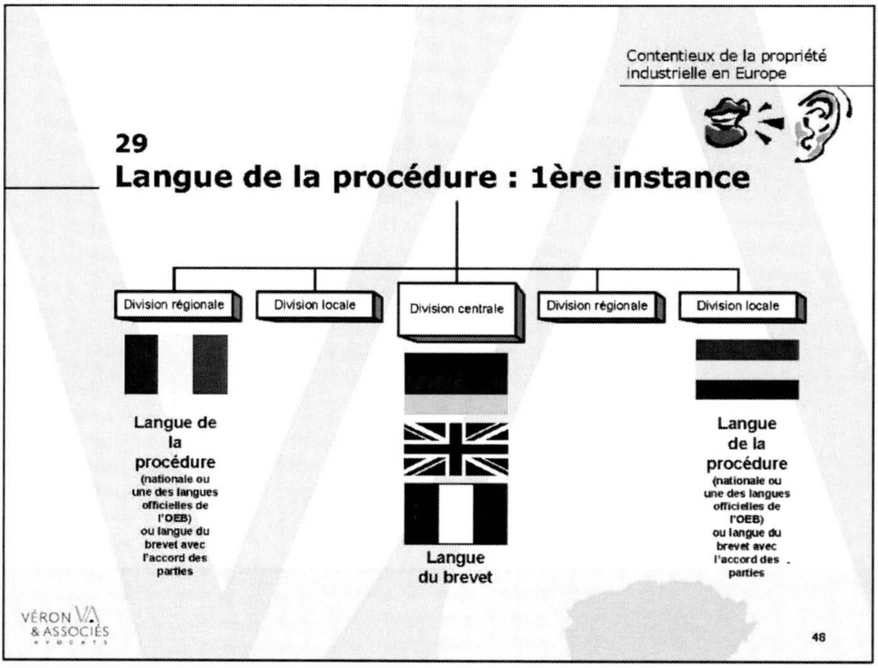

Devant les divisions régionales, on utilisera, en principe, la langue de la division nationale, mais l'usage de la langue du brevet sera possible, avec l'accord des parties et du tribunal.

Devant la division centrale, ce sera nécessairement la langue du brevet donc l'anglais, l'allemand ou le français.

En appel, la langue de première instance sera, en principe, utilisée ; la langue du brevet pourra toutefois adoptée sur accord des parties ; la juridiction pourra enfin choisir une langue qui, si elle est approuvée par les parties, sera utilisée.

Mais tout ceci n'est pas pour tout de suite, car le calendrier va impliquer d'abord un avis de la Cour de justice de l'Union européenne sur la compatibilité du projet avec les traités fondateurs de l'Union, puis des négociations internationales, un processus de signature et de ratification.

L'entrée en vigueur sera suivie d'une période transitoire, pendant lequel les titulaires de brevets européens demandés avant l'entrée en vigueur auront la faculté de dire « Pouce, je ne joue pas dans ce système » et de rester dans les systèmes juridictionnels actuels pendant 7 années : c'est ce qu'on appelle l'*opt-out*.

Le système sera au plus tôt en état de croisière dans les années 2020, mais vous serez prêts et vous en saurez déjà beaucoup sur le sujet.

Les litiges internationaux de propriété intellectuelle et le droit international privé

*Edouard Treppoz**

I. Introduction

L'internationalité du litige en PI. L'internationalité est au cœur de la propriété intellectuelle en raison de la nature immatérielle de ces biens particuliers objets de protection. Alors qu'un bien matériel a vocation à être physiquement appréhendé et donc fixé en un lieu, certes, pouvant être mobile, le bien immatériel, lui, peut être partout à la fois. Comme cela fut noté, il est doté d'ubiquité. Cette ubiquité est une force, mais aussi une faiblesse en ce qu'elle souligne les limites d'une protection simplement nationale de ces biens. Dès la fin du XIXième siècle, la réponse proposée fut la mise en place de conventions internationales tant en matière de propriété industrielle (Convention de Paris[1]) qu'en matière de droit d'auteur (Convention de Berne[2]). L'objetif de ces conventions était double : interdire toutes discriminations par la mise en place du principe du traitement national et imposer un minimum standard de protection, condition du traitement national. Un siècle plus tard, ce mouvement trouve son apogée avec l'accord sur les ADPIC de 1994 intégrant et modernisant ces conventions sous l'égide cette fois de l'Organisation Mondiale du Commerce.

Avec l'internet, les hypothèses d'internationalité du litige se multiplient. Structurellement, les causes de l'internationalité du litige sont triples. L'internationalité peut provenir de la création, du contrefacteur ou encore de la contrefaçon. La première hypothèse porte sur la contrefaçon dans un pays A d'une création étrangère à ce pays. On pense à l'article L. 335-2 du CPI français visant la contrefaçon des œuvres étrangères. La

* Agrégé des Facultés de droit, Professeur à l'Université Lyon 3.

1 Convention de Paris pour la protection de la propriété industrielle du 20 mars 1883, modifiée la dernière fois le 28 septembre 1979.

2 Convention de Berne pour la protection des œuvres littéraires et artistiques du 9 septembre 1886, modifiée la dernière fois le 28 septembre 1979.

deuxième hypothèse repose sur la nationalité étrangère d'une contrefacteur. Voici un brevet suisse contrefait en Suisse par une société française. Enfin, la contrefaçon peut, par ses dimensions, être plurilocalisée. Des copies sont faites dans un pays A pour être, ensuite, distribuées dans un pays B. L'internet ne modifie pas ces causes de l'internationalité. En revanche, d'exceptionnelles, elles deviennent presque normales. Ce renversement de la dialectique principe-exception est particulièrement visible quant à la troisième cause de l'internationalité. Une contrefaçon commise par l'internet est par essence internationale. L'affaire *Cristal*[3] témoigne à merveille de ce renversement de perspective. Avant l'internet, chaque marque, l'une espagnole pour du cava et l'autre française pour du champagne coexistait pacifiquement de chaque côté de la frontière. Avec l'internet, la coexistence est plus délicate, chaque marque étant accessible dans chacun des pays. Cette multiplication de l'internationalité des litiges se vérifie en jurisprudence et en doctrine par l'attrait croissant des intellectualistes aux thèses internationalistes.

Le recours au DIP. Pourtant, le recours aux méthodes du droit international privé pour résoudre cette dimension internationale des contentieux de propriété intellectuelle serait contesté et ce pour deux raisons. La première porte sur l'existence d'une harmonisation dans le cadre de ces grandes conventions internationales, aujourd'hui réunies au sein de l'accord sur les ADPIC. Cette harmonisation exclurait toute divergence et ainsi tout enjeu à la détermination de la loi applicable. Le conflit de lois se muerait en faux conflit en raison de l'équivalence substantielle des lois en présence. Cette présentation est évidemment excessive et accorde une bien trop grande importance à ces conventions. On notera d'abord que ces conventions n'imposent qu'un minimum de protection. Ainsi, malgré l'existence de l'article 6bis de la Convention de Berne sur le droit moral, le choix entre l'application de la loi française et de la loi américaine demeure un vrai conflit[4]. Ensuite, ces conventions n'harmonisent pas l'ensemble des questions de droit d'auteur ou de propriété industrielle. Ainsi et pour rester dans le registre du droit d'auteur,

3 Cass. civ. 1ère, 9 décembre 2003, *Cristal :* n° 01-03225 ; Rev. Crit. DIP, 2004, p. 632 note O. Cachard ; JDI 2004, p. 872, note A. Huet ; JCP 2004.II.10055 note C. Chabert ; D. 2004, p. 276 obs. C. Manara ; Procédures 2004, n° 52 obs. C. Nourissat ; RTDCom 2004, p. 281 obs. F. Pollaud-Dulian et LPA 23 février 2005, n° 38, p. 5 note C. Brière.

4 Voir notamment, *Dastar Corp. v. Twentieth Century Fox Film*, 539 U. S. 23 (2003) et Jane C. Ginsburg, The Right to Claim Authorship in US Copyright and Trademark Law, 41 Houston Law Review 2004, p. 263.

rien n'est dit quant à la détermination du titulaire originaire du droit. Le constat serait le même en matière de propriété industrielle. C'est donc reconnaître la persistance de vrais conflits de lois en matière de propriété intellectuelle, malgré ce travail d'harmonisation.

La seconde raison contestant le recours au droit international privé est plus profonde et repose sur le dogme, en la matière, du principe de territorialité. L'apparente internationalité de ces litiges serait contestée par une puissante doctrine italienne[5] mais aussi suisse[6], ne voyant là que des situations purement internes excluant ainsi tout recours au droit international privé. Selon cette doctrine, l'atteinte dans un pays ne pourrait porter que sur un titre de propriété de ce pays et non sur un titre de propriété étranger. L'explication proviendrait alors du principe de territorialité limitant territorialement l'application des lois de propriété intellectuelle. Toujours selon cette doctrine, la contrefaçon serait limitée aux frontières d'un pays et ne pourrait s'étendre sur plusieurs pays, à l'instar de la figure du délit dissocié. La prétendue contrefaçon internationale résultant de la fabrication dans un pays A d'un ouvrage contrefaisant et de la diffusion dans un pays B de cet ouvrage laisserait place à deux contrefaçons internes et distinctes, comme en témoigne d'ailleurs l'existence du délit de débit d'ouvrage contrefaisant. Impressionnante, cette thèse ne doit pas pour autant minimiser l'importance du droit international privé. D'abord, le principe de territorialité justifiant cette analyse interne de ces litiges est une réponse offerte par le droit international privé. Ensuite et surtout, le principe de territorialité ne constitue pas l'unique réponse offerte par le droit international privé à ces litiges. Nous pensons, au contraire, que ce principe de territorialité possède aujourd'hui « une légitimité déclinante »[7] pour reprendre l'expression de l'auteur d'un récent cours à l'Académie de droit international de La Haye sur ces questions. Nous verrons ainsi qu'un juge, autre que le juge du titre, peut être compétent pour se prononcer sur une contrefaçon qui ne s'est pas produite sur son territoire. Nous verrons aussi qu'une loi autre que la loi

5 Riccardo Luzzatto, Problemi Internazionalprivatistici del Diritto di Autore, Studio in Memoria di Mario Giuliano, Cedam, Padoue 1989 p. 589 et s.

6 François Perret, Territorialité des droits de la propriété industrielle et compétence « extraterritoriale » du juge de la contrefaçon, Etudes en l'honneur de J.-F. Poudret, Lausanne, 1999, p. 147.

7 Dario Moura Vicente, La propriété intellectuelle en droit international privé, Les livres de poche de l'Académie de droit international de La Haye, 2009, p. 24.

de protection peut être appliquée, dotant ainsi cette loi d'extra-territorialité tout en créant un principe de dépendance. Il reste, comme le notait Zwiegert qu'il existe « entre le conflit de lois et la territorialité le même rapport qu'entre l'eau et le feu : ou bien l'eau de la territorialité éteint le feu, ou bien le feu de ces dernières fait évaporer le principe de territorialité»[8]. Il est donc loin d'être certain que la territorialité ait éteint le feu du conflit de lois.

Vers des solutions uniformes de DIP ? Dès lors, si le recours aux méthodes de droit international privé s'impose, chaque pays aura vocation à reglementer ces litiges internationaux. Ainsi, si le juge français est compétent, le droit international privé français sera applicable, distinct de la loi suisse de droit international privé applicable à la suite d'une saisine du juge suisse. Là encore, il faudrait s'interroger sur une éventuelle harmonisation, non plus des règles internes, mais des règles de droit international privé. Cette harmonisation résulterait toujours des grandes conventions internationales, mais cette fois par l'intermédiaire du principe du traitement national lu comme consacrant une règle de conflit. Nous verrons pourtant que cette lecture du principe du traitement national consacrant une règle de conflit est aujourd'hui légitimement critiquée, excluant toute lecture conflictualiste de ces conventions. Si l'harmonisation existe, elle est aujourd'hui régionalement limitée notamment au sein de l'Union Européenne. On rappellera que, dans cet espace, la détermination du juge compétent dépend de critères harmonisés au sein du règlement Bruxelles I[9], tandis que la loi applicable dépend du Règlement Rome II[10]. Pourtant, là encore, les divergences, notamment quant à la place à accorder à la loi du droit, semblent perdurer[11]. L'harmonisation pourrait alors provenir de codifications savantes dont l'influence doctrinale n'est plus à prouver. Le scepticisme est, là encore, néanmoins de

8 Zweigert cité par Mercedes Novier, La propriété intellectuelle en droit international privé suisse, Droz, Genève 1996, p. 45, note 92.

9 Règlement (CE) n° 44/2001 du Conseil du 22 décembre 2000 concernant la compétence judiciaire, la reconnaissance et l'exécution des décisions en matière civile et commerciale.

10 Règlement (CE) n° 864/2007 du Parlement européen et du Conseil du 11 juillet 2007 sur la loi applicable aux obligations non contractuelles.

11 En ce sens, notamment : Nerina Boschiero, Infringement of Intellectual Property Rights – A Commentary of Article 8 of the Rome II Regulation, Yearbook of Private International Law, Volume 9, 2007, p. 103.

rigueur. L'explication est simple. Les Principes ALI[12] se voient aujourd' hui concurrencés par d'autres codifications au premier rang desquelles les Principes CLIP[13]. Or, ces codifications divergent quant à la détermination de la loi applicable et du juge compétent, soulignant d'autant les divergences nationales[14].

Nécessité de dissocier le *for* et le *legis*. Cette absence d'uniformité au stade des règles de droit international privé souligne l'importance de la détermination du juge. C'est en effet en déterminant le juge que les parties connaîtront le système de droit international privé qui s'appliquera à leur litige par essence international. Il est, en effet, bien connu aujourd'hui que la détermination du juge ne vaut application de loi matérielle de ce dernier. Comme le note opportunément la section 103 des Principes ALI « competence to adjudicate does not imply application of the forum State's substantive law». Les questions sont distinctes et appellent des méthodes distinctes. Tandis que l'une, la détermination du juge, est nécessairement unilatérale, l'autre, la détermination de la loi applicable, est, par principe, bilatérale. Distinctes, ces questions sont néanmoins soumises aux mêmes problématiques que sont la place du principe de territorialité ou encore l'analyse des délits complexes. Pour autant, si les problématiques sont communes, les réponses divergeront selon que la question porte au final sur la détermination du juge ou de la loi. La difficulté, classique du droit international privé, porte alors sur l'ordre de présentation. Faut-il débuter par la détermination du juge ou de la loi ? La question étant ici celle des litiges, la dimension contentieuse apparaît comme principale, justifiant dès lors de débuter par la détermination du juge pour envisager ensuite celle de la loi applicable.

12 Principes de l'American Law Institute relatifs à la compétence juridictionnelle, au choix du droit applicable et aux jugements dans les litiges transnationaux concernant la propriété intellectuelle. Une version française des principes établie par François Dessemontet a été publiée dans le Bulletin CEDIDAC n° 51 et est accessible à: http://www.unil.ch/webdav/site/cedidac/shared/Bulletins/Bulletin_no_5 1.pdf.

13 *Principles for Conflict of Laws in Intellectual Property* du Max-Planck Insitute.

14 Edouard Treppoz, Un autre regard : étude comparée des Principes de l'American Law Institute et du Max Planck Institute sur le droit international privé et la propriété intellectuelle, Droit international privé et propriété intellectuelle : un nouveau cadre pour de nouvelles stratégies, Kluwer 2010 (à paraître).

II. La détermination du juge compétent

La détermination du juge compétent est une question fondamentale de la propriété intellectuelle et hautement stratégique, comme en témoigne le développement d'actions torpilles et d'actions contre torpilles[15] au détriment sans doute des objectifs de simplicité et de rapidité portés par l'article 41 ADPIC.

Au-delà de ces questions stratégiques, deux difficultés doivent ici être envisagées. La première porte sur le domaine de l'exclusivité du juge du titre avec comme enjeu l'existence ou non d'une compétence extra-territoriale du juge de la contrefaçon. La seconde résulte de la détermination de ce juge de la contrefaçon lorsque cette dernière est commise par l'internet.

A. L'exclusivité du juge du titre

L'exclusivité du juge du titre suscite un abondant contentieux marquant une opposition nette entre les pays de *common law* et les pays de *civil law*[16]. Les uns adoptent une approche territorialiste, tandis que les autres se positionnent en faveur d'une approche universaliste. C'est finalement une approche mixte, et à nos yeux critiquable, qui semble se dessiner en droit communautaire.

La tendance territorialiste. Selon la tendance territorialiste, l'exclusivité du juge du titre s'étend aux actions en contrefaçon et ce, que l'action soit fondée sur un droit de propriété industrielle ou un droit d'auteur. Les conséquences d'une telle tendance sont profondes. Le juge du domicile du défendeur est incompétent pour se prononcer sur une contrefaçon commise dans un autre pays, la compétence du juge étant limitée aux contrefaçons commises sur son territoire. Cette exclusivité au stade du juge se répercute alors sur la loi applicable. En effet, comme nous le verrons, la solution encore dominante reste l'application de la loi de protection, soit la loi de la contrefaçon. En l'espèce, une telle loi sera celle du juge. On comprend dès lors que cette lecture territorialiste

15 Voir particulièrement, Mario Franzosi, Worlwide Patent Litigation and the Italian Torpedo, EIPR 1997, p. 382.

16 Pour une présentation en droit comparé: Laurence Brüning-Petit, Le contentieux judiciaire de la contrefaçon, Thèse Lyon 3, 2006, n° 115 ss et aussi Marta Petergas Sender, Cross-Border Enforcement of Patent Rights, Oxford, 2002, p. 164 ss.

puisse occulter l'intérêt du droit international privé, tant la situation semble finalement se décomposer en une multitude de situations internes.

Cette tendance connaît un succès croissant dans les systèmes de *common law*. On citera, en ce sens, une décision américaine *Voda v. Cordis Corporation*[17] refusant d'étendre la compétence des tribunaux américains à des contrefaçons de brevets commises en dehors des Etats-Unis. Toutefois, la décision la plus exemplaire reste la très récente et très riche décision anglaise opposant *Lucas Film* à un concepteur anglais de casque des troupes d'assaut du film *Star Wars*. Si en première instance[18], le juge avait accepté d'étendre sa compétence fondée sur le domicile du défendeur aux contrefaçons commises par ce dernier aux Etats Unis, le juge d'appel[19] s'y refuse limitant ainsi territorialement sa compétence, même en matière de droit d'auteur, aux contrefaçons commises sur son territoire. L'explication proviendrait de la nature locale de ces actions justifiant qu'elles soient traitées par un juge local. Sans doute aussi, ne faut-il pas sous-estimer dans cette affaire les réticences du juge anglais à s'octroyer unilatéralement une telle compétence, indépendamment de toute harmonisation en matière de reconnaissance et de litispendance. On notera d'ailleurs que, dans cette affaire, *Lucas Film* avait obtenu aux Etats-Unis un jugement par défaut condamnant le concepteur anglais. La reconnaissance de cette décision en Angleterre aurait dès lors dû justifier l'incompétence des tribunaux anglais sur cette portion du litige. Cette réticence à une extra-territorialité unilatérale permet alors de comprendre la distinction faite par le juge anglais entre cette affaire mettant en cause un demandeur américain et l'affaire *Pearce*[20] mettant en cause un demandeur hollandais. Dans cette dernière affaire et en raison de sa dimension communautaire, le juge anglais considère qu'il est compétent pour se prononcer sur cette contrefaçon commise en Hollande. On le voit, même les systèmes territorialistes s'ouvrent à l'universalisme.

17 *Voda v. Cordis Corporation* [2007] U. S. C.A. Fed. 29, 476 F.3d 887 (Fed. 2007).

18 *LucasFilm Limited v. A. Ainsworth*, High Court, 31 juillet 2008, (2008) EWHC 1878 (Ch).

19 *Lucasfilm Ltd and others v. Ainsworth and another*, [2009] EWCA Civ 1328; [2009] WLR (D) 368.

20 *Pearce v. Ove Aruo Partnership Limited and Others*, High Court, 7 mars 1997, IIC 1998, p. 833. Pour une confirmation de cette solution, voir: *Mother Bertha MusicLimited v. Bourne Music Limited*, High Court, 31 juillet 1997, IIC 1998, p. 613. Sur ces arrêts: LAWRENCE J. COHEN, Intellectual Property and the Brussels Convention, EIPR 1997, p. 379.

La tendance universaliste. La tendance universaliste suppose alors de circonscrire clairement le domaine de l'exclusivité du juge du titre. Le juge ne serait exclusivement compétent que pour les litiges portant sur la validité du titre ou l'inscription, limités dès lors à la propriété industrielle. En conséquence, le juge du domicile du défendeur serait compétent pour tous types de contentieux en matière de droit d'auteur, indépendamment de la localisation de ces contentieux. Mieux, même en matière de propriété industrielle, le juge du domicile serait compétent pour se prononcer sur une contrefaçon commise à l'étranger. Ce domaine attribué à l'exclusivité a pour avantage d'être cohérent avec la justification d'une telle exclusivité. On sait en effet que le principe de souveraineté postule la compétence exclusive du juge de l'Etat pour juger de l'activité des services publics de cet Etat[21]. Dès lors, l'intervention d'un service public au stade de l'enregistrement conduit à retenir une compétence exclusive des tribunaux de l'Etat du service public. Cette justification restreint d'autant le domaine de cette exclusivité qui doit être limité au fonctionnement du service public. Il semble ainsi juste qu'en droit d'auteur l'exclusivité ne soit pas justifiée, tout comme en matière de contrefaçon.

Telle est la position de la Cour de justice des communautés européennes. Cette dernière a pu juger que la notion de «litige en matière d'inscription et de validité de brevet» ne recouvre pas un différent sur la titularité[22]. Se faisant, la Cour confirme la nature restrictive de l'exclusivité du juge du titre, soulignant que pour »les autres actions, y compris les actions en contrefaçon, les règles générales de la Convention sont applicables»[23]. Ainsi, le juge français du domicile du défendeur serait compétent pour se prononcer sur une contrefaçon d'un brevet allemand commise en Allemagne, ce que reconnaît désormais même un juge anglais[24]. On citera, en ce sens, un arrêt du tribunal fédéral[25] suisse retenant

21 Dernièrement: Dominique Bureau & Horatia Muir-Watt, Droit international privé, PUF, 2007, T. I, n° 73 y voyant un défaut international de pouvoir juridictionnel

22 CJCE, 15 novembre 1983, Duijnstee: aff. 288/82, Rev. Crit. DIP, 1984.361, note G. Bonet.

23 Op. cit., n° 23.

24 *Pearce v. Ove Aruo Partnership Limited and Others*, High Court, 7 mars 1997, IIC 1998, p. 833.

25 ATF 129 III 295, JdT 2003 I 367.

sur le fondement de la Convention de Lugano la compétence des tribunaux suisses pour se prononcer sur une contrefaçon commise en dehors de la Suisse.

La tendance mixte. Si formellement, cette tendance universaliste perdure en droit communautaire, elle semblefragilisée en pratique. L'explication provient d'une difficulté courante en pratique, lorsque le défendeur soulève à titre d'exception la nullité du titre. Cette exception portant sur une matière objet de l'exclusivité justifie-t-elle la compétence du juge du titre et donc l'incompétence du juge du domicile ou doit-elle être considérée comme indifférente à l'égard de la compétence du juge du domicile ? Complexe, cette question a fait l'objet d'un traitement jurisprudentiel divergent par les juridictions nationales alimenté en grande partie par une différence terminologique entre les différentes versions linguistiques du règlement. Ainsi, alors que l'article 25 du Règlement Bruxelles I vise « le juge (...) saisi à titre principal » pour imposer à tout juge d'un autre Etat membre de se déclarer incompétent, le même article dans sa version anglaise retient *« which is principally concerned »*. Saisie de cette question dans l'arrêt *Gat*, la Cour de justice se prononce en faveur d'une large exclusivité en notant que « la règle de compétence exclusive (...) concerne tous les litiges portant sur l'inscription ou la validité d'un brevet que la question soit soulevée par voie d'action ou d'exception »[26]. C'est cette interprétation que consacrera la Convention de Lugano dans version révisée du 30 octobre 2007 retenant l'exclusivité du juge du titre aux questions de validité « que la question soit soulevée par voie d'action ou d'exception» (art. 22 al. 4).

En théorie, la Cour de justice et la Convention continuent ainsi à exclure du domaine de l'exclusivité le contentieux de la contrefaçon. Toutefois, en pratique, le juge de la contrefaçon qui ne serait pas le juge du titre dispose d'une compétence faible que le défendeur peut contester à tout moment en soulevant une exception portant sur la validité du titre. Ainsi, le titulaire d'un brevet européen contrefait dans chacun des pays couvert par ledit brevet par une même contrefacteur peut saisir les juridictions du domicile du contrefacteur pour l'ensemble du contentieux. Néanmoins, en pratique, il a désormais tout intérêt à fragmenter nationalement ses actions, et sans doute à les limiter là où les pertes sont les plus importantes. Le résultat pratique de cette interprétation est finalement proche de celui préconisé par la tendance territorialiste. Au delà

26 CJCE, 13 juillet 2006, GAT, aff. 4/03 : Rev. Crit. DIP, 2007, p. 777, article M. Wilderspin ; CCE, 2007, Etude 10, article M.-E. Ancel.

de sa faiblesse pratique, cette solution a pu être critiquée sur un plan théorique en raison des effets procéduraux distincts selon que la question est soulevée par voie d'action ou d'exception. Seule la réponse apportée à la première est en effet dotée d'effet *erga omnes*[27]. On comprend alors que la Convention de La Haye du 30 juin 2005 sur les accords d'élection de for (art. 2 al. 3) tout comme les Principes ALI (211(2)) retiennent une solution inverse. La question est à l'étude dans le cadre de la révision du Règlement de Bruxelles I, il serait sage que sur ce point le texte de révision vienne combattre la jurisprudence *Gat*[28].

B. Le juge de la contrefaçon et les cyber-délits

La seconde question délicate en matière de compétence porte sur la détermination du juge face à une hypothèse de contrefaçon plurilocalisée. La pluri-localisation résulte d'une dissociation entre le fait générateur, soit la fabrication des exemplaires contrefaisants, et le dommage, soit la distribution des exemplaires contrefaisants. Cette pluri-localisation est d'une actualité particulière lorsque le délit est commis par l'internet. Deux problématiques en découlent : celle de la qualification du délit et celle de la localisation des éléments constitutifs.

La qualification du délit. La qualification du délit est une problématique aussi délicate qu'importante. Elle suppose de revenir un instant sur une distinction fondamentale posée par un maître français du droit international privé, le Professeur Pierre Bourel, entre les parcelles d'activités délictuelles et les délits dissociés[29]. L'analyse en terme de parcelle décompose l'activité délictuelle en une pluralité de délits distincts, chacun de ces délits se localisant entièrement au sein d'un Etat. La conséquence de cette analyse porte sur la compétence juridictionnelle de chacun des Etats où se localise un des délits composant la parcelle d'activité délictuelle. Les tribunaux de l'Etat du lieu de fabrication sont compétents pour se prononcer sur la nature contrefaisante des fabrications

27 Voir déjà: Paul Lagarde, Application de la Convention d'exécution aux actions en contrefaçons de brevets nationaux, in Droit international et Actions en contrefaçons de brevet dans la CEE, PIBD, 1974.49.

28 En ce sens, notamment : James Fawcett, Special Rules of Private International Law for Special Cases : What Should We Do About Intellectual Property, Essay in Honour of Sir Peter North, Oxford University Press, 2003, p. 137 s.

29 Pierre Bourel, Les conflits de lois en matière d'obligations extracontractuelles, LGDJ Paris, 1961, p. 65 s.

commises dans ce pays. Tout comme les tribunaux de l'Etat du lieu de diffusion sont compétents pour se prononcer sur ces diffusions. A l'inverse, la seconde analyse appréhende la situation délictuelle unitairement, opérant une distinction entre son fait générateur et son dommage. L'analyse est alors celle de la Cour de justice des communautés européenne dans l'arrêt *Fiona Shevill*[30] qualifiant une hypothèse de diffamation transfrontalière de délit dissocié entre son fait générateur, l'édition et son (ou ses) dommage(s), la diffusion des journaux. Pour la Cour de justice, les tribunaux de l'Etat du fait générateur possèdent une compétence générale pour appréhender le délit dissocié, alors que les tribunaux du dommage ne sont compétents qu'à hauteur du dommage subi dans ce pays. Rapporté à la propriété intellectuelle, c'est reconnaître que le juge du lieu de fabrication possède une compétence extra-territoriale s'étendant à la fabrication et à la diffusion des marchandises contrefaisantes, tandis que le juge du lieu de diffusion verrait sa compétence limitée aux diffusions localisées dans ce pays. Le débat n'est donc pas que doctrinal et comprend des enjeux pratiques importants.

Or, sur ce point, la jurisprudence peine à se prononcer clairement comme en témoigne la position de la Cour de cassation française. Cette dernière s'est d'abord clairement prononcée en faveur d'une application de la matrice *Fiona Shevill* à ces hypothèses de contrefaçons. Ces dernières sont alors qualifiées de délits complexes justifiant de dissocier le délit entre le fait générateur et le ou les lieux de survenance du dommage. Si le domicile du contrefacteur localise le fait générateur, la diffusion des marchandises contrefaisantes marque la survenance du dommage. Cette solution sera confirmée et, ensuite, étendue aux contrefaçons commises par l'internet avec l'arrêt *Cristal* selon lequel « l'option posée par l'article 5-3, de la Convention de Saint-Sébastien du 26 mai 1989 applicable en la cause, doit s'entendre en ce que la victime peut exercer son action soit devant la juridiction de l'Etat du lieu d'établissement de l'auteur de la contrefaçon, compétente pour réparer l'intégralité du préjudice qui en résulte, soit devant la juridiction de l'Etat contractant dans lequel l'objet de la contrefaçon se trouve diffusé, apte à connaître seulement des dommages subis dans cet Etat»[31]. Il semble, pourtant, que la Cour ait

30 CJCE, 7 mars 1995 : C. 68/93 ; Rev. Crit. DIP, 1996, p. 487 note P. Lagarde ; JDI 1995, p. 543 obs. A. Huet ; *Europe* 6/1995, chron. n° 7, obs. L. Idot et D. 1996. J.61 note G. Parléani.

31 *Supra* note 3.

récemment marqué une évolution avec un arrêt *Saint Tropez*[32]. L'affaire portait sur une contrefaçon de vêtements protégés par le droit d'auteur. Une société française découvre, par l'entremise d'un de ses distributeurs, qu'une société danoise propose à la vente en Allemagne des modèles très proches de ses créations. Elle décide alors de faire commander en France, par une boutique, les modèles contrefaisants et, une fois les cartons de vêtements réceptionnés, d'assigner en contrefaçon la société danoise devant le tribunal de commerce de Paris. La Cour de cassation justifie la compétence des tribunaux français au motif que le fait dommageable, la commande de marchandises, s'était produit en France. Outre la question d'une éventuelle manipulabilité du critère de rattachement, l'arrêt est intéressant par la qualification retenue de la diffusion de fait dommageable et non plus de dommage. Autrement dit, en substituant le fait dommageable au dommage, la Cour de cassation passe d'une analyse en terme de délit dissocié à une analyse en terme de parcelles d'activités délictuelles. Il ne s'agit plus de localiser un délit pluri-localisé, mais de localiser une pluralité de délits omnilocalisés. La compétence des tribunaux français se déduit alors directement de l'article 5.3 localisant le fait dommageable, sans passer par le truchement de la jurisprudence *Fiona Shevill* localisant le dommage.

Que penser de ces évolutions ? La qualification de parcelles possède un certain nombre d'arguments non négligeables[33]. Elle repose, d'abord, sur la projection en droit international privé de l'analyse de droit interne, selon laquelle la copie et sa distribution constituent chacune un délit distinct. Dès lors, projeté en droit international privé, chacun de ces délits devrait être traité indépendamment. Ensuite, cette solution est présentée comme directement dictée par le principe de territorialité. Aucun délit n'aurait vocation à dépasser les frontières d'un Etat, puisque l'atteinte porterait sur le titre national de propriété intellectuelle limité aux frontières de l'Etat qui l'a délivré. Toutefois, selon nous[34], cette qualification

32 Civ. 1, 25 mars 2009 : n° 08-14.119, D. 2009. 1015, obs. X. Delpech ; Revue Procédures, 2009, comm. 151, obs. C. Nourissat ; JCP 2009. act. 194, obs. E. Cornut et Rev. Crit. DIP, 2009, p. 580, note E. Treppoz.

33 Voir particulièrement en matière de conflit de juridictions : Jérôme Passa, Droit de la propriété industrielle, LGDJ Paris, T. 1, n° 429.

34 Dans le même sens : marie-élodie ancel, Contrefaçon de marque sur un site web : quelle compétence intracommunautaire pour les tribunaux français, Etude à la mémoire du Professeur Xavier Linant de Bellefonds, Litec, 2007, p. 1-24 spéc. n° 11 et dans le même sens, Arnaud Nuyts, Suing At the Place of Infringement : The Application of Article 5(3) of Regulation 44/2001 to IP Matters and Internet

nationale n'exclut pas une qualification communautaire de délit complexe dissocié entre son événement causal et sa matérialisation au sens du Règlement de Bruxelles I. La qualification est autre simplement parce que les objectifs des textes diffèrent. L'un des objectifs du Règlement est d'harmoniser les différents droits nationaux. Or, cette harmonisation serait de pure façade si la qualification d'une situation délictuelle et donc, au final, les fors compétents, dépendaient des différentes lois nationales (voir en ce sens le point 19 de l'arrêt *Marinari*[35]). Il est donc cohérent que la Cour de justice mène une analyse matérielle et non juridique de la situation délictuelle, afin de localiser cette situation pour fonder la compétence du for délictuel[36]. Dès lors, la localisation du fait dommageable dépendrait non pas de l'atteinte portée au titre de propriété intellectuelle, mais de l'atteinte portée à l'objet de protection : le signe, l'invention ou encore l'œuvre. Ainsi comprise, l'atteinte peut s'analyser en un délit unique dissocié entre son fait générateur, la copie, et son dommage, la distribution, conformément à la « matrice »[37] *Fiona Shevill.*

La localisation des éléments constitutifs du délit. La problématique se déplace alors de la qualification à la localisation des éléments constitutifs du délit ainsi dissocié. La localisation du délit ne pose, en apparence, guère de difficulté pour des hypothèses de contrefaçon résultant de la distribution dans des pays B, C et D, de copies effectuées en A. La copie localiserait le fait générateur, tandis que chacune des distributions localiserait une partie du dommage. Il semble toutefois possible d'affiner ces localisation, afin notamment de prendre en compte les hypothèses de contrefaçons commises par l'internet.

La localisation du fait générateur par la copie serait, notamment, perfectible car trop fragile et manipulable. L'affinement proposé suppose de remonter à une localisation économique du fait générateur, au travers de l'établissement de son auteur. On notera, en ce sens, que dans l'arrêt *Fiona Shevill*[38], la Cour de justice localise le fait générateur, non par la publication, mais par l'établissement de l'éditeur de la publication.

Disputes, *in* International Litigation in Intellectual Property and Information Technology, A. Nuyts (éd.), Wolters Kluwer, 2008, p. 117.

35 CJCE, 19 sept. 1995, *Marinari :* aff. C-364/93.

36 Rapp. André Huet, L'incidence de la territorialité des marques et des brevets nationaux sur la compétence des tribunaux français en matière de contrefaçon, Mélanges offerts à Jean Jacques Burst, Litec, Paris 1997, p. 264.

37 Ancel, *supra* note 34.

38 *Supra* note 30.

Transposé à une hypothèse de contrefaçon, le rattachement ne dépend plus de la localisation de la copie, mais de l'établissement de l'auteur de la contrefaçon, comme l'a opportunément retenu la Cour de cassation française[39]. L'avantage de cette localisation repose sur sa pertinence lorsque le fait générateur est commis sur l'internet. En effet, le lieu de la copie sur le réseau est par trop manipulable pour offrir une localisation objective. En revanche, la localisation de l'auteur de la copie, parce qu'extérieure au réseau, limite les risques de manipulations.

Pour la localisation du dommage, l'affinement proposé par une partie de la doctrine supposerait, cette fois, de descendre de la localisation matérielle du dommage par la distribution à une localisation économique au domicile de la victime. Cet affinement aurait l'avantage d'éviter un éparpillement des dommages au profit d'un dommage unique. Surtout, il permettrait, lorsque la diffusion s'effectue par l'internet, d'offrir un rattachement extérieur au réseau. Pourtant, la jurisprudence communautaire ne semble pas favorable à une telle localisation, au motif qu'elle conférerait un *forum actoris*[40]. Il faut alors se résoudre à localiser le ou les dommages aux lieux de diffusions. Ce refus d'affinement et d'extériorisation par le domicile de la victime pose alors avec acuité la question de la localisation du dommage lorsque la diffusion s'effectue par l'internet. Deux thèses s'affrontent ! La première, défendue notamment par la Cour de cassation française avec constance[41], repose sur l'accessibilité du site. Selon cette thèse, le dommage se localiserait en tout point où le site internet serait accessible et ce, que le site soit ou non actif. Cette localisation large du dommage aboutit à conférer aux tribunaux français une compétence universelle en matière de cyber-délits, les sites internet étant par principe accessibles universellement. L'autre thèse suppose, au contraire, de prendre en compte l'activité du site et ainsi de subordonner la localisation du dommage dans un pays à l'activité de ce site vers ce pays. Toute

39 Cass. civ. 1ère, 9 décembre 2003, *Cristal:* n° 01-03225, *supra* note 3. et Cass. com., 20 mars 2007 : n° 04-19679 ; Rev. Crit. DIP, 2008, p. 322, note E. Treppoz ; JCP G 2007.II.10088, note M.-E. Ancel ; CCE 2007, comm 150, obs. M. Malaurie-Vignal ; CCE 2007, comm. 119, obs. C. Caron et Prop. Int., 2007, p. 349 obs. J. Passa.

40 CJCE, 11 janvier 1990, *Dumez*: aff C-220/88 ; point 16 ; Rev. Crit. DIP, 1990, p. 368, note H. Gaudemet-Tallon et JDI 1991, p. 467, obs. A. Huet ; CJCE, 19 sept. 1995, *Marinari :* aff. C-364/93 ; point 22 : JDI, 1996.562 obs. J.M. Bischoff CJCE, 19 juin 2004, *Kronhofer :* aff. C-168/02 ; point 21 ; Rev. Crit. DIP 2005, p. 326 note H. Muir-Watt et Procédures 2004, n° 236, obs. C. Nourissat.

41 Cass. civ. 1ère, 9 décembre 2003, *Cristal:* n° 01-03225, *supra* note 3.

compétence universelle est évitée au profit d'une certaine prévisibilité pour l'exploitant du site. Cette thèse a été retenue par les juridictions allemandes dans l'affaire de *l'Hôtel Maritime*[42]. La compétence des tribunaux allemands pour une contrefaçon commise par un site danois se justifiait alors par l'activité de ce site vers des utilisateurs allemands notamment au travers de la publicité rédigée en langue allemande.

Si la prise en compte de l'activité semble préférable, la difficulté porte néanmoins sur la caractérisation de cette activité, de ces liens suffisants, significatifs et substantiels pour reprendre la terminologie de la Cour d'appel de Paris[43] résistant à la Cour de cassation sur ce point. Simple lorsque le site propose à la vente des choses matérielles, l'activité pouvant dépendre des lieux de livraisons de ces marchandises, la caractérisation de l'activité devient particulièrement complexe lorsque la livraison est immatérielle. La disponibilité du bien risque alors de se confondre avec l'accessibilité du site[44]. Il nous semble pourtant que la confusion est loin d'être systématique. Le site peut, en effet, techniquement limiter l'opération de téléchargement à certains pays, alors même qu'il serait mondialement accessible. La volonté technique du propriétaire de n'offrir le téléchargement qu'à certains pays justifie alors de limiter la localisation de l'atteinte prétendue à ces seuls pays. L'activité et l'accessibilité se confondent par la mise en place de choix techniques par l'opérateur du site. Au-delà de cette volonté explicite d'autolimitation, il faut aussi, nous semble-t-il, prendre en compte la volonté implicite de l'exploitant du site. La langue, le mode de paiement, les bandeaux publicitaires utilisés par le site ou encore l'extension du site[45] offrent autant d'indices de la volonté de l'exploitant de diriger son activité vers certains pays ou au contraire de la limiter nationalement, comme l'illustre la jurisprudence *Hotel Maritime*[46]. On pourrait d'ailleurs se demander si le refus par certains sites d'instaurer un filtre par les adresses IP des utilisateurs, alors même que le site serait techniquement et financièrement en

42 *Hotel Maritime*, Bundesgerichtshof, 13 octobre 2004, GRUR Int. 2005, p. 433.

43 Notamment CA de Paris, 4e ch., 26 avril 2006 : CCE 2006, p. 106 obs. C. Caron et RLDI 2006, p. 523 chron. L. Pech ; CA de Paris, 4e ch., 6 juin 2007 : CCE 2007, comm. 119, obs. C. Caron et JCP G 2007.II.10151 M.-E. Ancel.

44 Hélène Gaudemet-Tallon, Droit international privé de la contrefaçon : aspects actuels, D. 2008, p. 735 et spéc. 737.

45 CA de Paris, P. 5, 2e ch, 25 septembre 2009, Prop. Int., 2010, p. 641, obs. A. Lucas notant que l'extension « *.com* » vise un public large.

46 *Supra* note 42.

capacité de le faire, ne témoignerait pas implicitement de sa volonté de viser un public mondial. Il reste néanmoins que cette technique du faisceau d'indices est plus délicate à mettre en œuvre pour les sites non commerciaux, comme en témoigne la récente décision de la Cour d'appel de Paris à propos du site d'un musée chilien diffusant des œuvres d'un artiste sans son autorisation[47]. La Cour a alors considéré que le site étant accessible en France à un public s'intéressant au peintre, il en résultait un lien de rattachement significatif, substantiel et suffisant avec les juridictions françaises. Comme cela a pu être écrit, « c'est donc que la seule possibilité pour le public français d'accéder au site suffit à caractériser le lien suffisant, substantiel ou significatif »[48], manière de reconnaître ici qu'accessibilité et activité se confondent. Il nous semble pourtant que l'assimilation n'est pas totale. La Cour vise en effet l'accessibilité à un public particulier, justifiant dès lors de refuser la compétence si ce public est inexistant et ce même si le site est accessible. L'hypothèse est celle d'un blog d'un écolier italien permettant à ces camarades de classe de télécharger les dernières chansons à la mode. Le site est accessible en France et pourtant aucun public français n'existe excluant de satisfaire au critère de l'activité. Le critère de l'activité nous semble donc pertinent et ce même lorsque le site est non commercial. On regrettera dès lors la position divergente du premier pôle de la Cour d'appel de Paris[49] s'alignant sur la position de la Cour de cassation et donc sur le critère de l'accessibilité. Un alignement inverse nous semblerait plus juste, soulignant la pertinence du critère de l'activité tant au stade de la compétence que du fond[50].

III. La détermination de la loi applicable

Longtemps, et particulièrement en propriété industrielle, la détermination de la loi applicable a pu sembler secondaire. La loi était celle du juge, lui même étant le juge du titre. Or, il a été, au contraire, montré que le juge n'était pas nécessairement le juge du titre, ce qui pouvait

47 CA Paris, pôle 5, 1re ch, 9 septembre 2009 : Gaz. Pal., 17 et 18 février, Chron. PLA, p. 23, obs. L. Marino et Prop. Int., 2010, p. 641, obs. A. Lucas.

48 Lucas, *supra* note 47, p. 642.

49 CA de Paris, 2 décembre 2009, *eBay c Maceo*, JCP, 2010, 22 février, 216, note C. Chabert.

50 En ce sens Edouard Treppoz, Rev. Crit. DIP, 2008, p. 336 s.

conduire à l'application d'une loi étrangère. Nous verrons, désormais, que cette loi peut être une loi autre que celle du titre.

Si les conflits de lois ne peuvent et ne doivent plus être occultés, leur résolution est néanmoins particulièrement complexe. L'explication provient de la pluralité de normes internationales potentiellement applicables à ces questions imposant un délicat travail d'identification de la règle de conflit avant de pouvoir envisager sa formulation.

A. L'identification de la règle de conflit

Identifier la règle de conflit de lois suppose d'avoir les idées claires sur ce qu'est une règle de conflit par opposition aux règles de conditions des étrangers. Une fois, cette distinction essentielle maîtrisée, il sera possible de résoudre les conflits de textes internationaux mis en évidence par la récente application du Règlement Rome II.

1. La distinction des règles de conditions des étrangers des règles de conflit de lois

Pour une part importante de la doctrine[51], la règle du traitement national présente à l'article 5.1 de la Convention de Berne, ainsi qu'à l'article 2 de la Convention de Paris était lue comme une règle de conflit de lois. Si le ressortissant étranger doit être traité comme le national, cela supposait, pour les tenants de cette doctrine, que la loi de ce dernier s'applique. Ainsi comprise la règle du traitement national aboutissait à l'application de la loi locale, comprise comme la loi du for. Cette lecture conflictualiste du traitement national a été critiquée[52]. La critique repose sur une confusion commune mais regrettable entre condition des étrangers et conflits de lois. Une chose est de pouvoir se prévaloir de droits dans un pays, une autre est de savoir selon quelle loi ces droits pourront être exercés. Or, le principe du traitement national ressortit uniquement à la

51 Voir dernièrement: NICOLAS BOUCHE, Le principe de territorialité de la propriété intellectuelle, L'Harmattan, Paris 2002, n° 913 et SAM RICKESTON & JANE C. GINSBURG, International Copyright and Neighbouring Rights, Oxford 2006, T. II, n° 20.08.

52 Voir notamment: JEAN-SYLVESTRE BERGÉ, La protection internationale et communautaire du droit d'auteur, LGDJ, Paris 1996, n° 391 et ANDRÉ LUCAS & HENRI-JACQUES LUCAS, Traité de propriété littéraire et artistique, 3ème éd., Litec, Paris 2006, n° 1288.

question de la condition des étrangers. Il vise à paralyser les discriminations au stade de la jouissance que connaisse la plupart des systèmes nationaux. On citera l'article L. 611-1 du Code français de propriété intellectuelle notant que, sous réserve des conventions internationales, les étrangers jouissent de la protection sous condition de réciprocité. La règle du traitement national énoncée à l'article 2 de la Convention de Paris exclut alors une telle discrimination à l'égard de l'étranger unioniste l'assurant de la jouissance de son droit, à l'instar d'un national. En revanche, cette règle reste muette quant à la détermination de la loi applicable. C'est d'ailleurs cette approche que semble retenir la Cour de justice des Communautés lorsqu'elle écrit dans son arrêt *TODS* « En effet, ainsi qu'il ressort de l'article 5, paragraphe 1, de la convention de Berne, celle-ci n'a pas pour objet de déterminer la loi applicable en matière de protection des œuvres littéraires et artistiques, mais elle instaure, en tant que règle générale, un système de traitement national des droits afférents à celles-ci.»[53].

La controverse est la même quant à la portée de la règle d'indépendance des droits que connaît la Convention de Paris. L'analyse conflictualiste proviendrait alors d'une lecture dynamique du principe d'indépendance retenu au paragraphe 1 de l'article 4bis et aux paragraphes 2 et 3 de l'article 6. Pour cette doctrine[54], ce principe d'indépendance « impliquerait » l'application de la loi du pays où la protection est réclamée. En effet, si un brevet demandé dans un pays est indépendant d'un brevet obtenu dans un autre pays, chaque brevet doit, en conséquence, être soumis à sa loi propre dont l'application est territorialement limitée. Bref, le principe d'indépendance vaudrait consécration implicite du principe de territorialité. Là encore, il nous semble que si ce principe d'indépendance va effectivement davantage dans le sens de l'application de la loi de protection que de la loi d'origine, ce principe ne peut néanmoins à lui seul valoir consécration du principe de territorialité. Nous verrons notamment que cette indépendance n'est pas nécessairement exclusive d'une certaine place laissée à la loi d'origine et donc à une certaine dépendance. Sans doute, faut-il alors conclure avec un auteur que « ces différentes

53 CJCE, 30 juin 2005, Aff. C-28/04: JDI, 2006, p. 639, note Bergé; CCE, 2005, comm. 133, note Caron; D. 2005, p. 2533, note Brière; Prop. Ind., 2005, comm. 67, note Kamina; Prop. Int., 2005, p. 442, obs. A. Lucas; JCP E 2006, p. 2178, n° 12, obs. H.-J. Lucas et RTDcom, 2005, p. 735, note Pollaud-Dulian.

54 Frédéric Pollaud-Dulian, Droit de la propriété industrielle, Montchrestien, 1999, n° 1582 et Moura Vicente, *supra* note 7, p. 262.

règles suggèrent par leur combinaison, la compétence de la *lex loci protectionis*, mais elles ne la prévoient pas expressément»[55]. Dès lors, formellement, il semble excessif de considérer que le principe d'indépendance, tout comme la règle du traitement national, s'analyse en une règle de conflit.

Ce débat quant à la distinction de ces questions de conflits de lois et de conditions des étrangers pouvait apparaître de pure méthode et par la même excessivement théorique. On verra, au contraire, que le Règlement Rome II en souligne l'intérêt pratique.

2. *La résolution des conflits de conventions*

Depuis le 11 janvier 2009, le Règlement Rome II sur la loi applicable aux obligations non contractuelles est applicable lorsqu'un juge communautaire est saisi d'un litige délictuel, ce ce qui comprend les litiges en matière de propriété intellectuelle faisant l'objet d'une règle de conflit spécifique à son article 8. Si ce règlement est d'une grande importance, sa portée en matière de propriété intellectuelle a pu être contestée. L'explication est simple et proviendrait particulièrement de l'existence en la matière des grandes conventions précitées. Dès lors, de l'application potentielle de l'article 8 du règlement et de la Convention de Berne ou de Paris découlerait un conflit de normes internationales. Si cette nouvelle figure conflictuelle met à l'épreuve l'inventivité de l'internationaliste, la solution est, en l'espèce, relativement simple. Elle résulte directement de l'article 28 du Règlement Rome II retenant la primauté des conventions internationales antérieures qui règlent les conflits de lois en matière délictuelle. Pour prendre un autre exemple, le juge français devra faire primer les Conventions de La Haye de 1971 sur la loi applicable en matière d› accidents de la circulation routière et de 1973 sur la loi applicable à la responsabilité du fait des produits sur le Règlement Rome II, ces conventions étant antérieures et énonçant des règles de conflits. On le voit en matière de propriété intellectuelle, la solution dépend de la question précédente quant à la lecture du traitement national et du principe d'indépendance. Il est donc clair, selon le point de vue que nous avons retenu, que la Convention de Paris ne peut primer le règlement. Pour la simple raison que la convention de Paris ne contient pas formellement de règle de conflit. Il faut alors conclure à l'application du règlement et de

55 Tristan Azzi, Atteintes aux droits de la propriété intellectuelle et conflits de lois – De l'utilité de l'article 8 du règlement Rome II, Prop. Int., 2009, p. 326.

son article 8 pour les contentieux de propriété industrielle. Le constat est distinct pour la Convention de Berne. Certes, l'article 5.1 ne peut pas davantage être compris comme une règle de conflit et ainsi primer le règlement. Néanmoins, l'article 5.2 est traditionnellement interprété comme une règle de conflit justifiant de primer sur le règlement conformément à son article 28[56].

En résumé et en droit communautaire, la règle de conflit siège désormais en matière de propriété industrielle à l'article 8 du règlement Rome II et en matière de propriété littéraire et artistique à l'article 5.2 de la Convention de Berne[57]. Il reste maintenant à préciser la formulation de ces règles.

B. La formulation de la règle de conflit

Envisager la formulation de la règle de conflit suppose de revenir, un instant, sur les irritantes questions soulevées lors de la détermination du juge compétent, mais cette fois, sous l'angle particulier du conflit de lois. Nous envisagerons, ainsi et d'abord, la place du principe de territorialité (ci-dessous 1), pour préciser, ensuite, la loi applicable en matière de cyber-délits (ci-dessous 2).

1. *La place du principe de territorialité*

La place du principe de territorialité est peu discutable, tant ce principe largement consacré en droit comparé semble dominer la matière. Nous verrons, pourtant, que des limites peuvent lui être apportées.

La consécration du principe. Une rapide étude de droit comparé du droit international privé de la propriété intellectuelle souligne l'importance du principe de territorialité au stade du conflit de lois. Inutile ici de revenir sur l'article 110 de la loi fédérale du 18 décembre 1987 soumettant l'ensemble des droits de propriété intellectuelle au droit de l'Etat pour lequel la protection est revendiquée. La règle vaut application de la *lex loci protectionis* dont la compétence est limitée territorialement au

56 Dans ce sens : Azzi, *supra* note 55 ; *contra* Nicolas Bouche, La loi applicable à la contrefaçon, in Droit international privé et propriété intellectuelle : un nouveau cadre pour de nouvelles stratégies, Kluwer 2010 (à paraître).

57 Comp. Nerina Boschiero, Infringement of Intellectual Property Rights – A Commentary of Article 8 of the Rome II Regulation, Yearbook of Private International Law, Volume 9, 2007, p. 99.

lieu de revendication de protection et dont l'application est indépendante d'autres *lege loci protectionis*. On citera, dans ce sens, le droit international privé italien et autrichien soumettant les droits de propriété intellectuelle, respectivement à la loi d'utilisation et d'exploitation. Sans vocation à l'exhaustivité, on ajoutera que la Cour suprême américaine a récemment rappelé l'importance de ce principe dans l'affaire opposant *Microsoft* à *AT&T*[58]. Le constat est le même si l'on passe des règles de sources nationales aux règles de sources internationales. Il est classique aujourd'hui de lire l'article 5.2 de la Convention de Berne visant textuellement la loi du pays où la protection est réclamée en une consécration de la loi du pays pour lequel la protection est réclamée[59]. La règle est alors la même que celle de la loi fédérale suisse. Enfin, l'article 8 du Règlement Rome II vise, à son tour, la loi du pays pour lequel la protection est revendiquée[60].

Cette consécration du principe de territorialité est trop souvent comprise comme la conséquence logique et par la même nécessaire de la nature particulière de la propriété intellectuelle. Il est, en effet, courant de déduire le principe de territorialité du rôle des Etats dans l'octroi du titre[61]. Sans doute, faut-il alors reconnaître que cette justification, à la supposer pertinente, se limiterait à la propriété industrielle. Surtout, il nous semble que cette intervention marque la revendication unilatérale de l'application de la loi du titre sur les question de validité et d'inscription, mais pas plus. Autrement dit, le domaine de l'exclusivité de la loi du titre devrait être le même que celui du juge du titre. Une puissante doctrine[62] a alors proposé de justifier ce principe de territorialité, non par l'intervention de l'Etat, mais par la qualification réelle de ces droits et par la localisation universelle qui en découlerait. En effet, la localisation universelle de l'objet de propriété intellectuelle commande l'application

58 *Microsoft v. AT&T Corp.*, 127 S. Ct. 1746 (2007): « *Foreign conduct is generally the domain of foreign law, and in the patent area, that law may embody different policy judgments about the relative rights of inventors, competitors, and the public.* ».

59 RICKESTON / GINSBURG, *supra* note 51, n° 20.09.

60 Pour une présentation de cet article : EDOUARD TREPPOZ, La lex protectionis et l'article 8 du règlement Rome II, D., 2009, p. 1643.

61 JEAN-PAUL NIBOYET, Traité de droit international privé, Sirey, 1941, T. IV, n° 1309 et encore HENRI BATIFFOL & PAUL LAGARDE, Droit international privé, LGDJ, 1983, T. II, n° 532.

62 MICHEL VIVANT, Juge et loi du brevet, Litec, 1977, n° 258 s. et JACQUES RAYNARD, Droit d'auteur et conflits de lois, Litec, 1990, n° 433 s.

de chacune des lois en tant que *lex rei sitae*. De manière paradoxale, la localisation universelle de l'œuvre commande le plus strict territorialisme des droits applicables[63]. Séduisante, cette thèse fait néanmoins l'objet de critiques. D'abord, elle repose sur une qualification qui, si elle semble légitime pour la propriété industrielle, est fortement contestée en droit d'auteur[64]. Ensuite, cette thèse retient des localisations multiples de l'objet de propriété intellectuelle, là où pour une partie de la doctrine il faudrait, au contraire, rechercher une localisation d'origine unique[65]. Enfin et surtout, cette solution serait « inopérante »[66], en ce qu'elle ne détermine non pas une loi, mais un ensemble de lois potentiellement applicables. Un choix serait donc nécessaire, afin de permettre l'application effective d'une loi parmi ces *leges rei sitae*. Finalement, le critère de rattachement ne serait pas la localisation de l'œuvre, mais son utilisation. Sans doute, faut-il alors reconnaître que le principe de territorialité n'est nullement une impérieuse nécessité tirée de l'enregistrement de ces biens ou de leur localisation, mais plus fondamentalement un choix d'opportunité[67] fondé sur des considérations économiques[68]. On comprend alors que ce principe, bien que largement consacré en droit comparé, puisse connaître des limites.

Les limites au principe. Sans doute, la limite la plus importante provient de la place qu'accordent certains pays à la loi d'origine en droit d'auteur. Selon ces systèmes, un dépeçage est organisé entre la loi d'origine applicable à l'existence du droit et la *lex loci protectionis* applicable au contenu. On citera en ce sens la jurisprudence française avec l'arrêt *Le Chant du Monde*[69], ainsi que le droit portugais ou le droit grec accordant

63 Raynard, *supra* note 62, p. 409.

64 Jean-Sylvestre Bergé, *supra* note 52, n° 102 s.

65 Voir notamment : Antoine Pillet & Georges Chabaud, Le régime international de la propriété industrielle, Sirey 1911, p. 5 s. et Emile Bartin, La localisation territoriale des monopoles intellectuels, JDI, 1934, p. 781.

66 Lucas / Lucas, *supra* note 52, n° 1209.

67 Louis d'Avout, Sur les solutions du conflit de lois en droit des biens, Economica, 2006, n° 75.

68 Mercedes Novier, La propriété intellectuelle en droit international privé suisse, Comparativa, 1996, p. 50.

69 Notamment : Joseph Drexl, The proposed Rome II Regulation, in Intellectual Property and Private International Law, J. Drexl et A. Kur (éd.), IIC Studies, 2005, p. 166 s.

une très large place à la loi d'origine[70]. Certes, le droit conventionnel viendrait harmoniser ces questions avec l'article 5.2 de la Convention de Berne imposant l'application de la *lex loci protectionis* au détriment de la loi d'origine. C'est pourtant une lecture inverse que retiennent les jurisprudences française[71] et américaine[72], excluant du domaine de la Convention de Berne les questions de titularité ressortissant à la loi d'origine. Réelle, cette limite serait néanmoins secondaire, car limitée au droit d'auteur considérée comme particulier, notamment en raison de son absence d'enregistrement.

Le constat est pourtant le même en propriété industrielle marqué par un déclin du principe de territorialité. On notera, en ce sens, que la loi d'origine n'y est pas inconnue. La plus éclatante de ces manifestations porte, sans doute, sur la question du droit au brevet européen tel que réglementé à l'article 60 de la Convention de Munich[73]. Alors que le strict respect du principe de territorialité suppose de soumettre la titularité d'une invention d'employé à chacune des lois de localisation, l'article 60 al. 1 dispose que « si l'inventeur est un employé, le droit au brevet européen est défini selon le droit de l'Etat sur le territoire duquel l'employé exerce son activité principale ». Il faut alors reconnaître, sur cette question spécifique de la titularité des inventions d'employés, que non seulement la loi applicable est dotée d'extraterritorialité, mais surtout que chaque loi nationale sera dépendante de cette loi unique. La règle de conflit de l'article 60 déroge ainsi clairement au principe de territorialité[74]. Le constat est le même en droit belge avec l'article 93 du Code de droit international privé notant que « la détermination du titulaire originaire d'un droit de propriété industrielle est régie par le droit de l'Etat avec lequel l'activité intellectuelle présente les liens les plus étroits ». Au delà de cette place accordée à la loi d'origine en matière de propriété

70 C. cass., 1e civ., 22 déc. 1959, *Soc. Fox. Europa c. Soc. Le Chant du Monde:* Rev. Crit. DIP, 1960, p. 361, note Terré; D.,1960, p. 93, note Holleaux; RTDCom, 1960, p. 351, obs. Desbois; JDI, 1961, p. 420, note Goldman.

71 CA de Paris, 4e ch., 14 mars 1991, *Sarl La Rosa c. Sté Almax International*, JCP G 1992 II 21780, note J.C. Ginsburg et JDI 1992, p. 149, note F. Pollaud-Dulian.

72 *Itar-Tass Russian News Agency v. Russian Kurier, Inc*, 153 F.3d 82 (U.S.C.A. 2d Cir. 1998).

73 Convention de Munich sur la délivrance de brevets européens du 5 octobre 1973, révisée à Munich le 28 novembre 2000.

74 En ce sens: François Dessemontet, Transfer of Technology under UNCTAD and EEC Draft Codifications: a European view on Choice of Law, Journal of International Law and Economics, 1977, vol. 12, p. 21.

industrielle, certains articles de la Convention de Paris postulent une application extra territoriale d'une loi créant ainsi un principe de dépendance, contraire au principe de territorialité[75]. On pense à l'article 6 *quinquies* imposant le point de vue de la *lex originis* quant à la nature du signe distinctif pouvant faire l'objet d'un dépôt. Une lecture identique a pu être proposée de l'article 4 de la Convention de Paris sur le délai de priorité. Enfin, et pour clore sur ces limites, certaines juridictions face à des délits complexes appliquent sans vergogne leur loi de manière extraterritoriale, dérogeant là encore au principe de territorialité. On citera en ce sens deux décisions, l'une américaine[76] et l'autre italienne[77] témoignant de la difficile localisation de l'atteinte lorsque cette dernière est pluri-localisée. Ces deux décisions témoignent alors d'une même tendance à localiser artificiellement l'atteinte aux Etats-Unis et en Italie, justifiant alors l'application de chacune de ces lois à des atteintes pourtant principalement commises au-delà de leur frontière. Sans doute, ces arrêts marquent la lente évaporation du principe de territorialité sous le feu du conflit de lois pour reprendre la belle image de Zweigert.

2. *La loi applicable au cyber-délit*

Ces derniers arrêts mettent en évidence la question de la loi applicable au cyber-délit. La problématique est commune à celle déjà envisagée en matière de conflit de juridiction. Toutefois, en matière de conflit de lois, un choix est nécessaire entre la loi du dommage et la loi du fait générateur.

Le rattachement par le fait générateur a suscité un véritable engouement jurisprudentiel en France à la suite d'un arrêt discuté de la Cour de cassation[78]. L'affaire portait sur un film américain diffusé en France et suspecté d'être tiré d'un livre lui même contrefaisant un autre livre. La Cour décide alors d'appliquer la loi américaine au motif que la loi applicable n'est pas la loi du dommage mais la loi du territoire des agissements délictueux. S'inscrivant dans cette lignée jurisprudentielle, le Tribunal de

75 Moura Vicente, *supra* note 7, p. 270.

76 *NTP Inc. v. Research in Motion LTD,* 418 F.3d 1282 (U.S.C.A. Fed. Cir. 2005). Plus généralement, lire David Baron, Cross-Border Infringement in High Tech Patent Cases, EIPR 2009, p. 31 ss, 31-36.

77 Corte di cassazionne, 3 avril 2003, *Omeprazol*, GRUR Int. 2004, p. 876.

78 Civ, 1ère, 30 janvier 2007, *Lamore :* n° 03-12354 ; Rev. Crit. DIP, 2008, p. 769, note T. Azzi ; Clunet, 2008, p. 163, note M.-E. Ancel ; Prop. Int., 2007, p. 337 obs. A. Lucas et Gaz. Pal. 2008, doct. p. 1291, chron. E. Treppoz.

grande instance de Paris[79] appliquera pour les mêmes raisons la loi américaine à une action en contrefaçon intentée par une société française de gestion des droits d'auteur de photographes contre *Google*. En conséquence, l'utilisation de ces photographies sans droit pour la fonction *Google images* sera considérée comme licite car conforme au f*air use* applicable en l'espèce. Une telle application de la loi du fait générateur a pu légitimement être critiquée. Deux raisons étaient particulièrement invoquées. Premièrement, un risque de manipulabilité excessive du critère de rattachement par le potentiel contrefacteur qui en choisissant le site choisirait la loi applicable. L'analogie avec l'application en droit communautaire de la loi d'émission pour les diffusions par satellites n'est donc pas pertinente, le point d'émission d'une diffusion par satellite n'étant pas manipulable à l'inverse d'une diffusion par l'internet. La seconde critique portait sur l'avantage donné par ce rattachement au potentiel contrefacteur, alors que le droit matériel de la propriété intellectuelle semble davantage s'intéresser aux titulaires.

Il semble donc préférable de retenir comme loi applicable la loi du dommage. On notera d'ailleurs que le Tribunal de grande instance de Paris a récemment opéré un revirement appliquant la loi française à une contrefaçon commise par *Google* à l'encontre d'un éditeur français, au motif que la loi française entretenait les liens les plus étroits avec le litige[80]. Cette solution serait d'ailleurs celle du Règlement Rome II pour des contentieux de propriété industrielle. Il nous semble, en effet, que le rattachement retenu par le Règlement impose une analyse des cyber-délits en une parcelle d'activité délictuelle. Chaque loi de protection est exclusivement compétente pour se prononcer sur les atteintes commises sur son territoire. C'est dire que face à une contrefaçon touchant plusieurs pays, la loi de chacun de ces pays est compétente en tant que loi dont la protection est revendiquée. En matière de cyber-délit, il faudrait alors appliquer chacune des lois de réception. La difficulté, sur laquelle le Règlement reste étonnamment silencieux, consiste à savoir si toutes les lois de réceptions sont applicables. Le risque évident, outre le vertige auquel pourrait succomber le juge, serait celui d'une application potentielle

79 TGI Paris, 3e ch., sect. B, 20 mai 2008, *SAIF c. SARL Google, Sté Google*: Juris-Data n° 2008-362899, RDTI, 2008, p. 501, note J.-C. Ginsburg – V. Y. Gaubiac, La Convention de Berne encore méconnue, CCE, 2008, étude 22.

80 TGI Paris, 3e ch, 2ième section, 18 décembre 2009, *Editions du Seuil et autres / Google Inc. et France*, RLDI, 2010, fév., p. 6, note A. Sing et S. Israel et Prop. Int. 2010, p. 644, obs. A. Lucas.

de toutes les lois du monde au détriment de toute prévisibilité. Il semble alors sage de subordonner l'application d'une telle loi à l'activité du site vers ce pays de réception[81]. La Cour de cassation française, retenant le critère de l'accessibilité au stade de la compétence, subordonne au contraire l'application de la loi de réception à l'activité du site vers ce pays. On citera les arrêts *Boss*[82] et *L'Oréal*[83]. Ce constat semble partagé si l'on en croit la jurisprudence allemande, mais aussi canadienne[84]. La solution paraît sage et juste. On peut toutefois se demander s'il ne faudrait pas reconnaître que le délit se localise à la résidence de la victime[85]. Extérieur à l'internet, ce rattachement est exclusif de toute manipulation. Il est prévisible pour l'utilisateur, ainsi que pour l'auteur justifiant, selon nous, de le retenir par préférence au fait générateur ou au dommage, même avec la limite de l'activité.

Cette étude des litiges internationaux de propriété intellectuelle montre que si la récurrence des problématiques des cyber-délits a ravivé le feu du conflit de lois, l'eau de la territorialité est loin d'être totalement évaporée. C'est finalement et paradoxalement d'une possible coexistence de ces deux éléments antagonistes dont témoigne cette étude.

81 Annette Kur, Trademark Conflicts on the Internet: Territoriality redefined, Intellectual Property in the Conflict of Laws, J. Basedow, J. Drexl, A. Kur et A. Metzger (éd.), 2005, p. 187.

82 Cass. com, 11 janvier 2005, *Boss:* n° 02-18381; JCP 2005 II 10055 note C. Chabert; Legipresse, 2005, mai, n° 221, III, n° 220-17, p. 77 chron. J. Passa; Prop. Ind., avril 2005, n° 4, p. 9 chron. J. Larrieu; Propr. int. 2005, n° 15, p. 203 obs. X. Buffet-Delmas et RLDI avril 2005, n° 4, p. 10 chron. G. Teissonnière.

83 Cass. com, 10 juillet 2007, *L'Oréal:* n° 05-18571; Rev. Crit. DIP, 2008, p. 322, note E. Treppoz; JCP G 2007 II 10161, note C. Chabert; JCP E 2007, p. 2269, note J. Passa et CCE 2007, comm. 119, obs. C. Caron.

84 Cour suprême du Canada, 30 juin 2004, Prop. Ind., 2004, p. 929, obs A. Lucas.

85 François Dessemontet, Le droit applicable à la propriété intellectuelle dans le cyber-espace, Commerce électronique et propriétés intellectuelles, Litec, coll. IRPI, Paris 2001, p. 117, n° 39 à 43.

La création de juridictions spécialisées : l'exemple du Tribunal fédéral des brevets

*Julie Bertholet & Pierre-Alain Killias**

I. Introduction

Le 1er janvier 2011, une nouvelle juridiction fédérale verra le jour dans le paysage de la propriété intellectuelle en Suisse. En effet, dès l'entrée en vigueur du nouveau code de procédure civile suisse[1], le 1er janvier 2011, un nouveau tribunal sera compétent pour connaître des litiges en matière de brevets à la place des tribunaux cantonaux[2].

La création du Tribunal fédéral des brevets s'insère dans une vaste réforme du droit des brevets en Suisse débutée vers la fin des années nonante. Initialement chargé d'harmoniser la loi fédérale sur les brevets et la Directive européenne relative à la protection juridique des inventions biotechnologiques[3], le Conseil fédéral a peu à peu élargi ce projet de révision à d'autres thèmes. La première procédure de consultation, qui s'est déroulée entre le 7 décembre 2001 et le 30 avril 2002, a tout d'abord révélé l'accueil favorable des milieux intéressés à la ratification des nouveaux instruments internationaux dans le domaine des brevets[4]. Lors de la deuxième procédure de consultation, qui s'est déroulée entre

* Me Julie Bertholet, avocate-stagiaire et doctorante à l'Université de Lausanne et Me Pierre-Alain Killias, Avocat, Docteur en droit, LL.M., Lexartis Avocats, Lausanne.

1 Code de procédure civile du 19 décembre 2008 (CPC), FF 2009, pp. 21-138.

2 Communiqué aux médias du 14 décembre 2009, « Tribunal fédéral des brevets : bientôt une réalité», disponible sur le site de l'Institut fédéral de la propriété intellectuelle.

3 Directive 98/44/CE du Parlement européen et du Conseil du 6 juillet 1998 relative à la protection juridique des inventions biotechnologiques, JOCE L 213 du 30 juillet 1998, p. 13.

4 Rapport sur les résultats de la procédure de consultation relative à l'avant-projet d'un arrêté fédéral concernant trois traités en matière de brevets et à la modification de la loi fédérale sur les brevets d'invention d'août 2002, établi par le Département fédéral de justice et police, disponible sur le site de l'Institut fédéral de la propriété intellectuelle.

le 1er juillet et le 31 octobre 2004, le Conseil fédéral a proposé la réglementation de la création d'un Tribunal fédéral des brevets[5]. Au regard des résultats également favorables à cette proposition, le Conseil fédéral a décidé d'échelonner la révision du droit des brevets en trois volets, en fonction de leur degré d'urgence : tout d'abord, l'approbation de la Convention sur le brevet européen révisée[6] et de l'Accord de Londres[7], ensuite la modification de la loi sur les brevets s'agissant de la protection des inventions biotechnologiques[8] et l'approbation du Traité sur le droit des brevets[9], et enfin l'adoption d'une loi sur les conseils en brevets[10] et d'une loi sur le Tribunal fédéral des brevets[11].

Alors que les deux premières parties de la révision générale du droit des brevets en Suisse sont entrées en vigueur, il reste aujourd'hui à achever la mise en œuvre du dernier volet. Les deux lois fédérales sur les conseils en brevets et sur le Tribunal fédéral des brevets, dont le délai référendaire expirait le 9 juillet 2009, n'ont donné lieu à aucun référendum. Le 1er mars 2010 sont entrées en vigueur les dispositions institutionnelles et organisationnelles de la loi sur le Tribunal fédéral des brevets, de sorte que cette autorité pourra commencer ses activités dès l'entrée en vigueur du nouveau code de procédure civile suisse.

Quand bien même ce dernier volet concerne également la réglementation fédérale sur les conseils en brevets, nous limiterons notre exposé à la réglementation relative au Tribunal fédéral des brevets.

Remplaçant les tribunaux cantonaux actuellement compétent en matière de brevets, le Tribunal fédéral des brevets, en tant que juridiction de première instance, disposera d'une compétence exclusive pour statuer sur les questions de validité et de violation dans ce domaine, pour octroyer des licences sur les brevets, ainsi que pour ordonner des mesures provisionnelles.

5 Modification du droit des brevets – Rapport sur les résultats de la procédure de consultation de janvier 2005, établi par le Département fédéral de la justice et police, disponible sur le site de l'Institut fédéral de la propriété intellectuelle.

6 Convention sur le brevet européen, révisée à Munich le 29 novembre 2000 (CBE 2000), RS 0.232.142.2.

7 Accord du 17 octobre 2000 sur l'application de l'article 65 de la Convention sur la délivrance de brevets européens (Accord sur les langues), RS 0.232.142.202.

8 Loi fédérale du 25 juin 1954 sur les brevets d'invention, RS 232.14 (ci-après LBI).

9 Traité du 1er juin 2000 sur le droit des brevets, RS 0.232.141.2.

10 FF 2009, p. 1725.

11 FF 2009, p. 1735.

II. Présentation

A. Contexte

Les litiges en matière de brevets sont souvent complexes, du fait de leur nature à la fois juridique et technique[12]; les juges appelés à en connaître doivent ainsi témoigner de connaissances spécialisées et de la capacité de pouvoir suivre les avancées technologiques.

Le système actuel de règlement des litiges en matière de brevets, qui s'appliquera jusqu'à ce que le nouveau Tribunal fédéral des brevets entre en fonction, ne permettait pas d'assurer que les juges saisis disposent des connaissances nécessaires. En effet, aux termes de l'article 76 al. 1 LBI, chaque canton désigne pour l'ensemble de son territoire un tribunal chargé de connaître en instance cantonale unique des actions civiles prévues par la loi sur les brevets. Il en résulte que pour toute la Suisse, il existe vingt-six tribunaux appelés à connaître des litiges en matière de brevets. Au regard du nombre restreint de procès en matière de brevets d'invention[13] et du nombre inversement proportionnellement élevé des tribunaux appelés à en connaître, ces derniers ne sont pas en mesure d'acquérir une expérience pratique suffisante[14]. S'il est vrai que quatre cantons (Aarau, Berne, St-Gall et Zurich) disposent d'un tribunal de commerce leur permettant d'assurer une certaine continuité jurisprudentielle, d'ailleurs reconnue dans les milieux intéressés[15], tel ne serait en revanche pas le cas des autres systèmes judiciaires cantonaux. Il existe par conséquent un risque d'insécurité juridique dans un domaine où les incidences économiques peuvent être considérables. A cela s'ajoute le fait que le Tribunal fédéral ne peut pas revoir les faits constatés dans le jugement cantonal[16]. Il en résulte que les litiges en matière de brevets ne relèvent de la compétence que d'une seule juridiction en ce qui concerne

12 Werner Stieger, Bundespatentgericht ante portas !, *in* M. Leupold et al. (éd.), Der Weg zum Recht : Festschrift für Alfred Bühler, Zurich 2008, pp. 182-183.

13 Selon le Message concernant la loi sur le Tribunal fédéral des brevets du 7 décembre 2007 (ci-après Message LTFB), environ trente litiges en matière de brevets sont jugés en Suisse par année, FF 2008, p. 382.

14 Stieger, *supra* note 12, p. 183.

15 Selon le Message concernant la LTFB, ces tribunaux de commerce tranchent environ 60 % des litiges en matière de brevets, FF 2008, p. 380.

16 Art. 105 al. 1 de la Loi du 17 juin 2005 sur le Tribunal fédéral, RS 173.110 (LTF).

les faits[17]. Il est donc impératif que celle-ci réponde à des exigences très élevées, en termes de connaissances techniques et d'expérience pratique[18].

B. Fondements d'une juridiction centralisée et spécialisée

La raison d'être de la création d'une juridiction centralisée et spécialisée en matière de brevets est double : d'une part, la mise en œuvre rapide du droit des brevets et, d'autre part, l'amélioration et l'unification de la jurisprudence dans ce domaine[19].

Comme cela a été évoqué ci-dessus, le droit des brevets se situe entre la technique et le droit. Au regard de l'évolution rapide des connaissances techniques et de l'émergence continue de nouvelles technologies, par exemple en matière de biotechnologie, une application également rapide du droit des brevets apparaît comme nécessaire pour assurer un parallélisme entre ces deux domaines et pour promouvoir l'innovation.

En second lieu, l'instauration du Tribunal fédéral des brevets répond à la volonté d'améliorer et d'unifier la jurisprudence en matière de brevets sur le territoire suisse. L'acquisition d'une jurisprudence de qualité est indispensable dans un tel domaine, au vu de l'importance économique tant des biens protégés par les brevets, tels que les produits pharmaceutiques, que du secteur, celui de la recherche et du développement, auquel il touche[20].

S'agissant de l'unification de la jurisprudence, elle répond, du point de vue interne, à un réel besoin en raison de la nature territoriale du droit des brevets. En effet, les droits issus d'un brevet étant soumis au principe de la territorialité, il en découle que leur acquisition, leur perte, mais aussi leur exercice sont en principe exclusivement régis par le droit de l'Etat pour lequel une protection est revendiquée[21]. Inversement, cela implique que l'application de ce droit concerne l'ensemble du territoire

17 Message concernant la LTFB, FF 2008, p. 380.

18 Stieger, *supra* note 12, p. 184.

19 Message concernant la LTFB, FF 2008, pp. 382-383.

20 Voir le Message concernant la modification de la loi sur les brevets et l'arrêté fédéral portant approbation du Traité sur le droit des brevets et du Règlement d'exécution du 23 novembre 2005 (ci-après Message LBI), FF 2006, pp. 129-131.

21 Kamen Troller, Précis du droit suisse des biens immatériels, 2ème éd., Bâle / Genève / Munich 2006, pp. 34-36 et pp. 431-433.

de protection. La mise en œuvre uniforme du droit des brevets constitue par conséquent un objectif impératif.

De plus, la création d'une juridiction centralisée est conforme à l'évolution européenne. A titre d'exemple, on peut signaler tout d'abord, même s'il n'a pas abouti, le projet d'Accord instituant un système de règlement des litiges en matière de brevets européens (EPLA)[22], mis en place sous l'égide de l'Organisation européenne des brevets, qui avait pour objet de créer un système judiciaire intégré comprenant des règles de procédures uniformes et une cour d'appel commune destiné au règlement des litiges en matière de brevet européen. Ensuite, on se doit de mentionner les travaux menés par l'Union européenne en vue d'introduire un brevet communautaire et une juridiction en la matière. Dans sa Communication du 3 avril 2007, intitulée « Améliorer le système des brevets en Europe »[23], la Commission européenne a tenu compte des travaux menés dans le cadre de l'Organisation européenne des brevets ; elle a proposé une structure juridictionnelle unifiée compétente pour connaître des litiges portant sur la validité et la violation des brevets européens et des futurs brevets communautaires, inspirée du modèle décentralisé de l'EPLA et pour laquelle la Cour de justice de l'Union européenne (ci-après la Cour de justice) assurerait une interprétation et une application homogène du droit communautaire[24]. Depuis juin 2009, la Cour de justice examine la compatibilité du projet d'accord avec les traités.

Au regard de ce qui précède, on constate que la création d'une juridiction centralisée et spécialisée répond à un réel besoin du point de vue suisse et qu'elle correspond à la tendance européenne.

22 Voir le Projet d'Accord instituant un système de règlement des litiges en matière de brevets européens, de décembre 2005, disponible sur : http://www.epo.org.

23 Communication de la Commission au Parlement européen et au Conseil, du 3 avril 2007, intitulée « Améliorer le système de brevet en Europe », COM(2007) 165 final.

24 *Cf.* COM(2007) 165 final, pp. 9-12 et la Recommandation de la Commission au Conseil visant à autoriser la Commission à ouvrir des négociations en vue de l'adoption d'un accord créant un système unifié de règlement des litiges en matière de brevets, du 20 mars 2009, SEC (2009) 330 final.

C. Modification de l'article 109 LDIP

Dans le cadre de la révision générale du droit des brevets, la modification de la loi sur les brevets du 22 juin 2007[25] a entraîné la modification des articles 109 et 111 de la loi sur le droit international privé[26], articles relatifs à la compétence internationale des autorités suisses et à la reconnaissance des décisions étrangères en matière de propriété intellectuelle[27]. Depuis l'entrée en vigueur du nouveau texte de l'article 109 LDIP, le demandeur a désormais le choix, en matière internationale et dans le cadre d'un litige portant sur la violation d'un droit de propriété intellectuelle, entre trois fors alternatifs, à savoir le for du domicile du défendeur, le for du lieu de l'acte ou du résultat et le for du lieu d'établissement. Cette nouvelle option en faveur du demandeur avait notamment pour objet de favoriser la compétence des tribunaux de commerce en Suisse[28]. Ainsi, lors de la consultation sur l'avant-projet de loi sur le Tribunal fédéral des brevets[29], certains participants ont estimé que la révision de l'article 109 LDIP rendait superflue la création d'un Tribunal fédéral des brevets[30]. A notre sens, même si la nouvelle teneur de l'article 109 LDIP permet de fonder dans la plupart des cas la compétence des tribunaux de commerce, soit de tribunaux plus expérimentés, elle ne constitue qu'une réponse partielle à l'ensemble des préoccupations actuelles[31]. La compétence des tribunaux de commerce n'est en effet rendue possible que dans les hypothèses où l'article 109 al. 2 LDIP est applicable, c'est-à-dire dans les litiges internationaux portant sur la violation d'un brevet, et non par exemple sur ceux portant sur la validité ou l'inscription d'un brevet.

25 RO 2008, p. 2551.

26 Loi fédérale du 18 décembre 1987 sur le droit international privé, RS 291 (ci-après LDIP).

27 Voir le Message LBI, FF 2006, pp. 37-38 et pp. 118-119.

28 Voir le Message LBI, FF 2006, p. 37.

29 La consultation sur l'avant-projet de loi sur le Tribunal fédéral des brevets s'est déroulée du 29 novembre 2006 au 30 mars 2007. Le rapport rendant compte des résultats de la consultation de septembre 2007, établi par le Département fédéral de justice et police est disponible sur le site de l'Institut fédéral de la propriété intellectuelle.

30 Rapport rendant compte des résultats de la consultation de septembre 2007, établi par le Département fédéral de justice et police, disponible sur le site de l'Institut fédéral de la propriété intellectuelle, p. 4.

31 En ce sens, STIEGER, *supra* note 12, p. 183.

En outre, s'il est vrai que la conservation de la compétence au sein de chaque canton d'une juridiction offre une certaine autonomie aux parties qui n'est pas négligeable, dès lors qu'elles ont la faculté de choisir la juridiction dont elles se sentent le plus proches, il ne faut pas négliger le fait que cette liberté est à double tranchant. D'une part, elle dessert la sécurité et la prévisibilité du droit, puisqu'elle rend possible le *forum shopping* et le *forum running*. D'autre part, elle pourrait favoriser celui qui, trouvant un intérêt dans l'ajournement de la procédure, tenterait de torpiller l'action en contrefaçon du titulaire d'un brevet par l'ouverture d'une action en constatation de non contrefaçon auprès d'une juridiction cantonale dont l'inexpérience en la matière est reconnue[32].

D. Création d'un Tribunal fédéral arbitral des brevets

En lieu et place du Tribunal fédéral des brevets, d'autres solutions ont été envisagées dans le Message concernant la loi sur le Tribunal fédéral des brevets ; l'une d'entre elles mérite d'être signalée, à savoir l'institution d'un tribunal fédéral arbitral. La création d'une telle autorité aurait rendu possible aussi bien la mise en œuvre rapide du droit des brevets, qu'une jurisprudence uniforme et de haut niveau. Cette option n'a toutefois pas été retenue en raison des problèmes constitutionnels qu'elle engendre et des frais élevés susceptibles de rendre l'accès à la justice difficile pour les inventeurs particuliers et les petites et moyennes entreprises[33].

III. Statut, composition et procédure applicable devant le Tribunal fédéral des brevets

Comme cela a déjà été indiqué, le Tribunal fédéral des brevets sera le tribunal de première instance en matière de brevets, alors que le Tribunal fédéral agira en tant que seconde instance (art. 1 LTFB).

Conçu sur le même modèle que les deux autres tribunaux fédéraux de première instance, le Tribunal fédéral des brevets revêt toutefois quelques singularités. Tout d'abord, son financement sera en principe assuré par les émoluments judiciaires. S'ils ne permettent pas de couvrir ses

32 Message LTFB, FF 2008, p. 383.

33 Message LTFB, FF 2008, pp. 383-384.

frais, le Tribunal fédéral des brevets recevra des contributions de l'Institut Fédéral de la Propriété Intellectuelle provenant des recettes générées par les taxes annuellement perçues sur les brevets (art. 4 LTFB). Ensuite, le Tribunal fédéral des brevets sera rattaché aux infrastructures du Tribunal administratif fédéral (art. 5 LTFB). Enfin, il est prévu que le Tribunal fédéral des brevets tienne, de manière générale, ses audiences au siège du Tribunal administratif fédéral. Ce ne sera que « lorsque les circonstances l'exigent » qu'il pourra tenir ses audiences dans un autre lieu (art. 7 LTFB). Le Message du Conseil fédéral fait en particulier référence à des raisons linguistiques et à des motifs d'économie de procédure (art. 6 et 7 LTFB)[34]. Qu'en est-il des procédures introduites devant les juridictions cantonales avant l'entrée en vigueur de la LTFB ? Ne devrait-on pas poursuivre celles-ci au lieu où elles avaient été introduites ? En outre, ne faudrait-il pas laisser aux parties la possibilité d'opter pour un lieu autre que le siège du Tribunal fédéral administratif lorsque les parties ou leurs conseils ont leur domicile ou leur siège en un même lieu ? Enfin, dans la mesure où une élection de for a été stipulée dans un contrat de licence, ne conviendrait-il pas d'en tenir compte afin de déterminer le lieu où le Tribunal fédéral des brevets tiendra ses audiences ? Dès lors que le législateur a fait des choix qui tenaient notamment compte de l'intérêt des PME et des individus de pouvoir disposer d'une justice qui ne soit pas excessivement onéreuse, il nous semblerait approprié que cette justice soit rendue dans un lieu qui n'impose pas aux parties des coûts injustifiés ou inutiles.

A l'instar des tribunaux de commerce[35], le Tribunal fédéral des brevets sera composé en partie par des juges ayant une formation juridique et en partie par des juges ayant une formation technique, qui devront dans les deux hypothèses disposer de connaissances attestées en droit des brevets (art. 8 al. 1 LTFB); au regard de la spécificité du droit des brevets, seule une telle composition permettra d'assurer l'établissement d'une jurisprudence de qualité. Les conditions formelles que doivent remplir les candidats ne sont pas définies dans la LTFB, laissant ainsi une certaine latitude à l'autorité d'élection. Le Message indique toutefois que le critère de la formation juridique et technique est réalisé si le candidat à l'élection a accompli des études de droit ou de sciences naturelles ou d'ingénierie sanctionnées par un diplôme dans une haute école suisse

34 Philippe Weissenberger & David Aschmann, Bundespatentgericht auf der Zielgeraden ? Fragen zum Gesetzesentwurf, sic ! 2008, p. 846 ss, p. 847.

35 Stieger, *supra* note 12, p. 186.

ou par un diplôme jugé équivalent dans une haute école à l'étranger et s'ils ont acquis une expérience pratique de plusieurs années dans une activité juridique, scientifique ou technique dans le domaine des brevets[36].

Compte tenu du nombre peu élevé de litiges en matière de brevets, il est prévu que le Tribunal fédéral des brevets ne soit composé que de deux juges ordinaires et d'un nombre suffisant de juges suppléants (art. 8 al. 2 LTFB). Ces juges seront élus par l'Assemblée fédérale (art. 9 al. 1 LTFB); elle procédera à la première élection des juges du Tribunal fédéral des brevets en été 2010[37]. La durée des fonctions est la même que pour tous les juges des tribunaux fédéraux, soit de six ans (art. 13 al. 1 LTFB).

En principe, le Tribunal fédéral des brevets statuera à trois juges, dont au moins un doit avoir une formation technique et un une formation juridique (art. 21 al. 1 LTFB). Exceptionnellement, si le président l'ordonne, le Tribunal fédéral des brevets statuera à cinq juges dans l'intérêt du développement du droit ou de l'uniformité de la jurisprudence et à sept juges lorsqu'un litige relève de plusieurs domaines techniques (art. 21 al. 2 et 3 LTFB). Le président du Tribunal fédéral des brevets statuera en tant que juge unique sur le refus d'entrer en matière sur des actions manifestement irrecevables, sur les mesures provisionnelles (sauf cas exceptionnels, cf art. 23 al. 3 LTFB, sur les demandes d'assistance judiciaire, sur la radiation du rôle des causes devenues sans objet ou closes et sur les actions en octroi d'une licence obligatoire pour l'exportation de produits pharmaceutiques.

Enfin, sauf dispositions contraires résultant de la loi sur les brevets[38] ou de la LTFB, la procédure applicable devant le Tribunal fédéral des brevets sera régie par le code de procédure civile du 19 décembre 2008 (art. 27 LTFB), dont l'entrée en vigueur aura lieu le 1er janvier 2011.

36 Message LTFB, FF 2008, p. 391.

37 Communiqué aux médias du 14 décembre 2009, « Tribunal fédéral des brevets : bientôt une réalité», disponible sur le site de l'Institut fédéral de la propriété intellectuelle.

38 Pour les exceptions prévues par la LBI, voir le Message LTFB, FF 2008, p. 401.

IV. Compétence exclusive du Tribunal fédéral des brevets

A. En général

Les différentes prérogatives du futur Tribunal fédéral des brevets sont énumérées à l'article 26 LTFB.

En premier lieu, le Tribunal fédéral des brevets est exclusivement compétent en matière d'actions en validité et en contrefaçon d'un brevet, ainsi qu'en matière d'actions en octroi d'une licence sur un brevet. Il dispose également d'une compétence exclusive pour ordonner des mesures provisionnelles en relation avec les actions susmentionnées et pour exécuter les décisions qu'il rend.

Le Tribunal fédéral des brevets dispose en deuxième lieu d'une compétence alternative pour juger d'autres actions civiles qui ont un lien de connexité avec les brevets, telles que les actions concernant la titularité ou la cession de brevets. Il partagera sa compétence avec celle des cantons.

Le sort des questions préjudicielles et des exceptions en matière de validité et de contrefaçon d'un brevet est traité par le troisième alinéa de l'article 26 LTFB.

Enfin, l'alinéa 4 de l'article 26 LTFB règle le cas des demandes reconventionnelles en nullité ou en contrefaçon d'un brevet déposées devant une instance cantonale en prévoyant leur transmission au Tribunal fédéral des brevets.

Il convient donc d'examiner plus en détail les compétences qui sont prévues à l'art. 26 LTFB.

B. Actions en validité, en contrefaçon et en octroi d'une licence sur un brevet

L'attribution d'une compétence exclusive au Tribunal fédéral des brevets s'agissant tant des actions en validité, que des actions en contrefaçon et en octroi d'une licence devrait assurément permettre de réaliser les objectifs poursuivis dans le cadre du dernier volet de la révision générale du droit des brevets, à savoir la mise en œuvre rapide du droit des brevets et l'établissement d'une jurisprudence de qualité et uniforme.

D'un point de vue pratique toutefois, force est de constater que ce système centralisé pourra engendrer certains inconvénients. On relèvera d'une part la localisation excentrée du Tribunal fédéral des brevets.

Disposant des infrastructures du Tribunal administratif fédéral, le siège du Tribunal fédéral des brevets à St-Gall désavantagera certainement le demandeur domicilié en région romande ou tessinoise. D'autre part, le haut degré de spécialisation des juges appelés à connaître des litiges en matière de brevets entraînera certainement une élévation parallèle des coûts des procès en matière de brevets.

1. *Les différentes actions concernées*

L'article 26 al. 1 let. a LTFB fonde la compétence exclusive du Tribunal fédéral des brevets s'agissant des actions en validité ou en contrefaçon d'un brevet et des actions en octroi d'une licence sur un brevet.

Sont considérées comme des actions en validité: les actions en nullité prévues par les articles 26 à 28 et 140k LBI, à savoir les actions en nullité totale ou partielle d'un brevet ou d'un certificat complémentaire de protection ; les actions en constatation de l'existence ou de la validité d'un brevet (art. 74 ch. 1 LBI); les actions en constatation de la violation de l'interdiction de la double protection (art. 20a, 125, 126 et 140 LBI); les actions en déchéance du brevet (art. 38 LBI).

Les actions en contrefaçon recouvrent les actions suivantes : l'action en cessation de l'acte ou en suppression de l'état de fait (art. 72 al. 1 LBI); l'action en dommages-intérêts (art. 73 LBI); l'action en remise du gain ; l'action en réparation du tort moral ; l'action tendant à la communication de certaines informations (art. 66 let. b LBI); l'action tendant à la publication du jugement (art. 70 al. 1 LBI); l'action tendant à la confiscation et à la réalisation ou celle tendant à la destruction des produits fabriqués illicitement ou des moyens destinés principalement à leur fabrication (art. 69 al. 1 LBI); l'action en constatation de la violation ou de la non violation d'un brevet (art. 74 ch. 2 et 3 LBI); l'action en constatation de ce que le brevet ne peut être opposé au demandeur en application d'une disposition légale (art. 74 ch. 4 LBI).

Les actions en octroi d'une licence visent en premier lieu les licences obligatoires prévues par la LBI. Il s'agit des actions qui tendent à l'octroi d'une licence non exclusive afin de pouvoir utiliser une invention dépendante (art. 36 LBI), à l'octroi d'une licence non exclusive tendant à assurer que l'invention soit suffisamment utilisée en Suisse (art. 37 LBI), à l'octroi d'une licence non exclusive fondée sur l'intérêt public (art. 40 LBI), à l'octroi d'une licence non exclusive dans le domaine de la technologie des semi-conducteurs afin de remédier à une pratique jugée contraire au droit de la concurrence (art. 40a LBI), à l'octroi d'une licence non exclusive sur une invention biotechnologique brevetée afin de permettre son utilisation comme instrument de recherche (art. 40b LBI), à l'octroi d'une licence non exclusive portant sur un produit ou un procédé de diagnostic dans le domaine humain afin de remédier à une pratique jugée contraire au droit de la concurrence (art. 40c LBI), à l'octroi d'une licence non exclusive en vue de la production et de l'exportation de produits pharmaceutiques (art. 40d LBI). Dans cette dernière hypothèse, il convient de signaler la compétence du juge unique pour trancher une demande fondée sur l'art. 40d LBI (art. 23 al. 1 let. e LTFB).

2. *La compétence exclusive du Tribunal fédéral des brevets dans un contexte international*

Selon le Message, le Tribunal fédéral des brevets pourra également connaître de litiges portant sur des brevets étrangers pour autant que la compétence internationale des autorités suisses soit établie[39]. Si l'on se place sous l'angle des litiges à caractère international, on ne peut s'empêcher d'observer que la nature exclusive de la compétence matérielle du Tribunal fédéral des brevets en matière d'actions en violation d'un brevet et d'actions en octroi d'une licence sur un brevet ne s'accorde pas entièrement avec les solutions qui prévalent en droit international privé. En effet, d'une part, l'article 16 ch. 4 de la Convention de Lugano[40] (art. 22 ch. 4 de la Convention de Lugano révisée) prévoit la compétence exclusive des tribunaux de l'Etat contractant sur le territoire duquel le dépôt ou l'enregistrement a été demandé, a été effectué ou est réputé avoir été effectué aux termes d'une convention internationale uniquement en matière d'inscription ou de validité des brevets. *A contrario*, dans le cadre de cette Convention, la compétence des Etats contractants en matière de contrefaçon d'un brevet est de nature dispositive. Quant à la nature de la compétence des Etats contractants pour octroyer une licence obligatoire sur un brevet, celle-ci ne tombe pas expressément sous le coup de l'art. 16 ch. 4 CL. Sous l'angle du droit international privé suisse, l'article 109 al. 1 LDIP fonde la compétence des tribunaux

39 Message LTFB, FF 2008, p. 400 ; *cf.* également WERNER STIEGER, Die Zuständigkeit der Schweizer Gerichte für Prozesse über und im Zusammenhang mit Patenten ab 2011, sic ! 2010 p. 3 ss, p. 4 ss.

40 Convention du 16 septembre 1988 concernant la compétence judiciaire et l'exécution des décisions en matière civile et commerciale, RS 0.275.11 (ci-après CL).

suisses pour connaître des actions portant sur la validité ou l'inscription en Suisse des brevets, sans en préciser toutefois expressément la nature exclusive. Quant aux chefs de compétence prévus par l'article 109 al. 2 LDIP en matière de violation d'un brevet, leur nature dispositive est incontestée.

Il découle des solutions prévues par le droit international privé conventionnel et suisse que la compétence du Tribunal fédéral des brevets ne pourra pas être assurée dans l'hypothèse d'un litige international portant sur la violation d'un brevet suisse, ou sur l'octroi d'une licence sur un brevet suisse. En effet, la compétence des tribunaux d'un autre Etat contractant de la Convention de Lugano ou d'un Etat tiers pourra être donnée tant sur la base d'un critère de compétence objectif, par exemple si le domicile du défendeur est à l'étranger, que sur la base d'une élection de for.

Bien sûr, la nouvelle loi sur le Tribunal fédéral des brevets n'a pas pour vocation de régler des questions de compétence internationale dans le cadre de litiges à caractère transnational. Elle ne s'intéresse d'ailleurs pas davantage à la répartition territoriale des litiges au sein de l'ordre judiciaire suisse. La loi sur le Tribunal fédéral des brevets a pour seul objet de régler la question de la compétence matérielle des tribunaux suisses dans l'hypothèse d'un litige relatif à un brevet. Cela étant, on peut s'interroger sur l'efficacité de la loi sur le Tribunal fédéral des brevets du point de vue des objectifs visés, si la compétence même des autorités suisses n'est pas garantie. En effet, les juridictions d'un Etat étranger saisies pour statuer sur la violation d'un brevet suisse pourront-elles assurer la mise en œuvre rapide du droit des brevets ou l'établissement d'une décision conforme à la pratique en Suisse ? Tel ne pourra être le cas que si les législations de l'Etat étranger concerné prévoient également la compétence de juridictions spécialisées et expérimentées en matière de brevets. Force est ainsi de constater qu'en raison des solutions actuelles issues des instruments de droit international privé les résultats attendus dès l'entrée en vigueur de la nouvelle loi sur le Tribunal fédéral doivent être relativisés.

Inversement, l'attribution au niveau interne d'une compétence exclusive à une autorité centralisée et spécialisée pour statuer sur les actions en validité et en violation d'un brevet, ainsi que sur les actions en octroi d'une licence sur un brevet est très favorable du point de vue du droit international privé. D'une part, la création du Tribunal fédéral des brevets permet de renforcer la position de la Suisse au sein de la communauté internationale[41]. On peut en effet imaginer que, dans le cadre de litiges internationaux portant sur des brevets étrangers, les décisions qui seront rendues par cette autorité spécialisée et expérimentée jouiront d'une meilleure reconnaissance. D'autre part, l'institution de cette instance spécialisée en matière de brevets devrait encourager les parties à convenir d'une élection de for en faveur des tribunaux suisses ; elle favorise en ce sens l'autonomie des parties.

C. Les mesures provisionnelles

Aux termes de l'article 26 al. 1 let. b LTFB, le Tribunal fédéral des brevets a la compétence exclusive pour ordonner des mesures provisionnelles avant litispendance d'une action visée à la lettre a, à savoir les actions en validité ou en contrefaçon d'un brevet et les actions en octroi d'une licence sur un brevet.

Ceci signifie que les cantons n'auront plus de compétence pour ordonner des mesures provisionnelles lorsque celles-ci sont rendues dans des domaines de la compétence exclusive du Tribunal fédéral des brevets.

D'après le Message, l'attribution d'une compétence exclusive au Tribunal fédéral des brevets s'impose également en matière de mesures provisionnelles pour des raisons d'économie de procédure, l'idée sous-jacente étant d'éviter le morcellement des procédures[42].

D. L'exécution des décisions rendues par le Tribunal fédéral des brevets en vertu de sa compétence exclusive

Le Tribunal fédéral des brevets aura enfin la compétence exclusive d'exécuter les décisions qu'il a rendues pour autant que celles-ci aient été rendues dans des cas qui sont de sa compétence exclusive.

L'article 26 al. 1 let. c LTFB constitue une exception à l'art. 339 al. 1 CPC, qui s'appliquera néanmoins lorsque la décision rendue par le Tribunal fédéral des brevets se fonde non pas sur l'article 26 al. 1 LTFB, mais sur l'article 26 al. 2 LTFB.

41 Stieger, *supra* note 12, p. 185, qui constate que la nouvelle attractivité d'un règlement des litiges en Suisse résultera non seulement de la création d'une autorité centralisée et spécialisée, mais aussi de l'entrée en vigueur d'un nouvel instrument de procédure civile modernisé.

42 Message LTFB, FF 2008, p. 400.

V. Compétence concurrente avec les tribunaux cantonaux

A. Autres actions civiles ayant un lien de connexité avec des brevets

L'article 26 al. 2 LTFB dispose que le Tribunal fédéral des brevets a la compétence de juger d'autres actions civiles ayant un lien de connexité avec des brevets, en particulier celles qui concernent la titularité ou la cession de brevets. Cette compétence n'est cependant pas exclusive, mais concurrente à celle des tribunaux cantonaux. La compétence exclusive du Tribunal fédéral des brevets se limitera aux actions qui impliquent l'application du droit matériel des brevets[43].

Avant d'aborder plus en détail cette norme, il convient d'observer qu'elle aura vraisemblablement pour effet à terme d'inciter les demandeurs à saisir directement le Tribunal fédéral des brevets plutôt qu'un tribunal cantonal du fait de l'article 26 al. 3 et 4 LTFB[44]. A ceci s'ajoute le fait que les élections de for prévues par des contrats de licence risquent bien de perdre en pertinence, si la validité du brevet est contestée par le biais d'une exception ou d'une demande reconventionnelle, les parties ne pouvant convenir que le Tribunal fédéral des brevets siégera dans une ville autre que St-Gall, l'article 7 LTFB laissant cette responsabilité au Tribunal fédéral des brevets et la loi ne prévoyant aucun moyen pour les parties de s'y opposer.

Les termes « d'autres actions civiles ayant un lien de connexité avec des brevets » sont illustrés par deux exemples non exhaustifs, les actions concernant la titularité et la cession de brevets.

Selon le Message, ce sont essentiellement les actions contractuelles relatives à un brevet qui sont visées par cette disposition. Les brevets pouvant donner lieu à toutes sortes d'engagements contractuels, les litiges qui en découlent auront souvent une nature contractuelle. A titre d'exemple, on peut mentionner les actions portant sur l'exécution d'un contrat de cession ou d'un contrat de licence, les actions portant sur la titularité d'un brevet ou encore, dans le cadre d'un contrat de travail, l'action du travailleur portant sur sa rétribution pour l'invention réalisée dans l'exercice de son activité au service de l'employeur, mais en dehors de ses obligations contractuelles[45].

43 FF 2008, p. 400.

44 *Cf. infra* ch. V.B. et V.C.

45 Message LTFB, FF 2008, p. 400 ; Stieger, *supra* note 12, pp. 192-195 ; Stieger, *supra* note 39, p. 11 ss.

Dans la mesure où ces actions relèvent avant tout du droit des contrats, il était logique que la loi sur le Tribunal fédéral des brevets se borne à fonder une compétence concurrente du Tribunal fédéral des brevets. Il en résulte que le demandeur pourra à sa convenance saisir le tribunal cantonal compétent *ratione materiae* et *ratione loci* ou s'adresser au Tribunal fédéral des brevets[46]. Les parties auront comme par le passé la faculté de déterminer librement le for de la procédure en convenant d'une élection de for, lorsque ces actions ne portent pas sur l'application du droit matériel des brevets.

Le texte de l'article 26 al. 2 LTFB ne faisant toutefois pas référence aux actions contractuelles mais aux actions qui ont un lien de connexité avec des brevets concernant en particulier la titularité ou la cession des brevets, qu'en est-il de ces actions lorsqu'elles ne découlent pas d'une relation contractuelle ? En effet, à défaut de rapports juridiques entre le prétendu titulaire d'un brevet et son véritable ayant droit, les actions portant sur la constatation de la titularité du droit de protection revêtiront un caractère délictuel. Au regard de l'article 26 al. 2 LTFB, ces actions ne seraient soumises qu'à la compétence dispositive du Tribunal fédéral des brevets, dès lors qu'elles concernent la titularité du brevet. Toutefois dans la mesure où elles impliquent l'application du droit matériel des brevets, en particulier de l'article 3 LBI relatif au droit à la délivrance du brevet, ces actions auraient dû être soumises à la compétence exclusive du Tribunal fédéral des brevets[47].

Encore plus délicate est la question du sort des actions en cession, au sens des articles 29 à 31 LBI. L'article 26 al. 2 LTFB semble indiquer que ces actions pourront être alternativement soumises à la compétence du Tribunal fédéral des brevets ou à celle des tribunaux cantonaux. Ce point de vue est d'ailleurs corroboré par le fait que les actions en cession ne figurent pas parmi les actions énumérées à l'article 26 al. 1 let. a LTFB. D'autres éléments nous conduisent cependant à considérer que les actions en cession devraient être soumises à la compétence exclusive du Tribunal fédéral des brevets. D'une part, l'article 29 al. 1 LBI prévoit que le véritable ayant droit à la délivrance du brevet peut intenter soit

46 Pour Weissenberger et Aschmann, la compétence concurrente des tribunaux cantonaux et du Tribunal fédéral des brevets ne constitue pas une solution suffisamment claire et prévisible ; selon ces auteurs la compétence exclusive du Tribunal fédéral des brevets aurait dû être étendue aux actions visées par l'article 26 al. 2 LTFB ; Weissenberger / Aschmann, *supra* note 34, p. 850.

47 FF 2008, p. 400.

une action en nullité, soit une action en cession. Il paraît par conséquent assez logique de ranger l'action en cession dans la même catégorie d'actions que l'action en nullité. D'autre part, l'action en cession étant à notre avis une action en constatation de droit, elle aura pour conséquence, en cas de succès, la modification par l'Institut Fédéral de la Propriété Intellectuelle du Registre des brevets. Compte tenu du fait que ces actions se fondent sur le droit matériel des brevets, elles auraient dû être soumises à la compétence exclusive du Tribunal fédéral des brevets[48].

Au regard de ce qui précède, il apparaît que la rédaction des articles 26 al. 1 let. a et al. 2 LTFB manque de clarté et qu'elle ne permet pas de déterminer avec exactitude quelles actions sont de la compétence exclusive du Tribunal fédéral des brevets et quelles actions pourront encore être tranchées par les tribunaux cantonaux. A l'avenir, il y aura ainsi lieu de préciser la nature exhaustive ou exemplative des actions énumérées dans le cadre de l'article 26 al. 1 let. a LTFB, afin de déterminer le sort de ces actions en zone grise qui ne sont ni des actions en validité, en contrefaçon ou en octroi d'un licence, ni des actions purement contractuelles. Cette incertitude ne peut qu'inciter les parties à une certaine prudence et à saisir directement le Tribunal fédéral des brevets, plutôt que de courir le risque de voir un tribunal cantonal décliner sa compétence, avec les frais que cela engendrerait nécessairement.

B. Question préjudicielle et exception de nullité ou de contrefaçon d'un brevet

L'art. 26 al. 3 LTFB dispose que : « [s]i un tribunal cantonal doit statuer sur la question préjudicielle ou sur l'exception de nullité ou de contrefaçon d'un brevet, le juge fixe un délai approprié aux parties pour intenter l'action en nullité ou en contrefaçon devant le Tribunal fédéral des brevets. Le tribunal cantonal suspend la procédure jusqu'à ce que la décision du Tribunal fédéral des brevets soit entrée en force. Si le Tribunal fédéral des brevets n'est pas saisi dans le délai imparti, le tribunal cantonal reprend la procédure, et la question préjudicielle ou l'exception n'est pas prise en compte. »

48 Stieger, *supra* note 39, p. 7 ; la situation est similaire en droit des marques : p. ex. Jacques de Werra, Des marques et des contrats : la marque d'agent et l'action en cession de marque, *in* Mélanges en l'honneur de François Dessemontet, Lausanne 2009, p. 71 ss.

A titre liminaire, il convient de préciser que le « tribunal cantonal » ne doit pas nécessairement être un tribunal civil, mais qu'il peut également s'agir d'un tribunal pénal, par exemple lorsque l'accusé soulève la question de la validité ou de la contrefaçon du brevet de la partie civile ou du plaignant.

La question de la compétence d'un tribunal saisi par voie préjudicielle ou d'exception pour se prononcer sur la nullité ou la contrefaçon d'un brevet a déjà beaucoup été discutée, notamment dans le cadre de la décision de la Cour de justice GAT / LuK rendue en 2006[49]. La loi sur le Tribunal fédéral des brevets traite expressément de la compétence en matière de question préjudicielle ou d'exception de nullité ou de contrefaçon d'un brevet à l'article 26 al. 3 LTFB. Ce dernier attribue d'une part la compétence au Tribunal fédéral des brevets pour en connaître. D'autre part, il pose les modalités de la répartition du litige entre le tribunal cantonal initialement saisi et la juridiction fédérale.

Pour que l'article 26 al. 3 LTFB trouve application, le tribunal cantonal doit être amené à devoir statuer sur la question préjudicielle ou sur l'exception de nullité ou de contrefaçon. Ceci implique que les faits permettant de fonder l'exception ou de poser la question préjudicielle devront avoir été allégués de manière précise, sans quoi il y aura lieu de considérer que le tribunal cantonal n'a pas à statuer sur ces questions ou exceptions. Le tribunal cantonal devra alors fixer un délai approprié aux parties pour intenter une action en nullité ou en contrefaçon devant le Tribunal fédéral des brevets. La formulation du texte légal est quelque peu maladroite, car l'on conçoit difficilement que des parties en litige soient à même d'intenter ensemble une action en nullité ou en contrefaçon de brevet devant le Tribunal fédéral des brevets. En fait, il faut considérer qu'il incombe à la partie à qui l'admission de l'exception profite d'ouvrir action devant le Tribunal fédéral des brevets[50].

L'ouverture d'action devra intervenir dans un délai approprié fixé par le Tribunal fédéral des brevets[51]. Il convient de considérer que le

49 CJCE, 13 juillet 2006, aff. C-4 / 03, GAT / LuK, Rec. 2006, p. I-6509.

50 Stieger, *supra* note 39, p. 14.

51 En effet, à l'instar d'une décision rendue dans le cadre d'un litige international par le Tribunal de commerce de Zurich, nous estimons utile d'accompagner le sursis à statuer de l'octroi d'un délai au défendeur pour introduire son action, à défaut duquel le tribunal saisi en premier lieu pourrait partir du principe que le brevet est valide ou non contrefait, *cf. Handelsgericht* de Zurich, cons. 2b, 13 octobre 2006, sic ! 2006, p. 854.

« délai approprié» ne saurait en principe excéder celui qui est généralement accordé pour déposer la demande reconventionnelle, puisqu'au terme du CPC la demande reconventionnelle doit être intentée dans le délai de réponse. Le tribunal cantonal devra alors suspendre la procédure jusqu'à ce que la décision du Tribunal fédéral des brevets entre en force. Si la partie concernée ne saisit pas le Tribunal fédéral des brevets, le tribunal cantonal pourra reprendre la procédure sans tenir compte de la question préjudicielle ou de l'exception initialement soulevée. Ceci n'empêchera cependant pas que la partie, à qui un délai a été fixé pour agir devant le Tribunal fédéral des brevets en nullité ou en contrefaçon, de le faire ultérieurement en saisissant directement le Tribunal fédéral des brevets d'une demande en ce sens. Se posera alors la question de savoir si la procédure en cours devant le tribunal cantonal devra être suspendue en application de l'art. 126 al. 1 CPC, dont la teneur est la suivante : « [l]e tribunal peut ordonner la suspension de la procédure si des motifs d'opportunité le commandent. La procédure peut notamment être suspendue lorsque la décision dépend du sort d'un autre procès ». A notre sens, la suspension devrait être refusée lorsqu'une partie s'est vu impartir un délai approprié pour faire valoir la nullité ou la contrefaçon du brevet et qu'elle a renoncé à agir devant le Tribunal fédéral des brevets dans ce délai. C'est sans doute la meilleure façon d'éviter que les procédures soient prolongées indéfiniment par des plaideurs de mauvaise foi.

L'attribution au Tribunal fédéral des brevets d'une compétence matérielle exclusive en matière de nullité et de contrefaçon, que la question soit soulevée à titre principal ou par voie d'exception, correspond aux récents développements en Europe.

En effet, depuis juillet 2006, la jurisprudence de la Cour de justice GAT / LuK retient que tous les litiges portant sur la validité d'un brevet sont soumis à la compétence exclusive des tribunaux de l'Etat d'enregistrement, indépendamment de savoir si la question est soulevée par voie d'action ou d'exception[52]. La teneur de la décision de la Cour de justice a ensuite expressément été reprise à l'article 22 ch. 4 de la Convention de Lugano révisée, dont l'entrée en vigueur aura lieu le 1er janvier 2011. Les tribunaux suisses n'ont toutefois pas attendu la modification formelle de cet instrument international ; en effet, dans une décision du

52 Sur cette décision, voir l'article de Wilderspin, La compétence juridictionnelle en matière de litiges concernant la violation des droits de propriété intellectuelle. Les arrêts de la Cour de justice dans les affaires C-4 / 03, GAT c. LUK et C-539 / 03, Roche Nederland c. Primus et Goldberg, Rev. Crit. DIP 2006, p. 777 ss.

13 octobre 2006 déjà, le Tribunal de commerce de Zurich s'était expressément référé à cette jurisprudence européenne pour suspendre une cause dans laquelle la validité d'une marque communautaire avait été soulevée par voie d'exception et fixer un délai aux parties pour saisir l'autorité communautaire[53].

La solution prévue par l'article 26 al. 3 LTFB a donc pour conséquence d'étendre au plan interne le principe selon lequel, en matière de brevet, l'attribution exclusive de certaines questions à la compétence d'une juridiction ne dépend pas de savoir si elles sont soulevées à titre principal ou à titre d'exception. Si l'on peut se réjouir de l'harmonisation réussie des règles de compétence internes et internationales, on doit néanmoins garder à l'esprit que le système qui prévaudra en Suisse, dès le 1er janvier 2011, revêt quelques inconvénients.

Le premier concerne la prévisibilité et la sécurité du droit. En effet, dès l'entrée en vigueur de la nouvelle loi sur le Tribunal fédéral des brevets, le demandeur à une action délictuelle ou contractuelle soumise à la compétence des tribunaux cantonaux courra toujours le risque que sa procédure soit paralysée par le défendeur qui soulèverait par voie d'exception la validité du brevet ou sa contrefaçon. Sous l'angle de l'autonomie des parties, l'intérêt d'une élection de for perdra également une très large partie de son intérêt en termes de prévisibilité, étant donné que les deux parties devront compter avec la possibilité que la nullité ou la contrefaçon soient invoquées par voie d'exception et que le juge élu suspende la cause.

En second lieu, l'attribution d'une compétence exclusive au Tribunal fédéral des brevets en matière de nullité et de contrefaçon dessert le principe de l'économie de procédure. En effet, à chaque fois que la nullité ou la contrefaçon d'un brevet sera contestée devant un tribunal cantonal, la compétence pour connaître du litige pourra se voir partagée entre la juridiction saisie de l'action délictuelle ou contractuelle et le Tribunal fédéral des brevets. Bien entendu, le demandeur souhaitant éviter les inconvénients liés à une scission et régler rapidement son différend pourra toujours saisir directement le Tribunal fédéral des brevets de son action délictuelle ou contractuelle.

En troisième lieu, il faut également clairement stigmatiser le texte légal dans la mesure où le défendeur ne pourra de fait plus soulever

53 *Handelsgericht* de Zurich, 13 octobre 2006, sic ! 2006, p. 854 ; DANIEL GIRSBERGER, Schutzrechte und Kollisionsrecht ? Echte oder nur Scheinprobleme ?, sic ! 2008, p. 47 ss, p. 53.

l'exception de nullité devant un tribunal cantonal et sera tenu d'agir en nullité devant le Tribunal fédéral des brevets[54].

A notre sens, il aurait été préférable que la loi sur le Tribunal fédéral des brevets adopte un système moins contraignant pour les parties et surtout plus respectueux non seulement des clauses d'élection de for stipulées dans les accords de licence ou de cession de brevets, mais aussi de la liberté du défendeur de soulever par voie d'exception la nullité du brevet, en prévoyant par exemple une compétence dispositive du Tribunal fédéral des brevets pour connaître des questions préjudicielles et des exceptions de nullité ou de contrefaçon ou en disposant d'un système tel que celui prévu par la Loi fédérale sur les cartels (art. 15 LCart)[55]. Le Tribunal fédéral des brevets aurait ainsi été appelé à rendre un avis sur la question préjudicielle ou sur l'exception de nullité ou de contrefaçon. Cet avis aurait lié l'autorité cantonale. Ainsi, il aurait été possible de répondre à l'objectif premier de la LTFB, qui est d'assurer aux plaideurs l'accès à une justice spécialisée en matière de brevets, tout en respectant pleinement la volonté des parties qui ont conclu ou qui concluent un accord sur une élection de for.

En ce qui concerne les modalités de la répartition de compétence entre les tribunaux cantonaux et la juridiction fédérale, la suspension du litige jusqu'à l'entrée en force de la décision du Tribunal fédéral des brevets nous paraît être la meilleure alternative. A la place, on aurait en effet pu envisager que le tribunal cantonal saisi de la question préjudicielle ou de l'exception de nullité ou de contrefaçon d'un brevet transfère l'entier de la cause au Tribunal fédéral des brevets. D'une part, la solution choisie dans le cadre de la nouvelle loi fédérale est celle qui respecte le mieux la volonté des parties dès lors que le for initialement saisi pour l'action principale est conservé. D'autre part, la marge de manœuvre de la partie mal intentionnée sera plus limitée ; celle-ci ne pourra en effet pas se contenter de soulever par voie préjudicielle ou d'exception l'invalidité du brevet ou sa contrefaçon pour mettre des bâtons dans les roues de l'autre partie, mais devra elle-même ouvrir action devant le Tribunal fédéral des brevets, en devant tenir compte notamment des frais engendrés par l'ouverture d'une telle action.

Une dernière remarque mérite d'être soulevée s'agissant du texte de l'article 26 al. 3 LTFB, qui n'évoque que la « nullité» et la « contrefaçon »

54 Stieger, *supra* note 39, p. 14 s.

55 Loi fédérale du 6 octobre 1995 sur les cartels et autres restrictions à la concurrence (LCart), RS 251.

d'un brevet. L'article 26 al. 1 let. a LTFB attribue une compétence exclusive au Tribunal fédéral des brevets en matière de validité, de contrefaçon et d'octroi d'une licence sur un brevet. On aurait ainsi pu s'attendre à ce que la compétence exclusive du Tribunal fédéral des brevets en matière préjudicielle et d'exception soit étendue à l'ensemble des actions visées par l'article 26 al. 1 let. a LTFB, comme le fait d'ailleurs l'article 26 al. 1 let. b LTFB, dans le domaine des mesures provisionnelles. En outre, la rédaction de l'article 26 al. 3 LTFB laisse ouverte la question de savoir si la constatation positive en validité d'un brevet pourra être examinée par les autorités cantonales lorsqu'elle est soulevée par voie préjudicielle ou d'exception ou si elle devra également être soumise au Tribunal fédéral des brevets, à l'instar de la nullité d'un brevet.

C. Demande reconventionnelle en nullité ou en contrefaçon d'un brevet

Au lieu d'être soulevée par voie préjudicielle ou d'exception, la nullité et la contrefaçon d'un brevet peuvent également faire l'objet d'une demande reconventionnelle. L'article 26 al. 4 LTFB a pour objet de garantir la compétence du Tribunal fédéral des brevets en ce qui concerne la nullité et la contrefaçon du brevet. Pour ce faire, il est prévu que le tribunal cantonal saisi d'une demande reconventionnelle en nullité ou en contrefaçon d'un brevet transmette non seulement la demande reconventionnelle, mais également la demande principale au Tribunal fédéral des brevets.

A notre sens, la solution de l'article 26 al. 4 LTFB répond non seulement à un souci d'économie de la procédure, mais apparaît également comme favorable au titulaire du brevet. Cela étant, on comprend mal pourquoi, dans l'hypothèse d'une demande reconventionnelle en nullité ou en contrefaçon, le tribunal cantonal devrait transmettre tant la demande reconventionnelle que la demande principale au Tribunal fédéral des brevets, alors que, dans l'hypothèse d'une exception de nullité ou de contrefaçon, le tribunal cantonal peut conserver sa compétence. Il aurait ainsi paru davantage logique de prévoir que le tribunal cantonal, certes incompétent s'agissant de la demande reconventionnelle en nullité ou en contrefaçon, puisse transmettre cette dernière au Tribunal fédéral des brevets tout en conservant sa compétence s'agissant de la demande principale et en suspendant la demande principale jusqu'à droit jugé sur la demande reconventionnelle.

En outre, à l'instar de l'article 26 al. 3 LTFB, on peut s'étonner du fait que le dernier alinéa de l'article 26 LTFB ne concerne que les demandes reconventionnelles de « nullité» et de « contrefaçon » de brevet. A notre avis, une simple référence aux actions prévues par l'article 26 al. 1 let. a LTFB aurait eu l'avantage de fournir une solution claire et complète.

D. Les conclusions civiles dans le cadre d'une procédure pénale ouverte contre le contrefacteur ?

L'article 122 al. 1 du nouveau code de procédure pénale suisse[56] donne en principe au lésé la possibilité de prendre des conclusions civiles dans le cadre d'une procédure pénale (*cf.* également art. 119 al. 2 CPP).

L'article 119 al. 2 CPP offre au lésé la faculté alternativement et cumulativement de conclure à la condamnation pénale du responsable de l'infraction et à la condamnation civile dudit responsable.

Or, du fait que le Tribunal fédéral des brevets a une compétence exclusive pour se prononcer sur la contrefaçon d'un brevet et sur les créances pouvant en résulter (dommages-intérêts, remise du gain), il apparaît que le lésé ne pourra plus prendre de conclusions civiles dans le cadre de la procédure pénale. Ceci est sans doute regrettable puisque le lésé devra consacrer davantage de temps et d'énergie pour obtenir un jugement condamnant l'auteur de la contrefaçon à le dédommager. Un dédommagement plus rapide ne pourra intervenir que dans le cadre d'une transaction portant en particulier sur les conditions de retrait de la plainte.

E. Les licences obligatoires fondées sur le droit de la concurrence

STIEGER considère que le texte de l'article 26 al. 1 let. a LTFB plaide en faveur de la compétence exclusive du Tribunal fédéral des brevets pour trancher une prétention tendant à ce qu'une licence obligatoire soit accordée sur la base de la loi sur les cartels[57].

56 Code de procédure pénale suisse du 5 octobre 2007 (CPP), FF 2007, pp. 6583-6752, qui entre en vigueur le 1er janvier 2011.

57 STIEGER, *supra* note 39, p. 9 s.

Il convient de se rallier à cette position, étant précisé que le Tribunal fédéral des brevets devra demander l'avis de la Commission fédérale de la Concurrence sur la question de savoir s'il y a une restriction illicite à la concurrence (art. 15 LCart).

VI. Tribunal fédéral des brevets et arbitrage

Avant de conclure, il reste à examiner les éventuelles conséquences de l'introduction de la nouvelle loi sur le Tribunal fédéral des brevets en matière d'arbitrage. En particulier, l'attribution d'une compétence exclusive au Tribunal fédéral des brevets aura-t-elle pour effet de soustraire de l'arbitrage les litiges portant sur la validité, la contrefaçon et l'octroi d'une licence sur un brevet ? A notre sens, compte tenu des critères d'arbitrabilité prévus tant en matière internationale qu'en matière interne, la réponse à cette question doit être négative.

En matière d'arbitrage international, l'article 177 al. 1 LDIP fixe un critère matériel d'arbitrabilité selon lequel « toute cause de nature patrimoniale peut faire l'objet d'un arbitrage »[58]. La loi sur le droit international privé suisse ne réserve pas expressément la compétence exclusive des tribunaux étatiques. Dans son arrêt Fincantieri, le Tribunal fédéral l'a confirmé et a précisé que l'arbitrabilité pourrait toutefois être niée «à l'égard des prétentions dont le traitement aurait été réservé exclusivement à une juridiction étatique par des dispositions qu'il s'imposerait de prendre en considération sous l'angle de l'ordre public »[59]. A notre sens, il découle tant de la loi sur le droit international privé, que de la jurisprudence du Tribunal fédéral que l'arbitrabilité d'un litige ne dépend que du caractère patrimonial de la cause, peu importe que la cause soit soumise à la compétence exclusive d'une certaine autorité, à moins que cette compétence exclusive ne soit dictée par des motifs d'ordre public international[60]. En droit des brevets, l'ensemble des prétentions que pourrait faire valoir le titulaire d'un tel droit, son partenaire contractuel ou un éventuel

58 Gabrielle Kaufmann-Kohler / Antonio Rigozzi, Arbitrage international – Droit et pratique à la lumière de la LDIP, Zurich 2007, N. 202 ; Jean-François Poudret / Sébastien Besson, Comparative Law of International Arbitration, 2ème éd., Zurich 2007, N. 338.

59 ATF 118 II 353, cons. 3c, confirmé dans l'arrêt 4A_370 / 2007 du 21 février 2008, cons. 5.2.2. Poudret / Besson, *supra* note 58, N. 345.

60 Briner, BaK 2007, *ad* art. 177, N. 12 et 13.

contrefacteur tendent à satisfaire un intérêt économique[61]. De telles prétentions ont par conséquent une nature patrimoniale et peuvent faire l'objet d'un arbitrage[62].

En matière d'arbitrage interne, le droit suisse est actuellement plus restrictif qu'en matière internationale. En effet, l'article 5 du Concordat intercantonal sur l'arbitrage[63] soumet l'arbitrabilité d'un litige à deux critères ; d'une part, le droit litigieux doit être librement disponible et, d'autre part, la cause ne doit pas relever de la compétence exclusive d'une autorité étatique. En droit des brevets, cette restriction supplémentaire n'empêche toutefois pas l'arbitrabilité des litiges ; en effet dans une décision de 1945, le Tribunal fédéral a jugé que la compétence de la juridiction cantonale unique prévue par l'article 76 LBI n'était pas exclusive[64]. Cette solution a été confirmée par la suite, notamment dans un avis du 15 décembre 1975 du Bureau fédéral de la propriété intellectuelle (actuellement Institut fédéral de la propriété intellectuelle), dans lequel il a établi que les tribunaux arbitraux étaient habilités à décider de la validité de droits de propriété intellectuelle[65].

Dès l'entrée en vigueur du nouveau code de procédure civile, la réserve en faveur des autorités étatiques exclusivement compétentes appartiendra au passé. En effet, l'article 354 CPC abandonne la limitation selon laquelle l'arbitrabilité d'un litige est exclue s'il est de la compétence exclusive d'une autorité étatique, en maintenant uniquement le critère de la disponibilité de la prétention litigeuse[66].

Ainsi, tant au regard du critère de patrimonialité, prévu par l'article 177 LDIP, que du critère de la libre disponibilité, selon le nouvel

61 Selon l'ATF 118 II 353, cons. 3b, peuvent être considérées comme patrimoniales « toutes les prétentions qui ont une valeur pécuniaire pour les parties, à titre d'actif ou de passif, autrement dit les droits qui présentent, pour l'une au moins de celles-ci, un intérêt pouvant être apprécié en argent ».

62 Bernard Dutoit, Droit international privé suisse, Commentaire de la loi fédérale du 18 décembre 1987, 4ème éd., Bâle / Genève / Munich 2005, *ad* art. 109, N. 13 ; Jegher, BaK 2007, *ad* art. 109, N. 59-60 ; Kaufmann-Kohler / Rigozzi, *supra* note 58, N. 204 ; Poudret / Besson, *supra* note 58, N. 355 ; Vischer, IPRG-Kommentar, *ad* art. 109, N. 19.

63 Concordat du 27 mars 1969 sur l'arbitrage, RS 279.

64 ATF 71 III 198 ; Pierre Jolidon, Commentaire du concordat suisse sur l'arbitrage, Berne 1984, p. 162, N. 422.

65 RSPIDA 1976, pp. 36-38 ; Jolidon, *supra* note 64, p. 162, N. 422.

66 Kaufmann-Kohler / Rigozzi, *supra* note 58, N. 195-199. Message relatif au code de procédure civile suisse, du 28 juin 2006, FF 2006, pp. 7000-7001.

article 354 CPC, l'introduction de la nouvelle loi sur le Tribunal fédéral des brevets n'aura aucune conséquence sur la faculté quasi illimitée des parties de soumettre un litige portant sur un brevet à la compétence d'un tribunal arbitral[67]. En effet, ce n'est que sous l'empire du Concordat sur l'arbitrage que l'on aurait pu craindre que, en matière d'arbitrage interne, l'attribution d'une compétence exclusive au Tribunal fédéral des brevets pour connaître de certains litiges ait pour effet de soustraire ces derniers à l'arbitrage. Dans la mesure où la nouvelle loi sur le Tribunal fédéral des brevets ne devrait pas entrer en vigueur avant le nouveau code de procédure civile suisse, un tel cas de figure sera heureusement évité.

Cela étant, l'arbitrage des litiges portant sur la propriété intellectuelle est sans doute appelé à se développer davantage encore du fait de certains inconvénients liés à la mise en place du Tribunal fédéral des brevets, par exemple le fait que les litiges seront à terme et selon toute vraisemblance traités à St-Gall, même si les parties ont pu convenir d'une élection de for.

VII. Droit transitoire

L'art. 41 LTFB dispose que « le Tribunal fédéral des brevets reprend, dans son domaine de compétence, le traitement des procédures qui, au moment de l'entrée en vigueur de la présente loi, sont pendantes devant les tribunaux cantonaux, pour autant que les débats principaux n'aient pas eu lieu ».

La LTFB ne définit pas ce qu'il faut entendre par débats principaux et ne précise pas quelle est la loi de procédure qu'il faut appliquer pour déterminer ce qu'il faut entendre par débats principaux. Logiquement, compte tenu du fait que le droit cantonal de procédure continuera de régir la procédure applicable aux litiges pendants au 31 décembre 2010, il faudra se fonder sur le droit de procédure du canton dont la justice est saisie.

Aux termes du Message du Conseil fédéral, le transfert des dossiers vers le Tribunal fédéral des brevets dépendra du stade d'avancement de la procédure devant le tribunal cantonal[68]. Si le litige fait déjà l'objet de

67 On constate d'ailleurs que le Message LTFB n'a pas du tout abordé la question de l'arbitrage.

68 FF 2007, p. 412.

l'administration des preuves (expertise ordonnée ; témoins auditionnés), l'économie de procédure devrait commander la poursuite du procès devant la juridiction cantonale.

Il convient de faire preuve de retenue dans le transfert des litiges vers le Tribunal fédéral des brevets dans la mesure où la solution légale va assez clairement à l'encontre des principes de droit transitoire généralement applicables aux modifications des règles de compétence matérielle[69].

VIII. Conclusions

La LTFB a l'avantage d'assurer une cohérence entre la réglementation de la compétence interne et la réglementation de la compétence internationale, en matière de brevet. La LTFB est conforme à la tendance européenne et communautaire, à savoir la compétence exclusive en matière de validité et de contrefaçon. En matière internationale, on peut attendre un impact positif de la compétence exclusive du Tribunal fédéral des brevets.

Au plan interne, on peut regretter que la LTFB prévoie encore des compétences concurrentes en faveur des tribunaux cantonaux. Ceci pourrait constituer à terme un handicap, notamment lorsque les parties cherchent à régler dans un contrat de licence la question de savoir si l'on choisit l'arbitrage ou si l'on opte pour une élection de for en faveur des tribunaux ordinaires. En effet, en portant leur choix sur une élection de for en faveur des tribunaux ordinaires, les parties s'exposent à devoir saisir dans un premier temps le tribunal cantonal compétent d'une action en paiement de redevances, puis à devoir accepter que cette procédure soit transmise au Tribunal fédéral des brevets ou soit suspendue dans l'attente d'une décision de ce tribunal. La solution retenue par la LTFB complique la procédure et la rendra nécessairement plus onéreuse. C'est pourquoi les parties auront intérêt soit à conclure une prorogation de for en faveur du Tribunal fédéral des brevets, soit à opter pour l'arbitrage. Une élection de for en faveur d'un tribunal cantonal ne présente en définitive que des inconvénients.

L'arbitrabilité des litiges est préservée. L'arbitrage constituera le seul moyen pour assurer l'autonomie des parties au plan interne. Le succès du Tribunal fédéral des brevets se mesurera également à l'évolution des litiges en matière de brevets qui sont soumis à l'arbitrage.

69 ATF 119 II 46, JdT 1994 I 109 ss.

ICANN's New gTLD Program: Applicant Guidebook and Dispute Resolution

Torsten Bettinger[*]

I. Introduction

The Internet Corporation for Assigned Names and Numbers (ICANN) dedicated to coordinating the domain name system, published on May 31, 2010 the 4th Draft of the Applicant Guidebook[1] (DAG 4) for new generic Top-Level-Domains (new gTLDs).

The gTLD Applicant Guidebook is the outcome of a detailed and lengthy consultation process with all constituencies of the global Internet community (registries, registrars, Internet service or access providers, commercial and non-commercial Internet users, trademark associations and holders of industrial property rights). The draft provides for an expansion of the domain name system to an unlimited number of new generic top-level domains (gTLDs) and constitutes a fundamental change in the present domain name system, which is limited to 21 gTLDs. The new gTLD Program is bound to have far-reaching consequences for the Internet and the brand name industries.

Once again, the global Internet community is called upon to contribute to the public discussion of the draft. The final version of the Applicant Guidebook is expected to be published in the fourth quarter of 2010. The exact opening date of the gTLD application submission period still remains to be fixed.

* RA Dr. Torsten Bettinger, LL.M., BETTINGER SCHNEIDER SCHRAMM, Patent- und Rechtsanwälte, München, www.bettinger.de.

1 Hereinafter referred to as « Version 4 DAG »; it is available at http://www.icann.org/en/topics/new-gtlds/comments-4-en.htm.

II. Assignment Criteria

A. Unlimited number of new TLDs

The Draft Applicant Guidebook provides for an unlimited expansion of the domain namespace. Upon completion of the first application round, ICANN is expected to assign up to 500 new top-level domains. Potential uses of the new gTLDs range from exclusively proprietary use by individual companies (e. g., .ibm, .sap, .allianz, .kpmg), the use of a gTLD by companies pertaining to a specific sector of industry (e. g., .travel, .hotel, .bank), members of social networks or gaming communities (e. g., .facebook, .xing, .PS3, .wii), special interest groups (e. g., .sport, .eco, .golf, .food, .wine), businesses or individuals of a specific geographic region (e. g., .berlin, .bayern, .nyc) or language communities [e. g., .cym (Wales), .gal (Galicia), .bzh (Brittany)] to the use of a gTDL for unrestricted assignment of second-level domains to enterprises across all industrial sectors, organizations or private individuals (e. g., .web, .shop, .buy).

B. Available characters and namespace structure

The gTLDs applied for may be written with ASCII characters or non-Latin letters (so-called internationalized gTLDs or IDNs). Consequently, transliterations of symbols of languages other than those using Latin letters (e. g., Chinese, Korean, Japanese, Cyrillic, Arabic) can also be registered.

Registrants of gTLDs are free to choose the structure of namespaces and design the terms and conditions of gTLD registration.

When a gTLD is assigned, the concept of use described in the application as well as the registration policy become subject matters of the registry agreement executed with ICANN and, therefore, may be amended only with ICANN's consent.

C. Eligibility requirements

As a rule, only corporations, organizations or institutions in good standing and established in accordance with the applicable law of their jurisdictions may apply for new gTLDs, while individuals or sole proprietorships are not eligible.[2] Proof of legal establishment or good standing may be furnished by submitting excerpts from public registers (commercial register, register of associations, etc.) or notarization.

ICANN may exclude applicants, their partners, managers or other executives from the application procedure if they have been convicted within the past ten years of a felony or a misdemeanor related to offences against property or tax offences or against whom disciplinary proceedings have been instituted on equivalent charges. This also applies to applicants and their partners, managers or other executives who have been the subject of a pattern of decisions indicating a practice of bad faith in respect of domain name registrations or uses.[3]

D. Assignment of gTLDs: ‹first come, first served›

gTLDs are assigned according to the principle of ‹first come, first served›. As a result, gTLDs that have already been assigned in the first application round can never be assigned to any third party thereafter. In the case that more than one applicant applies for the very same gTLD in the first application round (e. g., several corporations all having the same company logo applying for a domain name identical to such logo), the gTLD will be assigned by way of a comparative evaluation procedure or through an auction process (see Section VI herein below).

E. Distinction between ‹standard gTLD applications› and ‹community based gTLD applications›

The Draft Applicant Guidebook distinguishes two types of gTLD applications[4]:

(1) *Standard applications* relating to gTLDs that may be used for any purpose consistent with the requirements of the application and evaluation criteria and with the registry agreement to be entered into with ICANN (c.f. Section VII herein below) and that may be reserved for a specific user population or may be freely available to all Internet users.

2 See subsection 1.2.1, Module 1, DAG, Version 4.

3 See subsection 1.2.1, Module 1, DAG, Version 4.

4 See subsection 1.2.3, Module 1, DAG, Version 4.

(2) *Community-based gTLD applications* that are operated for the benefit of clearly delineated communities. An applicant who claims that its gTLD application relates to a specific community associated with the gTLD applied for must substantiate its status as a representative of such community and is expected to:

- demonstrate an ongoing relationship with a clearly delineated community;
- have applied for a gTLD string strongly and specifically related to the community named in the application;
- have proposed dedicated registration and use policies for registrants in its proposed gTLD commensurate with the community-based purpose it has named; and
- Have its application endorsed in writing by one or more established institutions representing the community it has named.

The designation as a standard gTLD application or as a community-based gTLD application will have implications in particular if contesting applications are filed for the same TLD (see the relevant passages in Section 5 herein below).

III. Stages of the Application Procedure

The times and dates of the opening and closing of the first application submission period have not yet been set. The first application submission period is expected to open no later than in the second half of 2010 and the period during which gTLD applications can be submitted to ICANN is expected to be no longer than 2 months. ICANN announced that upon completion of the application procedure of the first application submission round there would be a succession of subsequent application submission rounds.

A. Application Submission Period and Administrative Completeness Check

Application documents must be submitted through the TAS (Top-Level-Domain Application System), the TLD online application system provided by ICANN. Through the TAS, ICANN provides access to a set of more than 50 questions mainly relating to the applicant, the gTLD applied for, the proposed use of the gTLD, architecture and operation of the registry system as well as various financial aspects of the TLD application (budget, financial plan, etc.).[5] All application documents, including the required supporting documents, must be submitted electronically through the TAS exclusively.[6]

B. Payment of the Application Fees

Upon submission of an application, a gTLD evaluation fee in the amount of USD 185,000 has to be paid to ICANN. Receipt of payment in due time is prerequisite for participating in the new gTLD application procedure, for the applicant to be evaluated and for the gTLD applied for to be assigned (Evaluation Procedures).[7]

Part of the fee to be paid to ICANN will be refunded if an application for registration is withdrawn before the evaluation process is complete [if withdrawn after posting of applications until posting of initial Evaluation results: USD 130,000 refund (70 %); if withdrawn after posting Initial Evaluation results: USD 65,000 refund (35 %); after the applicant has completed Dispute Resolution Extended Evaluation or String Contention Resolution: USD 37,000 (20 %).[8]

Additional fees of USD 50,000 may be incurred if an extended technical evaluation by an expert panel is required (registry services technical evaluation panel).[9]

Upon the close of the application submission period, ICANN will check the application documents received for completeness and post those considered complete on the Internet. Answers to certain finance and security related questions, however, will not be posted.[10]

5 See subsection 1.4, Module 2, DAG, Version 4.
6 See subsection 1.5.2, Module 1, DAG, Version 4.
7 See subsection 1.5.1, Module 1, DAG, Version 4.
8 See subsection 1.5, Module 1, DAG, Version 4.
9 See subsection 1.5.2, Module 1, DAG, Version 4.
10 See subsection 1.1.2.2, Module 1, DAG, Version 4.

C. Initial Evaluation Phase

A prerequisite for being assigned a TLD, applicants must have successfully completed the evaluation procedure. During this procedure, ICANN will check whether

(1) the gTLD applied for is identical to an existing gTLD or another one applied for in the same application round or is likely to cause security or stability problems in the domain name system (string review),
(2) the applicant has the requisite technical and financial capability to operate a gTLD registry (applicant review), and
(3) the applicant's proposed registry services may have an adverse impact on security or stability of the domain name system (registry services review).

1. *String Review*

(1) As a prerequisite for a gTLD to be assigned, the gTLD applied for must not be identical with an existing gTLD or one applied for in the same application submission round[11] or a reserved name[12] and must not so nearly resemble another gTLD visually that it is likely to deceive or cause confusion. Mere association, in the sense that a gTLD brings another one to an Internet user's mind, is insufficient to create a likelihood of confusion.[13]

In a first step, an algorithmic score is used in a computer assisted process to check whether the gTLD applied for is likely to deceive or be confused with existing or applied-for gTLDs. This score provides a measure of similarity between gTLDs. Subsequently, an independent so-called String Similarity Panel appointed by ICANN will perform its own review of similarities.[14]

11 A list of existing TLDs is available at http://www.iana.org/domains/root/db /; in addition, the check includes IDN ccTLDs assigned in the so-called IDN ccTLD Fast Track process ; for more detail, see http://www.icann.org/en/topics/idn/fast-track/.

12 For the Top-Level Reserved Names List, see subsection 2.2.1.2, Module 2, DAG, Version 4.

13 For more detail, see subsection 2.2.1.1.1, Module 2, DAG, Version 4.

14 For more detail, see subsection 2.2.1.1.1, Module 2, DAG, Version 4.

If the panel finds that an applied-for gTLD is likely to deceive or cause confusion with an existing gTLD or one that has been reserved by ICANN, this will conclude the evaluation procedure and the gTLD application will be denied.[15]

If the panel finds that a gTLD applied for is at risk of deception or confusion with another gTLD applied for in the same application round, the evaluation procedure will continue and a decision on the gTLD application and the applicant to be assigned the gTLD applied for will be made in a so-called string contention procedure at a later stage of the application procedure (for details of the string contention procedure, see Section VI herein below).

(2) Furthermore, ICANN will review whether a gTLD applied for might expose the domain name system to security or instability risks, whether it is composed of the valid ASCII characters and symbols[16] as specified in the applicable technical standards and whether it complies with the standards for internationalized domain names.

(3) If an applied-for gTLD is considered a geographical name[17], special rules apply; in particular, the applicant must furnish proof in this case that its application is supported or at least not objected to by the relevant governments or public authorities having jurisdiction of the geographical region or place.[18] A Geographic Names Panel (GNP) will review whether these conditions apply.[19] If there is more than one application for a gTLD representing a geographical name in one application round and the required supporting documents have been submitted, the applications will be suspended and the applicants requested to settle the conflict by common consent.[20]

15 For more detail, see subsection 2.2.1.1.3, Module 2, DAG, Version 4.

16 Relevant standards are RFC 1035 and RFC 2181; for more detail, see subsection 2.1.1.3.1, Module 2, DAG, Version 4.

17 According to the DAB, Version 4, geographical names include (1) country names, (2) alpha-3 codes of country names and short-forms of country names listed in the ISO 3166-1 standard as well as names that are associated with a code designated as ‹exceptionally reserved› by ISO Code 3155.

18 See subsection 2.2.1.4, Module 2, DAG, Version 4.

19 See subsection 2.2.1.4.3, Module 2, DAG, Version 4.

20 See subsection 2.2.1.4.3, Module 2, DAG, Version 4.

2. *Applicant Review*

Furthermore, for an applicant to be assigned a gTLD, the applicant must demonstrate its technical (technical / operational review) and financial capabilities required to operate the registry. The requirements are specified in detail in subsection 2.1.2 of the DAG.[21] An expert panel (technical and financial panel of evaluators) will conduct the technical and financial evaluation based on the documents submitted by the applicants.[22]

3. *Registry Services Review*

Applicants are not required to demonstrate that they have a functioning registry service system in place already at the time of the evaluation stage. It will be sufficient for an applicant to demonstrate a clear understanding of the tasks and functions of a registry operation and some preparatory work for operating a gTLD registry, or to name a registry service provider offering the required registry services.[23] An expert panel will examine whether the registry services proposed in the application meet the requirements in terms of stability and security.[24]

4. *Extended Evaluation*

An applicant whose application has failed to pass the initial evaluation may object to ICANN's decision and request an extended evaluation against payment of an additional fee.[25]

IV. Third Party Objections to a gTDL Application

Module 3 of the Draft Applicant Guidebook provides that any third party may file an objection to the assignment of a gTLD to an applicant within 90 days of posting the applications in an ICANN report.[26]

21 The key technical questions to be answered by applicants concern connectivity, the registry system, nameservers, WHOIS database, payment system, but also matters such as IDN, DNSSEC and IPv6 support.

22 See subsection 2.2.2.3, Module 2, DAG, Version 4.

23 See subsection 2.2.3, Module 2, DAG, Version 4.

24 See subsection 2.2.3.4, Module 2, DAG, Version 4.

25 See subsection 2.3, Module 1, DAG, Version 4.

26 See subsection 3.1, Module 3, DAG, Version 4.

Whether or not an objection is justified will be determined by alternative dispute resolution proceedings. An objection may be filed on any one of the following four grounds:

- likelihood of confusion of the gTLD applied for with an existing or applied-for gTLD (string confusion objection);
- infringement of third-party rights recognized under international agreements or standards (legal rights objection);
- violation of generally accepted legal norms of morality and public order by the applied-for gTLD (morality and public order objection); or
- likelihood of negative impacts on a recognized community that is associated with the applied-for gTLD (community objection).

The procedural rules are set forth in the ‹New gTLD Dispute Resolution Procedure› (new gTLD DRP)[27], which is supplemented by the rules of procedure of the competent dispute resolution service provider (DRSP).[28] The language in all proceedings is English (Art. 5, New gTLD DRP). All communications in the proceedings must be submitted electronically (Art. 6, New gTLD DRP). Disputes are usually resolved without a hearing but the competent panel may decide in its sole discretion to hold a hearing under special circumstances (Art. 19, New gTLD DRP).

Before accepting the first dispute resolution proceedings, the competent DRSP will have published a schedule of fees specifying in detail the costs of the proceedings.

A. Likelihood of confusion of the gTLD with an existing or applied-for gTLD (string confusion objection)

Even if ICANN has not raised any objection in the evaluation procedure to a gTLD applied for on grounds of a likely confusion with another gTLD already existing or applied for in the same application round, gTLD operators previously accredited by ICANN or applicants of the same application round may initiate arbitration on the ground that the gTLD applied for is likely to be confused with an existing one or another gTLD applied for in the same application round. The competent body for administering such alternative dispute resolution proceedings is the

27 See attachment to Module 3 of the DAG, Version 4.

28 See subsection 3.2, Module 3, DAG, Version 4.

International Center for Dispute Resolution, a dispute resolution service provider established for international conflicts by the American Arbitration Association in the USA.[29] If the panel finds that the objection is well founded, ICANN will reject the application.

B. Infringement of third-party rights recognized under international agreements or standards (legal rights objection)

Holders of marks may object to gTLDs applied for by filing dispute resolution proceedings if the potential use of a gTLD applied for

- takes unfair advantage of the distinctive character or the reputation of the objector's trademark or service mark (‹ mark ›),
- unjustifiably impairs the distinctive character or the reputation of the objector's mark, or
- creates an impermissible likelihood of confusion between the applied-for TLD and the objector's mark).[30]

In interpreting the above elements, the panelists presiding over a legal rights objection will have to consider the following factors:

1. Whether the applied-for TLD is identical or similar, including in appearance, phonetic sound or meaning, to the objector's existing mark.
2. Whether the objector's acquisition and use of rights in the mark has been bona fide.
3. Whether and to what extent there is recognition in the relevant sector of the public of the sign corresponding to the TLD, as the mark of the objector, of the applicant, or of a third party.
4. Applicant's intent in applying for the TLD, including whether the applicant, at the time of application for the TLD, had knowledge of the objector's mark, or could not have reasonably been unaware of that mark, and including whether the applicant has engaged in a pattern of conduct whereby it applied for or operates TLDs or registrations in TLDs which are identical or confusingly similar to the marks of others.

29 See subsection 3.1.3, Module 3, DAG, Version 4.

30 See subsection 3.4.2, Module 3, DAG, Version 4.

5. Whether and to what extent the applicant has used, or has made demonstrable preparations to use, the sign corresponding to the TLD in connection with a bona fide offering of goods or services or a bona fide provision of information in a way that does not interfere with the legitimate exercise by the objector of its mark rights.
6. Whether the applicant has marks or other intellectual property rights in the sign corresponding to the TLD, and, if so, whether any acquisition of such a right in the sign, and use of the sign, has been bona fide, and whether the purported or likely use of the TLD by the applicant is consistent with such acquisition or use.
7. Whether and to what extent the applicant has been commonly known by the sign corresponding to the TLD, and if so, whether any purported or likely use of the TLD by the applicant is consistent therewith and bona fide.
8. Whether the applicant's intended use of the TLD would create a likelihood of confusion with the objector's mark as to the source, sponsorship, affiliation, or endorsement of the TLD.

Filing an objection under the above ADR procedure, does not preclude an objector from filing an action in a court of law.

C. Violation of generally accepted legal norms of morality and public order by the applied-for gTLD (morality and public order objection)

As a rule, anyone who feels that a gTLD applied for violates legal norms of public order and morality generally recognized in international law may file an objection to the application in dispute resolution proceedings. A so-called ‹ quick look procedure › is designed to dismiss frivolous and / or abusive objections right away.[31]

The grounds upon which an applied-for gTLD string may be considered contrary to morality and public order according to internationally recognized standards are:

- incitement to or promotion of violent lawless action,
- incitement to or promotion of discrimination based upon race, color, gender, ethnicity, religion or national origin,

31 See subsection 3.1.2.3, Module 3, DAG, Version 4.

- incitement to or promotion of child pornography or other sexual abuse of children, or
- a determination that an applied-for gTLD string would be contrary to equally generally accepted identified legal norms relating to morality and public order that are recognized under general principles of international law.[32]

Examples of such internationally recognized principles of law include, but are not limited to the Universal Declaration of Human Rights (UDHR), the International Covenant on Civil and Political Rights (ICCPR), the Convention on the Elimination of all Forms of Discrimination against Women (CEDAW), the International Convention on the Elimination of All Forms of Racial Discrimination, intellectual property treaties administered by the World Intellectual Property Organization (WIPO) and the WTO Agreement on Trade Related Aspects of Intellectual Property Rights (TRIPS).[33]

The competent body to administer such disputes is the International Center of Expertise of the International Chamber of Commerce of Paris.[34]

D. Likelihood of negative impacts on a recognized community that is associated with the applied-for gTLD (community objection)

Finally, established institutions related to clearly delineated communities may file an objection to an applied-for gTLD if the latter are clearly associated with this applied-for gTLD.[35]

For an objection to be successful, the objector must prove that:

- the community invoked by the objector is a clearly delineated community,
- community opposition to the application is substantial,
- there is a strong association between the community invoked and the applied-for gTLD string, and
- there is a likelihood of detriment to the community named.[36]

32 See subsection 3.4.3, Module 3, DAG, Version 4.

33 Explanatory Notes, Standards for Morality and Public Order Research, Fn. 2.

34 See subsection 3.1.3, Module 3, DAG, Version 4.

35 See subsection 3.4.4, Module 3, DAG, Version 4.

36 See subsection 3.4.4, Module 3, DAG, Version 4.

The competent body to administer such disputes is the International Center of Expertise of the International Chamber of Commerce of Paris.[37]

V. Independent Objector

Even though no complaint may have been filed by any other third-party, an « Independent Objector » (IO) acting in the public interest may still initiate dispute resolution proceedings against a gTLD string application.[38]

The IO does not act on behalf of any particular persons or entities, but acts solely in the best interests of the public who use the global Internet. In light of this public interest goal, the Independent Objector is limited to filing objections on the grounds of Morality and Public Order and negative impacts of a new gTLD on a recognized and clearly delineated Community. Neither ICANN staff nor the ICANN Board of Directors has authority to direct or require the IO to file or not file any particular objection. If the IO determines that an objection should be filed, he or she will initiate and prosecute the objection in the public interest.

The IO will be selected by ICANN, through an open and transparent process, and retained as an independent consultant. The Independent Objector will be an individual with considerable experience and respect in the Internet community, unaffiliated with any gTLD applicant.

VI. String Contention Procedure in the Case of Two or More Applicants for the Same gTLD String

If two or more applications for the same gTLD string have successfully completed the evaluation and objection stages, or if two or more gTLD strings applied for in the same application round cause confusion (string contention), it needs to be decided which of the contending applicants is to be allocated the gTLD applied for. In this case, the Applicant Guidebook provides that ICANN will first notify the applicants of the

37 See subsection 3.1.3, Module 3, DAG, Version 4.

38 See subsection 3.1.5, Module 3, DAG, Version 4.

contention occurred and request them to settle it by common consent.[39].

If the applicants fail to reach an agreement, the gTLD string applied for will be allocated either by means of a comparative evaluation or by an auction process.

If a contention set is composed exclusively of applications for a ‹standard gTLD›, allocation will be by means of an auction, i.e. the gTLD will be allocated to the applicant willing to submit the highest bid for the allocation.[40]

If one or more of the contending applicants have designated their applications as community-based[41], the respective applicants may elect to participate in a community priority (comparative) evaluation procedure where a comparative evaluation panel will review and score against the four criteria listed below whether an applicant can prove by clear and convincing evidence to have the support of the community invoked (qualified community application).[42]

(1) Community establishment,
(2) nexus between proposed string and community,
(3) dedicated registration policies, and
(4) community endorsement.

For each of the above criteria, applicants may score between 0 and 4 points on a scoring scale indicating to what extent an applicant meets the various criteria.[43]

If only one of the contending applicants scores 14 or more points, this applicant will be declared the winner of the comparative evaluation and prevail over those other contenders who have designated their applications as standard and those who have failed to score the minimum of 14 points required in the comparative evaluation of community-based applications.

39 See subsection 4.1, Module 4, DAG, Version 4.

40 For details of the auction procedure, see subsection 4.3, Module 4, DAG, Version 4.

41 The term « community » is broadly interpreted and may include, but not be limited to associations of legal entities (e.g., an association of providers of a particular service), of individuals (e.g.., a language community), or of an alliance of communities (e.g., an international federation of national communities of a similar nature); see Explanatory notes, subsection 4.2.3, Module 4, DAG, Version 4).

42 See subsection 4.2.2, Module 4, DAG, Version 4.

43 See subsection 4.2.3, Module 4, DAG, Version 4.

If more than one applicant having submitted an application designated as community-based score the required 14 points, the contention is resolved by way of auction for which only community-based applications having scored more than 14 points are eligible, as opposed to standard applications.

If none of the contenders score the required 14 points, all of the parties in the contention set (both standard and community-based applicants) will proceed to an auction.

As a rule, an application for a gTLD string that is identical with the company's mark or logo and that is intended exclusively for the company's proprietary use will not be considered a qualified community-based application; therefore, contentions among companies for the same gTLD string will usually be resolved by way of auction.

VII. gTLD Delegation and Execution of Contract with ICANN

At the end of an application procedure and prior to gTLD string delegation for its inclusion in the root zone, each applicant is required to complete pre-delegation testing where ICANN will review the applicant's DNS infrastructure and registry system. If the DNS infrastructure and the registry system meet the requirements specified in the DAG, the gTLD is delegated to the applicant and a standard-term registry agreement with ICANN is executed.[44] The term of the registry agreement is 10 years and may be renewed for successive periods of another ten years.[45]

VIII. Post-Delegation Dispute Resolution

Trademark industry repeatedly pointed out to ICANN that they would accept the expansion of the domain name system to an unlimited number of new TLDs only if rights protection mechanisms were implemented to prevent registration of domain names that abuse trademark rights.

44 The draft registry agreement is available as an attachment to Module 5, DAG, Version 4.

45 See Art. 4, subsection 4.2, New gTLD Agreement.

Against this backdrop, ICANN proposed already in its first two drafts of the Draft Applicant Guidebook that trademark holders may resort to alternative dispute resolution proceedings to defend themselves against registrations of their marks as gTLDs by any third party that violate or abuse their legal rights.

However, the trademark industry, in particular INTA and the WIPO Arbitration and Mediation Center[46], has made it clear in various comments on ICANN's new gTLD policy drafts that the proceedings proposed so far by ICANN are not suitable to effectively restrict the abuse of trademark rights and have, therefore, announced their opposition to the new TLD program unless additional effective rights protection mechanisms protecting trademark owners are established together with the introduction of the new TLDs.

In response to this criticism and after receiving extensive comments and consultation with the a broader community, ICANN decided to assemble an Implementation Recommendation Team (IRT) to develop various rights protection mechanisms able to restrict effectively any abuse in domain name registration under the new gTLDs.[47]

On May 29, 2009, the IRT published its recommendations[48] whose key elements were the :

(1) establishment of an Trademark Clearinghouse,
(2) special protection of globally protected marks in the areas of both top-level domains and second-level domains by drawing up a globally protected marks list,
(3) implementation of various pre-launch (prior to the TLD registration stage) and post-launch (after the commencement of the TLD registration stage) rights protection mechanisms and

ICANN then provided the GNSO council with the opportunity to offer input on the specific rights protection mechanisms as proposed by the IRT. The GNSO took on this task and established a « Special Trademark Issues Revue Team » (STI) to review the proposal and offer its input upon which the GNSO would be able to reach consensus.

46 See the WIPO correspondence with ICANN, related to the new gTLD program, at http://www.wipo.int/amc/en/domains/resources/icann/.

47 The IRT is group assembled by ICANN which is mostly comprised of U.S. corporate and trademark lawyers.

48 Available at http://www.icann.org/en/topics/new-gtlds/irt-final-report-trademark-protection-29may09-en.pdf (hereafter : the IRT Report)

On the basis of their recommendations the following proposals have been adopted by ICANN for inclusion in the fourth version of the new TLD Applicants Guidebook. Again, ICANN asks for community input on these issues before publishing the final version of the DAG probably in December 2010.

A. Establishment of a Trademark Clearinghouse

1. Purpose of Clearinghouse and Criteria for trademark inclusion in the Clearinghouse

DAG 4 proposes the creation of a Trademark Clearinghouse which is envisioned as a data repository enabling specific information collection and data validation functions for trademark information. Under the proposed model, trademark rights holders would voluntarily submit data regarding their trademarks to the clearinghouse. The Clearinghouse which shall be separated and independent from ICANN would validate all submitted data initially and on a regular basis thereafter and disseminate the information to the new gTLD registries for Sunrise Trademark Services or Trademark Claims services.

The proposed standards for inclusion of a trademark in the Clearinghouse are :

a) Nationally or multi-nationally registered text trademarks from all jurisdictions (including from countries where there is no substantive review).
b) Any text mark that has been validated through a court of law or other judicial proceeding.
c) Any text marks protected by a statute or treaty currently in effect and that was in effect on or before 26 June 2008.

No Common law rights will be included in the Trademark Clearinghouse Database, except for court-validated common law marks. This shall not preclude any gTLD registry from entering into a separate agreement with the Clearinghouse Service Provider to collect and verify other information for ancillary services, provided that any such information is held separate from the Trademark Clearinghouse Database.

The core function for inclusion in the Clearinghouse would be to authenticate that the data meets certain minimum criteria. As such, the following minimum criteria are suggested :

a) An acceptable list of data authentication sources, i. e. the web sites of patent and trademark offices throughout the world, third party providers who can obtain information from various trademark offices;
b) Name, address and contact information of the applicant is accurate, current and matches that of the registered owner of the trademarks listed;
c) Electronic contact information is provided and accurate;
d) The registration numbers and countries match the information in the respective trademark office database for that registration number.

For validation of marks by the Clearinghouse that were not previously validated at registration or protected via a court, statute or treaty, the trademark holder shall be required to provide evidence of continuous use of the mark in connection with the bona fide offering for sale of goods or services prior to application for inclusion in the Clearinghouse. Acceptable evidence of use might be labels, tags, containers, advertising, brochures, screen shots, and any other proof that evidences continued use.

2. *Trademark Claims Service und Sunrise Trademark Services*

All new gTLD registries will be required to use the Trademark Clearinghouse to support its pre-launch rights protection mechanisms (RPMs) that must, at a minimum, consist of either a **Sunrise Trademark Service** or **Trademark Claims Service**.

a) Trademark Claim Services

It is proposed that under the trademark claims service, when a registrant seeks to register a domain name, the registrar (through an interface with the Clearinghouse) will notify the registrant if one or more marks are considered an « identical Match » with the validated trademark[49].

49 « Identical Match » means that the domain name consists of the complete and identical textual elements of the trademark. In this regard: (a) spaces contained within a mark that are either replaced by hyphens (and vice versa) or omitted; (b) only certain special characters contained within a trademark are spelled out with appropriate words describing it (@ and &); (c) punctuation or special characters contained within a mark that are unable to be used in a second-level domain name may either be (i) omitted or (ii) replaced by spaces, hyphens or underscores and still be considered identical matches; and (d) no plural and no « marks contained » would qualify for inclusion.

After notice of the dispute the Registrant will be required to warrant that:

(i) the Registrant has received notification that the trademark(s) is included in the Clearinghouse;
(ii) the Registrants has received and understood the notice; and
(iii) to the best of the Registrant's knowledge, the registration and use of the requested domain name will not infringe on the trademark rights that are the subject of the notice.

If the domain name is registered, the registrar (again through an interface with the Clearinghouse) will notify the trademark holders(s) of the registration. This notification will not be before the registration is effectuated so as not to provide an opportunity for a trademark holder to inappropriately attempt to block a legitimate registrant from registering a name in which the registrant has legitimate rights.

These provisions are based on the experience that it is owners of large domain portfolios registering domain names on a massive scale by using automated processes who are frequently behind abusive domain name registrations. The requirement of the registrant representing and warranting that it will not infringe on the trademark rights that are subject of the notice is designed to prevent such automated registrations. In addition, this requirement is expected to have a deterrent effect.

b) Sunrise Registration Services

In cases where the registry opts to provide a Sunrise registration service, the Clearinghouse would also support any new gTLD registry during its initial launch phases by facilitating « Sunrise Period » registration procedures allowing trademark holders that have registered with the Trademark Clearinghouse an exclusive period of time, prior to general registration of domain names in the TLD, to register domain names matching their trademarks.

DAG 4 requires that each new gTLD registry operator be required to provide a sunrise registration process that applies sunrise eligibility requirements (SERs) as a floor, verified by Clearinghouse data, and incorporates a Sunrise Dispute Resolution Policy (SDRP).

The proposed SERs include: (i) ownership of a trademark of national effect that issued on or before the effective date of the registry agreement and was applied for on or before ICANN publishes new gTLD application list that is identical (as defined in section 6 above) to the applied for domain name; (ii) optional registry elected requirements re: international class of goods or services covered by registration; (iii) representation that all provided information is true and correct; and (iv) provision of data sufficient to document trademark registration or facilitate its authentication to the Clearinghouse.

The proposed SRDP must allow challenges based on at least the following four grounds: (i) at the time when the challenged domain name was registered, the registrant did not own a trademark registration of national effect; (ii) the domain name is not identical to the trademark on which the registrant based its Sunrise registration; (iii) the trademark registration on which the registrant based its Sunrise registration is not of national effect; and (iv) the trademark registration on which the domain name registrant based its Sunrise registration did not issue on or before the effective date of the Registry Agreement and was not applied for on or before ICANN announced the applications received.[50]

B. Uniform Rapid Suspension System (URS)

Furthermore, DAG 4 proposes the establishment of a mandatory Uniform Rapid Suspension System (URS) among the potential solutions to trademark protections in new gTLDs.[51] The URS is designed to supplement UDRP proceedings and to provide a faster and significantly less costly means of enforcing trademark rights against the trademark infringing use of domain names.

As with the UDRP, registrants accept the URS by entering into the registry agreement, which contains a standard clause providing that every registrant agrees to submit to the principles of the URS.

Unlike UDRP proceedings designed to result in the cancellation or the transfer of the domain name concerned, URS proceedings are designed to thwart quickly the infringement and abuse of a domain name by a specific website.

50 See Art. 9.1 of the Trademark Clearinghouse, DRAFT – MAY 2010, available at http://www.icann.org/en/topics/new-gtlds/trademark-clearinghouse-clean-28may10-en.pdf.

51 See also the WIPO Arbitration and Mediation Center's critical comments on the URS in its Letter of June 16, 2010 on Rights Protection Mechanisms found in version 4 of ICANN's Draft Applicant Guidebook, available at http://www.wipo.int/export/sites/www/amc/en/docs/icann160610.pdf.

As a rule, URS proceedings are available to all owners of trademark rights, but those trademark owners who have submitted their trademark data to the Trademark Clearinghouse have access to a simpler way of using the URS proceedings because they may submit their complaints electronically, they are offered a simpler way of payment and they may use the pre-filed registrant data when completing a complaint form. The fees amount to USD 200 for complaints challenging 1–25 domain name registrations and USD 250 for complaints challenging 25–100 domain name registrations, which is significantly less than the fees to be paid in UDRP proceedings.

However, the scope of application of URS proceedings is even more limited than the scope of application of UDRP proceedings. URS proceedings are designed to handle only clear-cut cases of domain name abuses. Forms are provided for stating the grounds for a complaint with the objective to simplify the effort involved significantly as compared to filing a UDRP complaint.

The substantive evaluation criteria are largely similar to those in UDRP proceedings, i. e. the complainant is required to prove that

(1) the domain name is identical or confusingly similar to a mark,
(2) the domain name registrant has no right to or legitimate interest in the domain name and
(3) the domain name has been registered and used in bad faith. However, the burden of proof of bad faith is to be higher than in UDRP proceedings. Clear and convincing evidence of bad faith has to be furnished.

The burden of proof shall be clear and convincing evidence. This burden of proof is intentionally higher than the UDRP given that the URS is meant only for the most clear-cut blatant case of infringing conduct.

If the registrant is in default, it will be prohibited from changing content found on the site to argue that it now amounts to a legitimate use and will also be prohibited from changing the WHOIS information. If the panel seized with the dispute issues a decision in favor of the objector, the domain name remains locked at the registry and cannot be transferred or assigned to any third party during the registration term.

All in all, despite some burdensome procedures of the URS in its current version, the URS appears to be an efficient and cost-effective supplement to the UDRP proceedings. Especially the abuse of domain names for parking websites attempted by filing for UDRP proceedings clearly falls within the scope of application of the new proceedings and may be prevented at a significantly lower cost by URS proceedings.[52]

C. Trademark Post Delegation Dispute Mechanisms (Trademark PDDRP)

In addition to the above rights protection mechanisms, the IRT and the WIPO recommend the implementation of dispute resolution proceedings where trademark owners may challenge gTLD abuse (Trademark Post Delegation Dispute Mechanism).[53] The background for these recommendations is the fear that it is to be expected in the course of the expansion of the domain name system to an unlimited number of new TLDs that some registry operators will abuse the gTLDs assigned to them by ICANN in order to profit from them by registering second-level domains in a systematic and abusive manner.

The mandatory administrative proceeding will commence when a third-party complainant (« Complainant ») has filed a Complaint with a Provider asserting that the Complainant is a trademark holder (which may include either registered or unregistered marks as defined below) claiming that one or more of its marks have been infringed, and thereby the Complainant has been harmed, by the registry operator's manner of operation or use of the gTLD.

According to the recommendations in DAG 4, in order to succeed the complainant has to prove, by clear and convincing evidence, that with respect to the

Top-Level

the registry operator's affirmative conduct in its operation or use of its gTLD string that is identical or confusingly similar to the complainant's

52 See the WIPO Arbitration and Mediation Center's criticism of several procedural aspects of the URS in its Letter of April 3, 2009 on WIPO Discussion Draft – Model Expedited (Domain Name) Suspension Mechanism and Letter of June 16, 2010 on Rights Protection Mechanisms found in version 4 of ICANN's Draft Applicant Guidebook.

53 Trademark Post-Delegation Dispute Resolution Procedure (Trademark PDDRP), REVISED – MAY 2010; see also the WIPO Arbitration and Mediation Center's critical comments on the PDDRP in its Letter to ICANN of June 16, 2010 on Rights Protection Mechanisms found in version 4 of ICANN's Draft Applicant Guidebook.

mark, causes or materially contributes to the gTLD doing one of the following:

a) taking unfair advantage of the distinctive character or the reputation of the complainant's mark; or
b) unjustifiably impairing the distinctive character or the reputation of the complainant's mark; or
c) creating an impermissible likelihood of confusion with the complainant's mark.

An example of infringement at the top-level is where a TLD string is identical to a trademark and then the registry operator holds itself out as the beneficiary of the mark.[54]

Second Level

(a) there is a substantial pattern or practice of specific bad faith intent by the registry operator to profit from the sale of trademark infringing domain names; and
(b) the registry operator's bad faith intent to profit from the systematic registration of domain names within the gTLD that are identical or confusingly similar to the complainant's mark, which:
    (i) takes unfair advantage of the distinctive character or the reputation of the complainant's mark; or
    (ii) unjustifiably impairs the distinctive character or the reputation of the complainant's mark, or
    (iii) creates an impermissible likelihood of confusion with the complainant's mark.

An example of infringement at the second level is where a registry operator has a pattern or practice of actively and systematically encouraging registrants to register second level domain names and to take unfair advantage of the trademark to the extent and degree that bad faith is apparent. Another example of infringement at the second level is where a registry operator has a pattern or practice of acting as the registrant or beneficial user of infringing registrations, to monetize and profit in bad faith.[55]

54 See Trademark Post-Delegation Dispute Resolution Procedure (Trademark PDDRP), REVISED – MAY 2010, para 6.

55 See Trademark Post-Delegation Dispute Resolution Procedure (Trademark PDDRP), REVISED – MAY 2010, para 6.

D. Registry Restrictions Dispute Resolution Procedure (RRDRP)

Finally, DAG 4 proposed the implementation of a Registry Restrictions Dispute Resolution Procedure (RRDRP).

The purpose of the RRDRP is to handle complaints from a harmed organization or individual alleging that a community-based restricted gTLD registry operator was not meeting its obligations to police the registration and use of domains within the restrictions stated in the terms of the gTLD registry agreement.

The need for such a procedure is based on the idea that it would not be fair to give a preference in the new gTLD Program allocation process to an applicant based on a commitment to restrict use of a TLD to a particular community, and then not require the applicant to keep its commitment.» The improper acts of the registry operator might result in harm to the community or its member organizations or groups.[56]

E. The Recommendations of the WIPO Arbitration and Mediation Center on the Implementation of an Expedited (Domain Name) Suspension Mechansim (ESM)

In addition to the IRT recommendations, a draft Expedited Domain Name Suspension Mechanism (ESM) published by the WIPO Arbitration and Mediation Center is currently under discussion. It is also designed to supplement the UDRP and provide for a quick and cost-effective defense of legal trademark rights against any clear-cut abuse of domain name registrations.[57]

This recommendation originated mainly from the experience that more than 60 % of registrants charged in UDRP proceedings do not respond to the complaint and, consequently, a decision is usually passed in favor of the objector based on the objector's submission. Therefore, in default cases, the ESM provides for expedited proceedings where either no opinion is given at all in the notice of Conclusion of Proceedings Following Respondent's Default or where only a prima facie decision is issued without a concluding consideration of evidence. The ESM was not adopted by ICANN in DAG 4.

56 See Registry Restrictions Dispute Resolution Procedure (RRDRP), available at http://www.icann.org/en/topics/new-gtlds/rrdrp-clean-28may10-en.pdf.

57 Available at http://www.wipo.int/export/sites/www/amc/en/docs/icann030409.pdf.

IX. Conclusion

All in all, the new gTLD application procedure developed by ICANN appears to be appropriate to prevent potential negative impacts that the expansion of the domain name system to an unlimited number of new gTLDs may have on the stability of the DNS. In particular, the comprehensive technical evaluation of the gTLD and their applicants will ensure that gTLD operators have the technical and financial capacity to safeguard long-term gTLD operation and thus protect assets underlying the registration and use of domain names.

Both the potential use of a « branded » gTLD for corporate purposes and the potential for advertising under new industrial-sector specific or generic top-level domains will inevitably force corporations to realign their marketing and registration strategies relating to their domain names and will have a significant impact on domain name management as well as on the monitoring and enforcement of intellectual property rights of domain name registrations that abuse their legal rights.

If the ‹ digital Klondike gold rush › feared by the trademark industry is to be avoided and the trademark owners› legal rights protecting them against abuse in the registration and use of domain names under the new gTLDs are to be ensured, it cannot be left to the registry Operators› discretion to establish systems of legal protection to prevent domain name registrations abusing other parties› legal rights; instead, comprehensive alternative dispute resolution mechanisms supplementing the UDRP that has proven its worth in practice are necessary. Registry operators must accept these legal protection mechanisms as binding prior to being assigned a new gTLD. Therefore, the trademark industry is well advised to avail itself of the opportunity to have an impact on the ongoing decision-making process by individual companies as well as their respective federations making public comments and thus to ensure protective mechanisms for trademark owners that are as comprehensive as possible.

L'arbitrabilité des litiges de propriété intellectuelle

*Bernard Hanotiau**

1. Les litiges en matière de propriété intellectuelle sont de plus en plus fréquents. L'objet de cet article sera d'examiner dans quelle mesure ils peuvent être traités par voie d'arbitrage[1].

* Professeur à l'Université de Louvain, Avocat aux barreaux de Bruxelles et Paris, membre du Conseil de l'ICCA, Membre du Conseil de l'Institut de la CCI, Vice-Président du CEPANI (Belgique) et de l'Institute for Transnational Arbitration (Dallas). Ancien Vice-Président de la LCIA.

1 Il existe de nombreux articles sur la question. On consultera en premier lieur l'excellente analyse d'ensemble qui a été faite par JEAN-BAPTISTE RACINE dans son ouvrage sur L'arbitrage commercial international et l'ordre public, Paris, L.G.D.J., 1999, p. 78 ss. L'on consultera également le rapport final de JULIAN LEW sur les litiges de propriété intellectuelle et l'arbitrage, établi dans le cadre de la commission de l'arbitrage international de la CCI, Bulletin de la Cour d'arbitrage internationale de la CCI, 1998, 38. Parmi les autres écrits, l'on relèvera en particulier DAVID W. PLANT, Resolving International Intellecutal Property Disputes, ICC Publications, Vienne 1999, et spécialement p. 30 ss (cité: PLANT, Resolving Disputes); le remarquable article comparatif de WILLIAM GRANTHAM, The arbitrability of international intellectual property disputes, Berkeley J. Int'L., 1996, p. 173; les articles publiés dans Creative Ideas for Intellectual Property: The ATRIP Papers 2000-2001, Cedidac, Lausanne, 2002 et notamment les rapports de PAUL M. JANICKE, Arbitration of disputes concerning patents of invention, p. 214; FRANÇOIS PERRET, Arbitration and Licensing Agreements: The Swiss Experience, p. 242; CHRISTIAN LE STANC, Arbitrage et Contrat de Licence: Expérience Française, p. 247; les rapports au séminaire tenu le 19 novembre 1993 à Zurich sous les auspices de l'Association Suisse d'Arbitrage, publiés dans ASA Special Series n° 6, mars 1994, sous le titre Objective arbitrability, antitrust disputes, intellectual property disputes et notamment les rapports de MARC BLESSING, Objective arbitrability – antitrust disputes – intellectual property disputes, p. 13; BERNARD HANOTIAU, Objective arbitrability, its limits, its problem areas, p. 26; JULIAN LEW, ICC Working party on intellectual property disputes and arbitration, p. 42; FRANÇOIS DESSEMONTET, Arbitrage, propriété intellectuelle et droit de la concurrence, p. 55; FRANCIS GURRY, Objective arbitrability, antitrust disputes, intellectual property disputes, p. 110; KAMEN TROLLER, Specific aspects of intellectual property disputes in arbitration, the Swiss perspective, p. 155; CORNELIS CANENBLEY, Intellectual property law and EC antitrust law in arbitration, p. 164; les rapports publiés dans un numéro spécial de l'American Review of International Arbitration de 1994, et notamment les rapports de DAVID W. PLANT, Arbitrability of intellectual property issues in the United States, p. 11; ROBERT BRINER, The arbitrability of intellectual property disputes with partic-

I. Principes généraux

2. La Convention instituant l'Organisation Mondiale de la Propriété Intellectuelle[2] définit en son article 2 la propriété intellectuelle comme étant « les droits relatifs :

ular emphasis on the situation in Switzerland, p. 28 ; JOCHEN PAGENBERG, The arbitrability of intellectual property disputes in Germany, The American Review of International Arbitration 1994, Vol. 5, p. 44 ; les articles publiés dans l'ouvrage édité par Loukas Mistelis et Stavros Drekoulakis, Arbitrability : International and Comparative Perspectives, Kluwer Law International, 2009 et notamment les rapports de KARIM YOUSSEF, Fundamental Observations and Applicable Law, Chapter 3 – The Death of Inarbitrability, p. 47 et de ANNA P. MANTAKOU, Substantive Rules on Arbitrability, Chapter 13 – Arbitrability and Intellectual Property Disputes, p. 263 ; l'article de MARC BLESSING, Arbitrability of intellectual property disputes, publié dans le numéro spécial d'Arbitration International sur l'arbitrabilité, 1996, p. 191 ; MURIEL JOSSELIN-GALL, Arbitrage et Propriétés intellectuelles, Droit et Patrimoine, 2002, p. 63 ; ROBERTO CECCON, Arbitration and intellectual property in the Italian legal system, Journal of International Arbitration 1996, n° 1, p. 65 ; GEORGES BONET & CHARLES JARROSSON, L'arbitrabilité des litiges de propriété industrielle en droit français, *in* Arbitrage et propriété intellectuelle, Colloque de l'IRPI, Librairies Techniques, Paris 1994, p. 61 ; C. JARROSSON, note sous Cour d'Appel de Paris, 24 mars 1994, Revue de l'Arbitrage, 1994, p. 520 ; FRANÇOIS PERRET, L'arbitrabilité des litiges de propriété industrielle en droit comparé: Suisse / Allemagne / Italie, *in* Arbitrage et propriété intellectuelle, Colloque de l'IRPI, Librairies Techniques, Paris 1994, p. 73 et L'arbitrabilité des contentieux en matière de brevets d'invention, Liber Amicorum Claude Reymond, Paris, Litec, 2004, p. 229 (cité: PERRET, L'arbitrabilité des contentieux); CHRISTINE LÉCUYER-THIEFFRY, Un nouveau domaine pour l'arbitrage aux Etats-Unis : la validité et la contrefaçon des brevets, Revue de l'Arbitrage, 1985, p. 405 ; ALBERT CHAVANNE, Arbitrage, propriété industrielle et ordre public, Mélanges J. Vincent, Paris, 1981, p. 51 ; BRUNO OPPETIT, L'arbitrage en matière de brevets d'invention après la loi du 13 juillet 1978, Revue de l'Arbitrage, 1979, p. 83 ss ; PHILIPPE FOUCHARD, Les conflits de lois en matière d'arbitrabilité des litiges de propriété industrielle, Revue de l'Arbitrage, 1976-77, p. 63 ss ; YVES DERAINS, Arbitrage et brevets d'invention, Droit et pratique du commerce international, 1975, p. 91 ; YVES DERAINS, L'expérience de la Cour d'arbitrage de la Chambre de Commerce Internationale en matière de propriété industrielle, Revue de l'Arbitrage, 1977, p. 40 ; ANDRÉ FRANÇON, L'arbitrage en matière de brevet et la jurisprudence, Revue de l'Arbitrage, 1975, p. 143 ; Extraits de sentences arbitrales CCI sur la propriété intellectuelle, 1ère et 2ème parties, Bulletin de la Cour internationale d'arbitrage CCI, 1993, p. 70 et 1994, p. 66 ; F. BACHAND, Note sous Cour suprême du Canada, 21 mars 2003, Revue de l'Arbitrage, 2003, p. 482 ; DANIEL P. SIMMS, Arbitrability of intellectual property disputes in Germany, Arbitration International, 1999, p. 193 ; T. AZZI, Note sous Paris, 28 février 2008, Revue de l'Arbitrage, 2008, p. 172.

2 Signée à Stockholm le 14 juillet 1967 et modifiée le 28 septembre 1979.

- aux œuvres littéraires, artistiques et scientifiques,
- aux interprétations des artistes interprètes et aux exécutions des artistes exécutants, aux phonogrammes et aux émissions de radio diffusion, aux inventions dans tous les domaines de l'activité humaine,
- aux découvertes scientifiques,
- aux dessins et modèles industriels,
- aux marques de fabrique, de commerce et de service, ainsi qu'aux noms commerciaux et aux dénominations commerciales,
- à la protection contre la concurrence déloyale,
- et tous les autres droits afférents à l'activité intellectuelle dans les domaines industriel, scientifique, littéraire et artistique ».

3. La propriété intellectuelle a pris une place considérable dans le commerce international. Depuis vingt ans, la technologie informatique a connu un développement sans précédent et l'évolution des systèmes de télécommunications a été fulgurante. Il en est résulté une multiplication des contrats en la matière et, avec eux, une multiplication des litiges[3].

4. Les litiges en matière de propriété intellectuelle peuvent concerner la matière des brevets, des dessins et modèles, les droits d'auteur, le droit des marques, les secrets industriels et le savoir-faire (« know-how ») ou encore le domaine de la concurrence déloyale. Les litiges trouvent leur source dans différents types de contrats : contrats de licences de propriété intellectuelle, contrats de transfert de propriété intellectuelle (généralement dans le contexte d'un rachat d'entreprise), contrats relatifs au développement de la propriété intellectuelle (contrats de recherche ou contrats d'emploi).

5. La plupart des litiges trouvent leur source dans des contrats de licence, aux termes desquels le licencié se voit conférer pour une durée et un territoire déterminés l'exploitation des droits de propriété intellectuelle. Les litiges concernent le règlement des royalties, la détermination de leur montant, l'étendue des droits concédés, les motifs justifiant la

3 C'est la raison pour laquelle l'OMPI a créé un centre d'arbitrage, doté d'un règlement propre, pour la résolution des litiges en matière de propriété intellectuelle. Voyez sur la question CAMILLE A. LATURNO, International Arbitration of the Creative : A look at the World Intellectual Property Organization's New Arbitration Rules, Transnational Lawyer 1996, p. 357 et ROBERT H. SMIT, General commentary on the WIPO Arbitration Rules, American Review of International Arbitration 1998, p. 3.

rupture du contrat, les indemnités à verser en cas de violation des obligations contractuelles, l'impact d'une infraction aux dispositions légales impératives, notamment en matière de droit de la concurrence.

6. D'autre part, lors des transferts d'entreprise, il est courant que le vendeur donne à l'acheteur des garanties sur l'étendue et la validité des droits de propriété intellectuelle, l'existence et la portée des licences détenues par la société ou accordées par celle-ci et l'état des enregistrements ou demandes d'enregistrement des droits de propriété intellectuelle concernés. Une procédure d'indemnisation est prévue au cas où les garanties s'avéreraient totalement ou partiellement inexactes. Les arbitres seront alors chargés de déterminer le cas échéant l'existence des droits, qui en est propriétaire, l'étendue des droits, sous réserve des questions d'arbitrabilité que nous examinerons ultérieurement, ainsi que les conséquences de leur décision sur les garanties et l'obligation éventuelle d'indemniser.

7. Enfin, les contrats de recherche et développement génèrent également un contentieux spécifique, généralement lié à un manque de précision des dispositions contractuelles définissant les droits de l'employé, du chercheur ou de la société qui finance et en tout cas bénéficie des travaux de développement.

8. Il existe beaucoup d'autres situations dans lesquelles les parties peuvent recourir à l'arbitrage pour déterminer leurs droits respectifs en matière de propriété intellectuelle, notamment en cas de concurrence déloyale dans le contexte d'un contrat de distribution, ou en cas de contrefaçon, lorsque celle-ci est contestée.

9. Les domaines concernés par les litiges de propriété intellectuelle sont nombreux et variés. Ces litiges peuvent revêtir un caractère technique extrêmement prononcé, ainsi, par exemple, lorsqu'il s'agit de savoir si les pièces industrielles fabriquées et commercialisées par un ex licencié constituent une contrefaçon et dès lors une violation des obligations résultant du contrat de licence résilié, ou dans le domaine pharmaceutique lorsqu'il s'agit de déterminer si le produit commercialisé par un laboratoire pharmaceutique respecte ou non les termes d'une transaction intervenue entre deux concurrents ou constitue une nouvelle contrefaçon.

10. Les litiges en matière de propriété intellectuelle ont suscité traditionnellement un problème d'arbitrabilité à différents niveaux :

- D'une manière générale, la législation applicable admet-elle l'arbitrabilité des litiges en matière de propriété intellectuelle ? Dans toutes les matières ou dans certaines d'entre elles uniquement ? Au plan strictement juridique, cela impliquera éventuellement qu'on se demande si les droits de propriété intellectuelle sont disponibles.
- Si l'arbitrabilité est généralement reconnue, quelles en sont les limites ? En particulier, les arbitres ont-ils le pouvoir de trancher les litiges relatifs à la validité du titre de propriété intellectuelle ? Dans l'affirmative, cette compétence est-elle limitée à une décision à titre incident ou préalable ? Ou le Tribunal Arbitral peut-il également trancher la question à titre principal ? Et dans l'affirmative, sa décision est-elle limitée aux parties à l'arbitrage ou a-t-elle également un effet *erga omnes*?

11. Les raisons qui justifient l'attitude totalement ou partiellement restrictive de certains Etats relativement à l'arbitrabilité des litiges en matière de propriété intellectuelle relèvent juridiquement de l'ordre public et ont une double origine : d'une part, les titres, brevet ou marque, sont délivrés par une autorité publique et l'arbitre n'aurait pas le pouvoir de déclarer nul ou inexistant un acte de puissance publique ; d'autre part, ils ont pour objet de conférer à leur titulaire un monopole et donc de restreindre la liberté du commerce et de l'industrie[4]. Ils ont été analysés en détail par Francis Gurry, l'actuel directeur général de l'Organisation Mondiale de la Propriété Intellectuelle à Genève[5]. L'auteur démontre que les différentes raisons invoquées ne résistent pas à l'analyse, qu'il s'agisse du fait que les droits de propriété intellectuelle sont des monopoles[6] ou que certains droits sont consignés dans des registres destinés à

4 Racine, *supra* note 1, p. 78.

5 Objective arbitrability, antitrust disputes, intellectual property disputes, *supra* note 1.

6 «*... intellectual property rights are monopolies in a very restricted sense. They are not monopolies over anything that already exists in the public domain. Rather, they consist of exclusive rights granted in return for the disclosure of something which, by definition, must not have been in the public domain ... In addition, ... the State displays a very ambivalent attitude toward arrogating to itself the power to determine the limits of the so-called monopoly. In some cases, it does not examine the subject matter as to conformity with the statutory criteria of grant before allowing the creation of the monopoly. It allows the owner of the monopoly rights to*

informer le public de l'existence de droits exclusifs relativement à l'objet du titre[7] ou du fait que les litiges les concernant doivent relever de la compétence exclusive des tribunaux étatiques en raison du caractère *erga omnes* des décisions rendues. Et l'auteur de conclure qu'une fois reconnu le droit du propriétaire du titre de propriété intellectuelle d'en disposer librement, il est difficile d'identifier des motifs d'ordre public qui exigeraient que la question d'opposabilité du titre entre parties soit soustraite à la matière arbitrable[8].

12. En ce qui concerne l'argument selon lequel seule une décision d'un tribunal étatique peut affecter la validité *erga omnes* du titre qui a été accordé par l'autorité étatique et enregistré dans le registre public, l'on fait valoir qu'un arbitrage est une procédure initiée par contrat entre les parties, et qui va donner lieu à une décision liant ces parties uniquement. Lorsque la validité du titre est en cause, la question n'est donc pas sa validité *erga omnes* mais plutôt l'opposabilité du titre entre parties[9]. Comme l'ont très bien fait remarquer Messieurs Bonet et Jarrosson en France[10], il ne faut en effet pas confondre validité et opposabilité du titre. La validité est un état de l'acte apprécié au moment de sa formation. Si l'arbitre devait statuer sur la validité d'un titre de propriété industrielle,

restrict them in secret by entering licensing agreements. It allows pre-trial settlements. Why should … the State … take the position that the owner cannot agree to have a third party, the arbitral tribunal, decide that the owner cannot enforce the title against another party ?», p. 117.

7 *« Another possible reason for excluding arbitrability is the fact that, in the case of titles granted pursuant to a statutory application procedure, there is a public record of the title which serves to inform the public of the existence of exclusive rights in respect of the subject matter of the title. A decision on the conformity of that subject matter to the statutory criteria … should not be made privately … But again, this reason does not seem to reflect a consistently applied policy on the part of the State. The State tolerates license contracts to be made in respect of a patent, often without any requirement of registration of the fact that such contracts involve an agreement not to enforce exclusive rights conferred by the patent between the parties to the license contract. In addition, parties are free to make pre-trial settlements … The terms of settlement may involve a license given by the title owner to the other party, a private recognition of the non enforceability of the title between the parties. There is no requirement that such pre-trial settlements be registered as a matter of public record »*, p. 116.

8 p. 117.

9 Gurry, *supra* note 1, p. 115.

10 L'arbitrabilité des litiges de propriété intellectuelle en droit français, *supra* note 1, p. 64.

sa décision ne pourrait alors avoir qu'un effet *erga omnes* car « dire qu'un acte n'est pas valable entre parties, mais valable en dehors d'elles, n'a en effet juridiquement aucun sens »[11]. En revanche, un arbitre peut déclarer opposable ou inopposable entre les parties un titre de propriété industrielle. C'est donc « d'efficacité du titre entre les parties (notion qui renvoie à la force obligatoire du contrat portant sur le titre) qu'il faut parler »[12]. Et il n'est incontestablement pas choquant qu'un arbitre décide que le titre litigieux ne lie pas les parties entre elles[13]. D'où la conclusion de la doctrine que rien n'empêcherait que tous les litiges de propriété intellectuelle soient arbitrables, mais uniquement *inter partes*. Les sentences tranchant par exemple la question de la validité du droit[14] ne lieraient évidement pas les autorités publiques qui l'auraient accordé, ni les tiers[15]. Les arbitres pourraient par ailleurs toujours, s'ils l'estimaient judicieux, suspendre la procédure d'arbitrage jusqu'à ce que les autorités ou les tribunaux compétents aient statué sur la validité du droit. Par ailleurs, selon Böckstiegel, même lorsque les Etats se réservent une compétence exclusive en la matière, l'arbitrabilité n'est pas pour autant exclue, l'intérêt public n'étant pas suffisant pour considérer la règle comme étant d'ordre public. Elle est simplement impérative. L'article V (2)(b) de la Convention de New York ne pourrait donc être appliqué pour refuser l'exequatur de la sentence[16].

13. L'on peut citer à titre d'exemple une sentence CCI n° 6097 de 1989[17] qui a admis en application du droit allemand la possibilité de se prononcer sur la validité *inter partes* d'un brevet. Le litige opposait un demandeur japonais à un défendeur allemand et concernait l'exécution d'un

11 *Ibidem* et Racine, *supra* note 1, p. 86.

12 *Ibidem.*

13 Jarrosson, note sous Paris, 23 mars 1994, *supra* note 1, p. 524.

14 Ainsi, dans un litige entre le détenteur d'un brevet et un de ses licenciés, si ce dernier invoque la nullité du brevet, entraînant corrélativement la nullité du contrat de licence.

15 Voyez notamment François Perret, L'arbitrabilité des litiges de propriété industrielle en droit comparé, *supra* note 1, p. 82 et Philippe Fouchard, Rapport de synthèse, Colloque de l'IRPI, *supra* note 1, *supra* note 1, p. 143.

16 Karl-Heinz Böckstiegel, Arbitrability and public policy, Comparative Arbitration Practice and Public Policy in Arbitration, ICCA Congress Series n° 3, p. 198.

17 Bulletin de la Cour internationale d'arbitrage de la CCI, octobre 1993, p. 80.

contrat de licence d'exploitation dudit brevet, déposé en Allemagne Fédérale. Le défendeur soulevait la nullité du brevet. Le Tribunal Arbitral siégeant à Zurich s'est déclaré compétent pour statuer sur la validité du brevet *inter partes*. Il fit notamment valoir que « ce pouvoir de décision n'affecte pas la valeur formelle du brevet accordé en Allemagne Fédérale par acte de souveraineté de l'Etat, et il ne produit pas d'effet à l'égard des tiers. Par ce transfert de compétence, les parties ont voulu donner au Tribunal Arbitral, conformément au sens et au but de la procédure d'arbitrage, la possibilité de régler ce litige inter partes de façon simple, rapide et définitive ». Et les arbitres d'ajouter : « D'après l'opinion générale, il n'est pas possible en droit positif allemand ... de donner compétence à un Tribunal Arbitral pour déclarer nul un brevet. Mais les juristes sont de plus en plus nombreux à considérer dans la doctrine que cette conception stricte n'est plus défendable, et que l'on peut admettre qu'un Tribunal Arbitral statue, avec effet entre les parties, sur la validité d'un brevet invoqué par le demandeur ». Il semble néanmoins que cette position ne soit aucunement acquise en Allemagne[18].

II. L'arbitrabilité dans les droits nationaux

14. Dans son rapport final sur les litiges de propriété intellectuelle et l'arbitrage pour la Commission de l'arbitrage international de la CCI[19], le Professeur Lew range les pays en quatre catégories :

- ceux qui refusent totalement l'arbitrabilité des litiges de propriété intellectuelle ;
- ceux qui l'acceptent sous des réserves justifiées par l'ordre public ;
- ceux qui reconnaissent la totale arbitrabilité des litiges en la matière et
- ceux où la question reste incertaine dès lors qu'elle n'a été traitée ni par la législation ni par la jurisprudence[20].

15. Le Professeur Lew indique que l'approche restrictive qui tend à refuser la soumission à l'arbitrage des litiges de propriété intellectuelle n'est plus que le fait d'une minorité de pays, tels certains pays

18 Voyez *infra*, n° 27.

19 *Supra* note 1.

20 *Supra* note 1, p. 43.

d'Amérique Latine, la Corée du Sud, l'Afrique du Sud et Israël. Dans les autres systèmes juridiques, l'arbitrabilité est reconnue plus ou mois largement, les pays les plus libéraux étant d'une part les Etats-Unis mais, plus encore, la Suisse et la Belgique, comme nous le verrons ci-après.

16. Avant d'examiner un certain nombre de législations nationales, l'on abordera la question de savoir quelle doit être l'attitude du Tribunal Arbitral lorsqu'il est confronté en matière de propriété intellectuelle à des questions arbitrables et d'autres qui ne le sont pas. Il devra bien entendu se déclarer incompétent pour les questions non arbitrables et traiter celles dont il peut connaître. La situation devient toutefois plus compliquée lorsque la question non-arbitrable est préliminaire à la détermination d'une question arbitrable. Dans ce cas, le Tribunal Arbitral doit-il suspendre la procédure et attendre la décision d'un tribunal étatique sur la question préliminaire ? Des éléments de réponse à cette question nous ont été donnés par la Cour d'Appel de Paris dans une décision *Société Deko c / G. Dingler et Société Meva*[21] du 24 mars 1994. En France, la question de la validité d'un brevet n'est pas arbitrable à titre principal. Elle n'était par ailleurs pas non plus considérée comme arbitrable à titre incident à l'époque où cette décision a été rendue[22]. En revanche, sont arbitrables les questions concernant l'exécution et l'interprétation des contrats conclus relativement aux droits dérivés du brevet. La Cour d'Appel de Paris a décidé qu'en l'espèce, le Tribunal Arbitral, saisi d'un litige relatif au contrat d'exploitation de brevets conclu entre leur titulaire, Mr. Dingler et la société Meva et, d'autre part, la société de droit français Deko, avait, à bon droit, refusé de surseoir à statuer jusqu'à la décision du Tribunal de Grande Instance saisi d'une demande d'annulation des brevets. La Cour d'Appel de Paris a jugé que les actions soutenues devant le Tribunal Arbitral et devant le Tribunal de Grande Instance avaient des objets différents : d'une part l'exécution d'un contrat et d'autre part la validité des brevets. Elle a ajouté que si la nullité des brevets était prononcée, il n'en resterait pas moins qu'une situation contractuelle aurait existé entre les parties et que la juridiction ayant à apprécier l'exécution du contrat peut être distincte de celle qui se prononce sur

21 Revue de l'arbitrage, 1994, p. 515 et note Ch. Jarrosson.

22 Voyez *infra*, n° 20.

la validité des brevets. Il reste que cette distinction est extrêmement délicate.

17. En Belgique, la loi sur les brevets d'invention du 28 mars 1984[23] reconnaît l'arbitrabilité des litiges en la matière[24]. L'article 51 § 1 de la loi admet en outre qu'une sentence arbitrale peut annuler totalement ou partiellement un brevet et qu'une telle décision bénéficie de l'autorité de la chose jugée *erga omnes*, sous réserve de la tierce opposition.

18. L'application de la loi belge sur les brevets d'invention est limitée à un brevet belge ou à la fraction belge d'un brevet européen. Qu'en est-il dès lors de l'arbitrabilité en Belgique d'une question de validité d'un brevet étranger ? En Belgique, comme dans de nombreux pays, et à la différence de la Suisse, c'est le critère du caractère disponible du droit qui est retenu comme critère d'arbitrabilité. L'arbitre siégeant en Belgique devra donc déterminer quelle est la loi applicable au concept de disponibilité, soit probablement la *lex causae*, c'est-à-dire la loi régissant les droits litigieux. Il va donc en résulter que l'arbitre international siégeant en Belgique pourra se prononcer sur la nullité d'un brevet suisse[25] mais devra s'abstenir si le brevet en cause est un brevet français alors même que la loi belge est très libérale en la matière[26].

19. Les litiges concernant les marques de fabrique, les dessins et les modèles sont également arbitrables en Belgique. Bien que la loi uniforme Benelux sur les marques et celle sur les dessins et modèles ne fassent référence qu'aux tribunaux étatiques, les commentateurs s'accordent à conclure que ces articles n'affectent pas l'arbitrabilité des litiges. La même solution s'impose en ce qui concerne le droit d'auteur[27].

23 Pasin., 1983, n. 1, p. 165.

24 L'article 73 de la loi stipule que les règles qu'il compte ne font pas obstacle à ce que les contestations relatives à la propriété d'une demande de brevet ou d'un brevet, à la validité ou à la contrefaçon d'un brevet ou à la fixation de l'indemnité visée à l'article 29 ainsi que celles relatives aux licences de brevets autres que les licences obligatoires soient portées devant les tribunaux arbitraux.

25 Voyez *infra*, n° 34.

26 PERRET, L'arbitrabilité des contentieux en matière de brevets d'invention, *supra* note 1, p. 237.

27 MARCEL HUYS & GUY KEUTGEN, L'arbitrage en droit belge et international, Bruxelles, Bruylant, 1981, p. 104 ss; PHILIPPE DE BOURNONVILLE, L'arbitrage, Larcier, 2000, p. 128 ss; LOUIS VAN BUNNEN, Six ans d'expérience de la loi

20. En France, les litiges en matière de brevet sont arbitrables, dans les conditions prévues aux articles 2059 et 2060 du Code civil, ainsi que le prévoit le texte de l'article 68 de la loi du 2 janvier 1968 relative aux brevets d'invention, telle qu'elle a été modifiée par la loi du 13 juillet 1978[28]. Toutes les questions relatives au brevet (portée, copropriété, contrefaçon et droits contractuels[29]) peuvent donc être soumises à la décision d'un tribunal arbitral, à l'exception du pur statut des brevets, c'est-à-dire la question de leur validité[30]. Mais la solution doit être nuancée, depuis l'arrêt du 28 février 2008 de la Cour d'Appel de Paris dans l'affaire *DOO c / SA Diebolt*[31].

21. Dans cette affaire, une société française et une société slovène avaient conclu un accord de distribution ainsi qu'un contrat de licence autorisant la seconde à exploiter un brevet appartenant à la première. Les

uniforme Benelux sur les marques, J.T., 1977, p. 288; JACQUELINE LINSMEAU, L'arbitrage volontaire en droit privé belge, Bruylant, Bruxelles 1991, p. 25 ss.

28 Actuel article L615-17 du Code de la propriété intellectuelle.

29 En effet, seuls les intérêts privés des parties en cause forment, dans cette hypothèse, l'objet de la contestation. Les parties ont donc la libre disposition de leurs droits et le litige est arbitrable en application de l'article 2059 du Code civil. RACINE, *supra* note 1, p. 80. Voyez notamment les sentences CCI n° 1912 de 1974 et 2048 de 1972 citées par YVES DERAINS, L'expérience de la Cour d'arbitrage de la Chambre de Commerce Internationale en matière de propriété industrielle, Revue de l'Arbitrage, 1977, p. 40; sentence CCI n° 6709 de 1991, JDI 1992, p. 998, obs. D. Hascher, et Bulletin de la Cour internationale d'arbitrage de la CCI 1994, p. 69 et DOMINIQUE HASCHER, La pratique de la Chambre de Commerce Internationale, in Arbitrage et propriété intellectuelle, Colloque de l'IRPI, Librairies Techniques, Paris 1994, note 552, p. 23. Voyez également l'arrêt de la Cour d'Appel de Paris du 24 mars 1994, *société TEKO c. G. Dingler et société Meva*, Revue de l'Arbitrage, 1994, 515 et note Ch. Jarrosson et le commentaire de Racine, *supra* note 1, p. 81.

30 LE STANC, *supra* note 1, p. 247. L'auteur se réfère à un cas pratique dans lequel, d'une part, une sentence arbitrale a été rendue condamnant le licencié au versement de redevances impayées et où, d'autre part, les tribunaux français, saisis avant l'introduction de la procédure arbitrale, ont finalement déclaré le brevet nul, le licencié se voyant en conséquence dispensé de payer les redevances qu'il avait retenues. La solution mixte arbitrabilité-inarbitrabilité et l'absence d'obligation de sursis à statuer en droit français ont abouti dans le cas d'espèce à deux décisions totalement contradictoires.

31 *Liv Hidravlika DOO c / SA Diebolt*, Revue de l'Arbitrage 2009, p. 168 et note T. Azzi.

deux contrats contenaient une clause d'arbitrage CCI. Un différend est né, la société française reprochant à la société slovène de ne pas s'être conformée aux conditions fixées par la licence. La société slovène, assignée en arbitrage, a contesté la validité du brevet, concluant donc à la caducité du contrat de licence faute d'objet. La défenderesse a parallèlement soulevé l'exception d'incompétence, au motif que la validité d'un brevet n'est pas une question arbitrable. L'arbitre s'est déclaré compétent, a admis la validité du brevet et a condamné la société slovène à payer une somme importante à son cocontractant. Le recours en annulation formé par la défenderesse a été rejeté par la Cour d'Appel de Paris, laquelle a décidé que la question de validité du brevet débattue de manière incidente à l'occasion d'un litige de nature contractuelle pouvait être soumise à l'arbitre, l'invalidité éventuellement constatée n'ayant, pas plus que s'il s'agissait de la décision d'un juge, d'autorité de chose jugée, car elle ne figure notamment pas au dispositif et n'a d'effet qu'à l'égard des parties, de même d'ailleurs qu'une décision en faveur de la validité, les tiers pouvant toujours demander la nullité du brevet pour les mêmes causes.

22. Il résulte donc de cette décision que la question de validité d'un brevet n'est pas arbitrable à titre principal mais l'est à titre incident, dès lors qu'elle n'a d'effet qu'entre parties et que la décision de l'arbitre sur la validité du titre de propriété industrielle n'a d'incidence que sur le sort du contrat qui forme l'objet du litige. Il reste que la décision de la Cour d'Appel quant à l'absence d'autorité de chose jugée de la sentence relativement à la validité du brevet, n'est pas pleinement convaincante. L'autorité de chose jugée s'applique en effet d'abord au dispositif mais aussi aux motifs décisifs de la décision. Or, dès lors que l'application du contrat dépend de l'existence du brevet, le motif par lequel un arbitre se prononce sur sa validité est un motif décisif. La décision de la Cour d'Appel n'est pas davantage exempte de problèmes, dans la mesure où elle laisse la porte ouverte aux contradictions de décisions si, par exemple, un arbitre admet la validité d'un brevet dans le cadre d'un litige contractuel et que par la suite, un juge en prononce la nullité. L'on reconnaitra néanmoins que cette décision est une avancée importante puisqu'elle admet l'arbitrabilité partielle en France des litiges relatifs à la validité des brevets.

23. Est également arbitrable en France le contentieux d'exploitation d'une marque[32] et le contentieux de la contrefaçon[33]. En ce qui concerne ce dernier, la compétence de l'arbitre est limitée à l'action civile, en ce compris les intérêts civils consécutifs à l'infraction de contrefaçon. Elle ne s'étend pas en revanche à l'action publique, la matière pénale échappant à l'arbitrabilité[34].

24. En revanche, dans le domaine du droit d'auteur, il semble que l'arbitrage soit exclu en ce qui concerne le droit moral de l'auteur, droit extra-patrimonial et non disponible, dans un souci de protection de l'auteur et de l'œuvre[35], encore qu'il existe au moins une décision de la Cour d'Appel de Paris où l'arbitrabilité du droit moral de l'auteur a été reconnue et où la Cour – confirmant une décision du Tribunal de Grande Instance – a renvoyé les parties à l'arbitrage[36].

25. En Italie, les litiges concernant la validité des brevets et des marques ne sont pas arbitrables dans la mesure où ils mettent en cause l'octroi des droits dérivés et dans tous les cas où l'intervention du Ministère public est prévue par les lois spéciales concernant ces droits de propriété intellectuelle[37]. En revanche, sont arbitrables les litiges concernant les droits contractuels librement convenus par les parties et qui ne mettent pas en cause la validité du brevet ou de la marque[38].

26. En Allemagne, il est acquis que les litiges en matière de propriété intellectuelle sont arbitrables, sous certaines réserves cependant. Le mémorandum[39] du Gouvernement annexé à la nouvelle loi sur l'arbitrage (en vigueur en Allemagne depuis le 1er janvier 1998) fait une réserve pour le

32 Actuel article L716-4 du Code de la propriété intellectuelle. RACINE, *supra* note 1, p. 81 et références citées.

33 *Ibidem.*

34 RACINE, *supra* note 1, p. 82.

35 RACINE, *supra* note 1, p. 55

36 Zaldin c / Sté Editions Recherches, Cour d'Appel de Paris, 1ère Ch., 26 mai 1993, Revue Internationale du Droit d'Auteur 1994, Vol. 1, p. 292.

37 Arrêté Royal du 29 juin 1939 n° 1127, article 78 dans le cas des brevets ; Arrêté Royal du 21 juin 1942 n° 929, article 59 dans le cas des marques.

38 International Handbook on Commercial Arbitration, V° Italy, commentaire de P. Bernardini, p. 13.

39 Bundestag-Drucksache No. 13 / 5274 (juillet 1996).

cas où le législateur donne compétence exclusive à certains tribunaux pour des litiges spécifiques, telles que des demandes de déclaration de nullité ou de révocation d'un brevet. Il précise que ces procédures affectent des droits qui ont été octroyés par un acte de l'administration étatique et ne sont donc pas à la disposition des parties par voie d'accord. En conséquence, ces droits doivent être tranchés par voie d'une décision judiciaire susceptible d'établir ou de modifier une relation juridique (*Gestaltungsurteile*) n'ayant pas seulement effet entre les parties, mais à l'égard de tous[40].

27. Une fois l'enregistrement d'un brevet effectué, un droit de propriété intellectuelle est présumé valable en Allemagne jusqu'à ce qu'il soit déclaré nul en appel par le tribunal des brevets. Il résulterait du mémorandum précité que même si la validité des droits de propriété intellectuelle n'est soulevée qu'*inter partes*[41], elle doit être tranchée par les tribunaux étatiques. En conséquence, les arbitres saisis d'une telle question doivent en déférer au tribunal allemand compétent. La procédure arbitrale pourra reprendre son cours une fois que la question aura été tranchée. Si d'autre part la validité d'un droit de propriété intellectuelle est la seule question litigieuse, l'arbitre doit se déclarer incompétent[42]. En revanche, l'arbitrabilité des garanties concernant les droits de propriété intellectuelle serait pleinement acquise.

28. Aux Etats-Unis, tous les litiges en matière de propriété intellectuelle sont arbitrables[43]. Le Parlement a expressément prévu dans l'article 35 U.S.C. §294, l'arbitrage volontaire et obligatoire des litiges en matière de validité, d'opposabilité et de contrefaçon des brevets[44]. Il est toutefois prévu dans la loi que la sentence rendue relativement à la validité d'un brevet n'a qu'un effet relatif entre parties[45]. Dans le contexte des litiges

40 *Idem*, p. 35.

41 La question semble toutefois controversée. Ainsi, Jochen Pagenberg *supra* note 1, p. 48, estime que selon le droit allemand, un tribunal arbitral peut très bien déclarer un brevet sans valeur (*unenforceable*) entre parties et rejeter dès lors la demande introduite par le propriétaire du brevet contre un prétendu contrefacteur.

42 Voyez aussi Julian Lew, *supra* note 1, p. 45.

43 Voyez toutes les références et détails dans David W. Plant, Arbitrability of Intellectual Property Issues in the United States, *supra* note 1, p. 11 s.

44 Lew, *supra* note 1, p. 46 et Plant, Resolving Disputes, *supra* note 1, p. 121.

45 Racine, *supra* note 1, p. 84.

en matière de *patent interference*, l'article 35 U.S.C. § 135 (d)[46] réserve au *Commissioner of patents and trademarks*[47] le droit de déterminer la brevetabilité. La même réserve est inscrite dans l'article 37 C.F.R. § 1690 (d). Il faut toutefois préciser qu'afin d'éviter une contrariété de décisions, l'article 35 U.S.C. § 294 précise que si un brevet dont la validité a été affirmée par une sentence arbitrale est ensuite annulé par une décision définitive émanant d'une cour étatique, la sentence pourra être modifiée par le juge, à la condition que les parties l'aient expressément convenu. L'autorité de la chose jugée de la sentence arbitrale sera ainsi remise en cause, ce qui conduit à qualifier de révision la voie ouverte par cette disposition[48]. Enfin, l'arbitrabilité des litiges en matière de marques relevant d'un *federal trademark statute* semble aussi généralement admise[49].

29. Le Parlement américain n'a pas légiféré dans le domaine du droit d'auteur. La jurisprudence admet néanmoins que les contrats de licence de droit d'auteur[50] peuvent contenir une clause d'arbitrage. L'arbitrabilité s'étend à la violation du *copyright*, ainsi qu'à sa validité lorsqu'elle est soulevée à titre incident. Comme l'a souligné la Cour d'Appel du 7ème Circuit[51], « il n'y a pas de raison de considérer que des arbitres ont plus de chance de se tromper dans des affaires de droit d'auteur que des juges étatiques ou fédéraux ; la Cour Suprême a récemment rejeté un tel argument en décidant que l'arbitrage de litiges antitrust dans le cadre d'opérations internationales n'est pas contraire à l'ordre public ». Se

46 « *Interferences*

d) Parties to a patent interference, within such time as may be specified by the Commissioner by regulation, may determine such contest or any aspect thereof by arbitration … Nothing in this subsection shall preclude the Commissioner from determining patentability of the invention involved in the interference ».

47 Plant, Arbitrability of Intellectual Property Issues in the United States, *supra* note 1, p. 12 et 14.

48 Perret, L'arbitrabilité des contentieux en matière de brevets d'invention, *supra* note 1, p. 233.

49 *Idem*, p. 19.

50 Selon Robert Briner, *supra* note 1, p. 33, les litiges en matière de droits d'auteur sont aussi généralement arbitrables, avec certaines réserves pour la Hongrie, la Roumanie, l'Italie, Israël et l'Espagne.

51 *Saturday Evening Post Co. v. Rumbleseat Press*, Inc., 816 F. 2d 1191, 1198-99 (7 Cir. 1987).

référant de la sorte au célèbre arrêt *Mitsubishi*[52], l'argument de la Cour est que dès lors que l'arbitrage d'un litige mettant en cause un monopole économique (l'antitrust) n'était pas considéré par la Cour Suprême comme une menace pour l'ordre public, il n'y avait pas de raison d'empêcher l'arbitrage d'un litige mettant en cause un monopole légal beaucoup moins dangereux (le droit d'auteur)[53]. La Cour a par ailleurs fait valoir que le danger d'atteinte à l'ordre public était largement atténué par le fait que les décisions des arbitres ne lient que les parties en présence et n'ont aucune valeur de précédent[54]. Enfin, la Cour a également relevé que le danger de monopole était beaucoup plus important dans le domaine des brevets et pourtant le Parlement a expressément autorisé l'arbitrage des litiges relatifs à leur validité.

30. Au Canada également, l'arbitrabilité des litiges en matière de propriété intellectuelle est généralement acceptée. En particulier, toutes questions concernant les brevets, y compris la validité du brevet, peuvent être soumises à arbitrage[55].

31. Il en est de même en matière de droit d'auteur depuis un important arrêt du 21 mars 2003 de la Cour Suprême, que la doctrine canadienne compare à l'arrêt *Mitsubishi* aux Etats Unis[56]. Le différend soumis à l'arbitrage était issu de difficultés d'interprétation d'un contrat de licence d'exploitation de *Caillou*, un personnage de bande dessinée pour enfants. Ce contrat avait pour objet la cession par deux personnes, qui l'avaient signé à titre de co-auteurs, de certains droits de reproduction pouvant être exercés à l'échelle mondiale par les éditions Chouette. Le différend avait d'abord était soumis à la Cour supérieure du Québec, mais celle-ci l'avait renvoyé à l'arbitrage. La sentence arbitrale a fait

52 « *But there is no reason to think that arbitrators are more likely to err in copyright cases than state or federal judges are; the Supreme Court recently rejected such an argument in holding that the arbitration of antitrust claims arising out of international transactions is not contrary to public policy. See Mitsubishi Motors Corp. v. Soler Chrysler-Plymouth, Inc.* », 816 F. 2d, 1198.

53 816 F. 2d, 1198-99.

54 816 F. 2d, 1199.

55 Briner, *supra* note 1, p. 32. En Hollande, la validité d'un brevet relève de la compétence exclusive du Tribunal de 1ère instance de La Haye. *Idem*, p. 33.

56 Cour Suprême du Canada, 21 mars 2003, *Editions Chouette Inc., C / Desputeaux*, Revue de l'Arbitrage, 2003, p. 473 et note F. Bachand.

l'objet d'un recours et en un premier temps, la Cour d'Appel du Québec, district de Montréal, a décidé, dans un arrêt du 18 avril 2001[57], que l'article 37 de la loi sur le droit d'auteur conférait une compétence exclusive aux tribunaux étatiques, à l'exclusion des tribunaux arbitraux, à l'égard de toute procédure relative à l'application de cette loi. Le raisonnement de la Cour était notamment que le droit moral de l'auteur présentait des liens avec la personnalité, l'honneur et la dignité de ce dernier, justifiant son appartenance aux questions qui intéressent l'ordre public visé par l'Article 2639 du Code civil du Québec. Sans le dire explicitement, la Cour d'Appel avait retenu comme critère général d'inarbitrabilité celui de la disponibilité des droits en litige et avait jugé que le droit moral de l'auteur était indisponible.

32. Saisie d'un recours contre cet arrêt, la Cour suprême a jugé ce raisonnement incorrect car même si le droit moral est incessible en droit canadien, l'auteur peut néanmoins y renoncer et il peut même le faire à titre onéreux. La question ne relevait donc pas de l'ordre public. La Cour d'Appel avait aussi décidé qu'une décision portant sur la titularité, l'étendue ou la validité du droit d'auteur était opposable à tous et ne pouvait pour cette raison être rendue que par un tribunal judiciaire. La Cour d'Appel confondait de la sorte l'opposabilité de la sentence et ses effets sur les tiers. Or, s'il est vrai qu'une sentence arbitrale est opposable à tous en ce qu'elle modifie l'ordonnancement juridique et que cette modification doit être reconnue et respectée par tous, elle ne peut en principe avoir d'effets, au plan juridique, et sauf législation contraire, qu'à l'égard des parties. Il n'y avait donc pas de raison de décider, sur cette base, que les litiges en matière de droit d'auteur étaient inarbitrables[58].

33. Enfin, le droit suisse reconnaît totalement l'arbitrabilité des litiges de propriété intellectuelle. L'article 177 de la loi suisse sur le droit international privé admet en effet l'arbitrabilité de tous litiges ayant un caractère patrimonial, entendant par là « toutes les prétentions qui ont une valeur pécuniaire pour les parties, à titre d'actif ou de passif »[59]. Ainsi, tous les aspects de la propriété intellectuelle, en ce compris les droits moraux ou

57 [2001] J.Q. n° 1510, [2001] R.J.Q. 945, 16 C.P.R. (4th) 77.

58 Bachand, op.cit., p. 487.

59 ATF 118 II 356 cons. 3b; Bulletin ASA 1993, p. 59 et Dessemontet, *supra* note 1, p. 65.

la validité d'un titre de propriété industrielle, peuvent faire l'objet d'un arbitrage.

34. Il en est ainsi notamment de tous les litiges[60] concernant la validité d'un brevet suisse. En outre, si un tribunal arbitral déclare un brevet suisse nul parce qu'il ne respecte pas les conditions de brevetabilité, la sentence arbitrale constitue un titre valable pour obtenir l'annulation et la suppression du brevet du registre[61]. Toutefois, il semble que l'Office suisse des brevets n'a jamais été invité à ce jour à annuler sur la base d'une sentence arbitrale un brevet suisse enregistré.

35. Qu'en est-il des brevets étrangers ? En principe, la validité d'un tel brevet est arbitrable en Suisse. Cette conclusion est-elle susceptible d'être remise en cause du fait de l'existence dans le pays du brevet concerné, d'une compétence exclusive des tribunaux étatiques ? L'on a vu que dans une sentence CCI, précitée[62], rendue sous l'empire du Concordat, les arbitres, siégeant en Suisse, ont décidé que la question de la validité d'un brevet allemand était arbitrable, nonobstant le fait qu'en Allemagne, cette question relevait de la compétence exclusive du *Patentgericht*. Les arbitres ont en effet décidé que leur décision sur la question ne liait que les seules parties à l'arbitrage et n'était donc pas de nature à affecter les droits et obligations de tiers. Jusqu'il y a peu, l'on pouvait considérer que cette solution d'arbitrabilité pouvait être paralysée par le jeu de l'article 9 de la loi de droit international privé[63]. Conformément à cet article, un tribunal suisse saisi en second lieu d'une action déjà pendante dans un Etat étranger, devrait surseoir à statuer si l'on peut s'attendre à ce que le tribunal étranger saisi rende dans un délai raisonnable une décision susceptible de reconnaissance en Suisse. Or, le tribunal fédéral suisse a décidé le 14 mai 2001[64] que cette disposition s'imposait

60 Voyez les contributions de Georges Bonet, Charles Jarrosson et François Perret, *supra* note 1.

61 Feuille suisse des brevets, dessins et marques 1976, I, 9 / 10. Perret, *supra* note 1, p. 56, Troller, *supra* note 1, p. 159; Lew, *supra* note 1, p. 15; Racine, *supra* note 1, p. 87.

62 *Supra* note 17 et § 13.

63 Perret, L'arbitrabilité des contentieux, *supra* note 1, p. 238 et Jean-François Poudret & Sébastien Besson, Droit comparé de l'arbitrage international, LGDJ, 2002, n° 512.

64 ATF 127 III 279.

également aux arbitres. En conséquence, dès lors qu'un tribunal allemand était saisi en premier lieu de la question de validité du brevet, un tribunal arbitral siégeant en Suisse, saisi ultérieurement par l'autre partie, devait surseoir à statuer, voire se dessaisir selon le cas, sur base de l'article 9 de la loi de droit international privé. Cette limitation aux pouvoirs des arbitres tombait toutefois si, pour juger de l'exception d'arbitrage soulevée devant elle, la Cour étatique étrangère appliquait non pas la *lex fori* mais la loi d'arbitrage du siège[65]. L'arrêt précité du Tribunal Fédéral a suscité un tel émoi qu'une nouvelle disposition a été introduite ultérieurement par le législateur suisse pour éviter l'application de l'article 9 LDIP en matière d'arbitrage international, à savoir l'article 186 alinéa 1bis, en vigueur depuis le 1er mars 2007[66]. Cet article précise que le tribunal arbitral « statue sur sa compétence sans égard à une action ayant le même objet déjà pendante entre les mêmes parties devant un autre tribunal étatique ou arbitral, sauf si des motifs sérieux commandent de suspendre la procédure ».

36. Le Professeur Perret fait également état de ce que les membres de la Convention sur le brevet européen ont saisi leurs bureaux de brevets de la question de l'arbitrabilité des litiges relatifs à la validité d'un brevet européen et que des recommandations sur cette question ont été émises lors d'une conférence gouvernementale qui s'est tenue les 16-17 octobre 2000. Lesdites recommandations préconisent que la validité du brevet européen soit déclarée arbitrable, la question de savoir si elle devrait l'être uniquement entre parties ou devrait également avoir un effet *erga omnes* – cette dernière solution étant préconisée par la délégation suisse – restant néanmoins ouverte[67].

37. L'on peut dire en conclusion que les litiges en matière de propriété intellectuelle sont arbitrables dans une très large mesure[68]. D'une part, les droits patrimoniaux découlant des droits de propriété intellectuelle sont disponibles. Un arbitre peut donc en principe connaître d'un litige relatif à la mauvaise exécution, à l'inexécution ou à la résiliation d'un

65 Perret, L'arbitrabilité des contentieux, *supra* note 1, p. 238.

66 Cet article a été introduit par le chapitre I de la loi fédérale du 6 octobre 2006 (RO 2007, 387, 388 ; FF, 2006, 4469, p. 4481).

67 *Idem*, p. 241.

68 Sur la jurisprudence arbitrale en la matière, voyez les sentences citées par Blessing, Arbitrability of Intellectual Property Issues, *supra* note 1, p. 206 et 215.

contrat portant sur des droits de propriété industrielle, par exemple un contrat de licence. Il peut aussi généralement déterminer qu'il y a eu violation des droits du titulaire de brevet et condamner en conséquence à des dommages-intérêts. D'une manière générale, un nombre croissant de systèmes juridiques autorisent l'arbitrabilité de la plupart des litiges en matière de propriété intellectuelle. En d'autres termes, le domaine réservé de l'inarbitrabilité ne cesse de se réduire, au point de ne plus laisser subsister, au titre de « noyau dur », que l'arbitrabilité *erga omnes* de la validité du titre.

Designing Tailored Alternative Dispute Resolution in Intellectual Property: the Experience of WIPO

*Sarah Theurich**

I. Introduction

Disputes in Intellectual Property (IP) are as multifaceted as the subject itself. To name only a few, they can range from the most complex patent infringement, technology transfer and research and development cases, over software licensing, IP financing, trademark coexistence and design issues, to questions of art resale rights or the use of traditional knowledge.

IP disputes often have specific needs that require tailored resolution methods. First and foremost, the specificity of the subject matter demands legal and technical expertise from involved dispute resolution facilitators. Second, IP controversies are increasingly played out on an international level and need global solutions. Further, market cycles are rapidly evolving, which makes time and cost effective dispute resolution paramount. Finally, there may be know-how and trade secrets involved and hence confidentiality would be key.

These are some of the reasons why the international IP community advocated in the early 1990s[1] in favor of the creation of a tailored international dispute resolution service to be provided by the World Intellectual Property Organization (WIPO)[2], which led to the establishment of

* Legal Staff, WIPO Arbitration and Mediation Center.

1 For example, the International Association for the Protection of Intellectual Property (AIPPI), the International Federation of Industrial Property Attorneys (FICPI), and the Licensing Executives Society International (LESI). For more details on the history of the creation of the WIPO Arbitration and Mediation Center, see: Development of WIPO's Dispute Resolution Services, World Intellectual Property Organization, 1992-2007, Part III, pp. 93-104, www.wipo.int/amc/en/history/.

2 WIPO is an intergovernmental organization dedicated to developing a balanced and accessible international intellectual property system, which rewards creativity, stimulates innovation and contributes to economic development while safeguarding the public interest. It currently has 184 Member States and administers 24 international Treaties. For more information on WIPO, please see www.wipo.int.

the WIPO Arbitration and Mediation Center (WIPO Center)[3]. Francis Gurry, the Director General of WIPO, explained « [t]he underlying reason for the establishment of the Center was a belief in the specificity of intellectual property as a subject matter, and, thus, of disputes concerning intellectual property, coupled with the conviction that arbitration and other dispute-resolution alternatives offered particularly suitable means of accommodating the specific characteristics of intellectual property disputes ».[4]

As an international service provider, the WIPO Center promotes, on a not-for-profit basis, the neutral cost and time effective alternative dispute resolution (ADR) of international commercial disputes between private parties through procedures such as arbitration, mediation and, since 2007, expert determination. While its procedures are appropriate in all types of commercial disputes, the WIPO Center specializes in particular in cases arising out of intellectual property and technology transactions, such as licensing, research and development and distribution agreements, as well as entertainment related matters.

The standard WIPO Mediation, Expedited Arbitration, Arbitration[5] and Expert Determination Rules (WIPO Rules) provide in themselves a tailored tool for IP disputes. Developed by leading international dispute resolution specialists and IP experts, they contain specific provisions that are particularly adapted to IP disputes (e. g., on technical evidence, expert appointment, interim measures, trade secrets and confidentiality). To date, the WIPO Center has administered more than 220 mediations and arbitrations under WIPO Rules, most of which have been filed in the last five years.

The role of the WIPO Center is twofold :

First, as an administering authority it administers disputes under WIPO Rules through an active case management system (including procedural rules and model clauses in a variety of languages ; a database, open to further expansion, of over 1,500 qualified international mediators, arbitrators and experts specialized in different IP related fields ;

3 The WIPO Center's website is available at : www.wipo.int/amc.

4 Francis Gurry, The WIPO Arbitration and Mediation Center and its Services, The American Review of International Arbitration, Vol. 5, No. 2, 1994, pp. 197-201.

5 For a commentary on the WIPO Arbitration Rules, see « WIPO Arbitration Rules : Commentary and Analysis », Juris Publishing, Juris Net, New York, 2000.

management of case related fees; electronic case communication tools; and procedural model documents).

Second, it also acts as a resource center. In addition to providing ADR training and publications, it advises parties and entities, upon request, on existing WIPO ADR procedures and how they can be customized to specific needs. It also develops tailored dispute resolution policies that are adapted to the particular needs of certain business sectors, or specific associations of right holders, that face recurrent disputes.

As varied as IP disputes are, the dispute resolution needs of disputing parties or specific business and industry sectors can be equally diverse. Through its flexible character, ADR lends itself to adaption to the concrete needs of parties involved in a case (II), or to be the basis for the development of tailored dispute resolution systems for specific recurring types of disputes in selected sectors (III). The following explains the WIPO Center's commitment to designing tailored ADR methods on both fronts.

II. Tailoring Standard WIPO ADR to Party Needs – or How to « Make it Fit »

If parties opt for ADR, they have great latitude to adapt the features of the process to their specific needs, which goes from selecting the adequate procedure, to tailoring the ADR clause, to selecting appropriate remedies.

A. Party Autonomy

The WIPO Rules are based on party autonomy, a recognized principle in international commercial arbitration[6], and applicable to ADR in general. As a private and consensual mechanism, ADR is based on the concept of a contract between the parties by which they agree to submit all future or existing disputes to resolution through ADR. Hence, the contractual character gives parties the power to determine the specific

6 Julian D. M. Lew, Loukas A. Mistelis, Stefan M. Kröll, Comparative International Commercial Arbitration, Kluwer Law International, The Hague, 2003, Section 17-8 f.

elements of the ADR process. The parties are the « masters » of their ADR process and can « make it fit » their concrete needs.

The first crucial point to decide for parties is whether the ADR process should be administered by an institution or *ad hoc*. While *ad hoc* ADR leaves it to parties to design the entire ADR process, institutional ADR, such as the procedures available through WIPO, already provides a frame for the procedure including timelines and procedural steps. While institutional ADR has the advantage of an established basic procedural structure, it still leaves a lot of flexibility to parties to adapt the procedure to their needs. This can save considerable time and costs, as it is extremely difficult and time consuming for parties to agree on anything, including on procedural rules, once they are in dispute.

In WIPO ADR, and subject to mandatory provisions in applicable national law, parties can agree on elements such as the law applicable to the substance of the case, the arbitration law, the place of arbitration or mediation, the appointment (including number and person) of the mediator or arbitrator, the language of the procedure, and other procedural elements. Such elements should ideally be determined in the ADR clause already. If no such contract clause exists, they can also be later defined in an ADR submission agreement. Parties in WIPO procedures can also agree on procedural elements at different stages during the ADR process. This principle is, for example, expressed in Article 2 of the WIPO Mediation, Arbitration, Expedited Arbitration and Expert Determination Rules under the scope of application, establishing that these rules apply « unless the parties have agreed otherwise ».

B. Selecting Appropriate ADR Procedures

ADR offers a wide range of options and selecting the appropriate procedure(s) is paramount. In WIPO ADR, apart from mediation and expert determination, parties can choose between standard arbitration and expedited arbitration (see below 1 on fast track arbitration). Combining procedures can also be a particularly advantageous option.

Mediation[7] is an informal procedure, in which parties ask a neutral intermediary, the mediator(s), to assist them in reaching a settlement of the dispute. The mediator(s) have the necessary skills and expertise to

7 See for example Guide to WIPO Mediation available at: www.wipo.int/freepublications/en/arbitration/449/wipo_pub_449.pdf.

help parties identifying the issues in dispute, their underlying interests and to determine a range of alternative options. Mediation helps to find business-oriented solutions and to preserve long-term relationships. Any settlement which parties achieve is enforceable as a contract between them.

Arbitration[8] is a procedure in which the dispute is submitted to one or more independent arbitrators who render a binding decision, the arbitral award, which is normally final and not subject to appeal. The award is internationally enforceable under the New York Convention for the Recognition and Enforcement of Foreign Arbitral Awards of 1958.

Expert Determination[9] is a procedure in which a specific matter is submitted to one or more experts who make a determination on the issue referred to them. It is particularly appropriate for technical or specific issues, such as the determination of a royalty amount. The determination is binding unless the parties have agreed otherwise.

1. Considering Fast Track Arbitration

Standard WIPO Arbitration with the possibility of a three-member arbitral tribunal may well be appropriate in certain cases. This may, for example, be the case in complex patent disputes with patents protected in different jurisdictions, and involving lengthy evidence and expert reports. In other disputes, parties may have an interest in arbitration under the WIPO Expedited Arbitration Rules[10], providing for a sole arbitrator.

The WIPO Expedited Arbitration Rules provide for one exchange of pleadings in comparison to two exchanges of pleadings under the standard WIPO Arbitration Rules. In WIPO Expedited Arbitration, the Statement of Claim is to be submitted together with the Request for Arbitration in order to commence the arbitration (Article 10 WIPO Expedited Arbitration Rules) and the Statement of Defense is to be submitted together with the Answer to the Request (Article 11 WIPO Expedited Arbitration Rules). In standard WIPO Arbitration, the Statement of

8 See for example Guide to WIPO Arbitration, available at: http://www.wipo.int/freepublications/en/arbitration/919/wipo_pub_919.pdf.

9 For more information on WIPO Expert Determination, see www.wipo.int/amc/en/expert-determination.

10 For a comment on WIPO Expedited Arbitration, see Jan Paulsson, The WIPO Expedited Arbitration Rules: Fast-Track Arbitration I., World Arbitration and Mediation Report, Vol. 6, No. 11, 1995, pp. 255-258.

Claim can be submitted after the Request for Arbitration (Article 10 WIPO Arbitration Rules) and the Statement of Defense after the Answer to the Request (Article 12 WIPO Arbitration Rules).

Further, in WIPO Expedited Arbitration, the timelines are shorter and the fees are reduced.[11] For example, a fixed fee applies for the arbitrator's fees in cases where the amount in dispute does not exceed 10 million USD.

WIPO Expedited Arbitration may be appropriate when the value in dispute does not justify the cost of more extensive procedures, or when the number of issues in dispute is limited. It may also be that parties wish to commence with an ambitious time or cost frame, subject to future case developments. In specific instances parties may need a particularly urgent final and enforceable decision.

In practice, WIPO Expedited Arbitration has often been used in trademark and software related disputes, and also in disputes relating to artistic productions.

a) Example: WIPO Expedited Arbitration of a Trademark Coexistence Dispute[12]

In this case, a European company had registered a trademark for luxury goods in different countries. An Asian manufacturer started to sell fashion products under a similar registered trademark. The Asian company filed a court case and administrative cancellation proceedings in two European countries alleging non-use by the European company of its trademark. After the court case went to appeal, the parties settled their dispute by concluding a trademark coexistence agreement which included a WIPO expedited arbitration clause. When the European company used its trademark in a trade fair, the Asian company initiated WIPO expedited arbitration proceedings claiming infringement of the coexistence agreement.

Following consultations between the parties and the Center, a European trademark specialist was appointed as sole arbitrator. After two rounds of pleadings, the arbitrator conducted a one-day hearing in

11 On cost-efficiency in WIPO ADR, see also Berly Acosta-Lelievre, A Cost-Effective Alternative, WIPO Magazine, February 2010, www.wipo.int/wipo_magazine/en/2010/01/article_0008.html.

12 This and other anonymized case summaries are available at the WIPO Center's website at: http://www.wipo.int/amc/en/arbitration/case-example.html.

a European country and issued an award six months after the commencement of the proceedings. Finding partial infringement of the co-existence agreement, the arbitrator granted the primary remedy claimed and ordered the European company to refrain from such infringing behavior.

b) Example: WIPO Expedited Arbitration Relating to an Artistic Production Finance Agreement[13]

A producer of artistic performances entered into an agreement with an insurance company to finance arbitration proceedings. The finance agreement included a WIPO expedited arbitration clause. The producer brought arbitration proceedings against an Asian entity in Singapore. The producer claimed the costs of the Singapore arbitration under its finance agreement. Faced with the financing company's apparent refusal to make such payment, the producer filed WIPO expedited arbitration proceedings indicating that, as a result of the deadline imposed by the arbitral tribunal in Singapore, it required that a final award be issued within six weeks after the commencement of the WIPO expedited arbitration. Following consultations with the parties, the WIPO Center appointed a sole arbitrator. After a one-day hearing in a European country, the sole arbitrator issued a timely arbitral award within five weeks.

2. *Combining ADR Procedures*

ADR procedures can also be combined together in order to cumulate the advantages of the different procedures, by having for example a first mediation phase, followed in the absence of settlement by arbitration. Such « multi-tiered » dispute resolution processes can help avoid an escalation of mechanisms while combining their benefits where necessary. To date, over 20% of the cases submitted to the WIPO Center were based on a combined clause providing for mediation followed, in the absence of settlement, by (expedited) arbitration.

a) The Advantages of Combining Procedures

Providing for an initial mediation phase has the advantage of increasing settlement chances while keeping the risk for parties low. Mediation is an

13 This and other anonymized case summaries are available at the WIPO Center's website at: http://www.wipo.int/amc/en/arbitration/case-example.html.

informal and flexible procedure, allowing either party to withdraw from the procedure.

To date, 73 % of WIPO mediations have settled. Even in arbitration, which normally ends with a final and binding award, parties still have the possibility to explore settlement at any stage of the arbitration process. In WIPO arbitration, to date so far, 58 % of cases have settled.[14]

Also, the mediation phase may allow parties to be better prepared for the arbitration phase and to have a clearer understanding of the issues in dispute. Some of the issues may already have been resolved in the mediation, which allows the resolution of the remaining issues in arbitration to occur faster.

For purposes of neutrality, impartiality and independence, the arbitrator appointed in the arbitration phase would normally be a different person from the mediator in the mediation phase. In exceptional instances, and provided the parties explicitly agree, they may also ask the mediator to act as arbitrator. In WIPO cases, this has only occurred once upon the parties› explicit request.

b) Drafting Multi-Tier Clauses

When drafting a clause combining different ADR procedures, it is important to define time-limits for each phase, so as to avoid undue delay in the resolution of the dispute.

As indicated above, there are different options available to parties in WIPO ADR. They may combine mediation with (expedited) arbitration and expert determination in different constellations.

The most frequently used WIPO ADR clause is « Mediation Followed, in the Absence of a Settlement, by [Expedited] Arbitration ». It provides that

> « *Any dispute, controversy or claim arising under, out of or relating to this contract and any subsequent amendments of this contract, including, without limitation, its formation, validity, binding effect, interpretation, performance, breach or termination, as well as non-contractual claims, shall be submitted to mediation in accordance with the WIPO Mediation Rules. The place of mediation shall be*

14 On settlement see also, WIPO Arbitration and Mediation Center, Update on the WIPO Arbitration and Mediation Center's Experience in the Resolution of Intellectual Property Disputes, in Les Nouvelles, Journal of the Licensing Executives Society International, March 2009, pp. 49-54.

[specify place]. The language to be used in the mediation shall be [specify language].
If, and to the extent that, any such dispute, controversy or claim has not been settled pursuant to the mediation within [60][90] days of the commencement of the mediation, it shall, upon the filing of a Request for Arbitration by either party, be referred to and finally determined by arbitration in accordance with the WIPO [Expedited] Arbitration Rules. Alternatively, if, before the expiration of the said period of [60][90] days, either party fails to participate or to continue to participate in the mediation, the dispute, controversy or claim shall, upon the filing of a Request for Arbitration by the other party, be referred to and finally determined by arbitration in accordance with the WIPO [Expedited] Arbitration Rules. [The arbitral tribunal shall consist of [a sole arbitrator][three arbitrators].] The place of arbitration shall be [specify place]. The language to be used in the arbitral proceedings shall be [specify language]. The dispute, controversy or claim referred to arbitration shall be decided in accordance with the law of [specify jurisdiction]. »*
(The WIPO Expedited Arbitration Rules provide that the arbitral tribunal shall consist of a sole arbitrator.)*

C. Tailoring the ADR Clause

It is generally advised to use model ADR clauses and submission agreements[15] in order to provide for the principal elements and to avoid any ambiguity which may later lead to difficulties and delays in the dispute resolution process. As indicated above, WIPO model clauses and submission agreements, allow parties to define elements such as the place of arbitration or mediation, applicable law, language of proceedings, appointment of mediator or arbitrator.

Where necessary, model clauses and submission agreements may be adapted to the specific needs of parties and include further provisions.

For example, in certain instances where specialized expertise is needed, parties have indicated in the ADR clause the qualifications required from the mediator or arbitrator. They have also set specially

15 For example, the WIPO Center makes available model ADR clauses and submission agreements in different languages on its website at: www.wipo.int/amc/en/clauses.

reduced timelines for certain stages of the ADR process and excluded discovery (see case example under Section II.C.1 below).

In the ADR clause, parties may also determine the degree of confidentiality. By selecting certain institutional rules and the place of arbitration, parties agree on applicable confidentiality provisions. For example, the WIPO Mediation Rules provide for confidentiality and prohibit in particular the disclosure of information exchanged in the mediation to any outside party or in subsequent proceedings (Articles 14-17). The WIPO Arbitration (Articles 73-76) and Expedited Arbitration (Articles 66-69) Rules provide in particular for the confidentiality of the existence of the arbitration, any disclosures made during the arbitration, and of the arbitration award. Beyond that, parties can also stipulate specific confidentiality safeguards in the ADR clause. For example, in one WIPO Arbitration, the clause provided that « [a]ll proceedings, submissions, and decisions related to the arbitration shall be confidential and held in confidence, except as otherwise required to be disclosed by law or to enforce the Arbitrator's award ».

Further, in addition to provisions on available interim relief in institutional Rules (such as Article 46 WIPO Arbitration Rules), parties may also provide for specific interim relief in the ADR clause itself. This was the case in a WIPO Arbitration clause, which stipulated that « [n]either party shall be precluded hereby from seeking provisional remedies in the courts of any jurisdiction including, but not limited to, temporary restraining orders and preliminary injunctions, to protect its rights and interests, but such shall not be sought as a means to avoid or stay arbitration ».

1. *Example : Tailored ADR Clause in a WIPO Expedited Arbitration Relating to a Banking Software Dispute*[16]

In this case, a US company providing data processing software and services and an Asian bank concluded an agreement regarding the provision of account processing services. The parties agreed that the US company was to be the exclusive service provider for certain of the bank's affiliates in North America and Europe. The agreement contained

16 Part of this case summary, as well as other anonymized case summaries are available at the WIPO Center's website at : www.wipo.int/amc/en/arbitration/case-example.

a WIPO Expedited Arbitration clause, tailored to the parties› specific needs by reducing timelines and excluding discovery:

« Any dispute or controversy arising out of this agreement shall be submitted to and resolved by arbitration under the WIPO Expedited Arbitration Rules. [...] The arbitrator will be selected from a panel of persons having experience of information technology. Discovery shall not be permitted. A hearing on the merits of all claims for which arbitration is sought by either party shall be commenced not later than 60 days from the date of the Request for Arbitration is filed. The arbitrator must render a decision within 10 days after the conclusion of such hearing. The place of Arbitration shall be New York City. The applicable substantive law shall be that of the State of New York. »

Four years after the conclusion of their agreement, the US company alleged that the bank had violated the agreement by using processing services offered by third parties in the countries covered by the agreement. When the parties failed to settle the dispute, the US service provider commenced WIPO expedited arbitration proceedings claiming infringement of the agreement and substantial consequential damages. The parties agreed upon a sole arbitrator specialized in IT dispute resolution.

The parties further agreed to use the WIPO Electronic Case Facility (WIPO ECAF), an online case communication system that can be used in cases filed under WIPO Rules if parties opt for it.[17] Submissions and communications are thereby filed into an online case docket, providing an electronic case record available to the parties, the arbitrators or mediators, and the WIPO Center. In order to protect the confidentiality of the procedures and to provide full security, WIPO ECAF is secured by a firewall, user names, changing passwords and a RSA SecurID card.

The sole arbitrator in this case held a two-day hearing in New York City. Three months after the request for expedited arbitration, the

17 More information on WIPO ECAF is available at www.wipo.int/amc/en/ecaf. WIPO ECAF was also used in the 32nd America's Cup, an international sailing competition. Disputes arising in relation with this competition were to be resolved by a jury under specific rules of procedure. As the jury members were based in different countries, an international flexible communication system was needed. See Dina Leytes, America's Cup – WIPO Provides Online Dispute Resolution Facility, WIPO Magazine, Issue 3, June 2007, www.wipo.int/wipo_magazine/en/2007/03/article_0009.html.

arbitrator rendered a final award finding partial infringement of the agreement and granting damages to the US service provider.

2. *Example: Tailored ADR Clause in a Complex Pharma Patent Dispute*

In another WIPO arbitration, the parties had opted for a different arbitration model. The dispute involved US and Asian parties, and concerned US and European patents in the area of pharmaceutical products.

Following prior litigation in US and Europe, the parties concluded a worldwide settlement agreement in the form of a patent license with a tailored WIPO Arbitration clause, deviating from the standard WIPO Arbitration procedure. The clause provided for a Trial Tribunal, consisting of a sole US Arbitrator with jurisdiction for issues relating to US Patents, and a sole European Arbitrator with jurisdiction for issues relating to the European Patents. The clause further provided for an Appeal Tribunal consisting of three arbitrators. New York was agreed as the place of arbitration and as applicable law.

Once the arbitration had started, the parties' counsel agreed on a timetable for the proceedings, the scope of the discovery, preliminary claim construction of the US and European patents, a protective order and a hearing schedule. They also agreed on using WIPO ECAF.

A one-week hearing took place in New York at which both the US Arbitrator and the European Arbitrator were present and heard all the witnesses and issues.

Thanks to the collaborative approach of the parties› counsel in organizing the procedure, a complex patent arbitration could be conducted in an efficient manner. Eighteen months after the commencement of the arbitration, the US and the EU arbitrators rendered separate awards dealing with the respective patents under their jurisdiction. The parties also agreed not to start the appeal procedure.

D. Tailoring the Remedies

Parties in ADR can obtain remedies that are tailored to their particular needs and may not always be available in court.

As mediation is an interest-based procedure, parties can agree on creative and business-oriented solutions. Any remedies they agree on in the settlement agreement will be binding as an enforceable contract.

In arbitration, it is up to the arbitrator to issue a particular remedy in the award, depending on what relief was requested by the filing party and if that party has established its case. Also, there may be a counterclaim from the defendant party requesting certain relief as well.

While monetary relief remains the most common form sought in WIPO cases, parties often also request specific actions as a remedy, such as a declaration of non-performance of contractual obligations, or of infringement of rights. Other forms of remedies sought are, for instance, further safeguards for the preservation of confidentiality of evidence, the provision of a security, the production of specific data, the delivery of a specific good or the conclusion of new contracts.

For example, in a WIPO arbitration relating to an artist promotion dispute, the parties settled their dispute and agreed that the artist would provide a number of its works to the gallery.[18]

III. Tailoring Specific ADR Services for Recurring Disputes or Selected Sectors

A. Why Tailored ADR Services ?

While the standard WIPO Rules are generally appropriate for all commercial disputes, there are certain business sectors that experience specific recurring types of disputes with particular features and needs that can best be addressed by specially tailored ADR services. The WIPO Center therefore works with IP owners and users and their representative organizations and associations, as well as with other interested private or public entities, in order to facilitate or establish specially adapted ADR schemes.[19]

When developing tailored ADR services, the WIPO Center works in consultation with relevant experts and entities. The service may include specifically tailored ADR rules, clauses and schedule of fees. Typically, a specialized Panel of mediators, arbitrators and experts is set up.

18 This and other anonymized case summaries are available at the WIPO Center's website at: www.wipo.int/amc/en/arbitration/case-example.

19 See also SARAH THEURICH, Efficient Alternative Dispute Resolution in Intellectual Property, in WIPO Magazine, Issue 3, June 2009, www.wipo.int/wipo_magazine/en/2009/03/article_0008.html.

Further, specialized training may be provided on ADR in the specific sector.

B. Tailored Domain Name Dispute Resolution

A prominent example of WIPO's tailored ADR efforts is the WIPO-initiated and ICANN mandated Uniform Domain Name Resolution Policy (UDRP). The UDRP was launched in 1999 for the resolution of disputes between trademark owners and domain name registrants over the abusive registration of domain names. To date, the WIPO Center has administered nearly 17,000 domain name disputes under the UDRP.[20]

The WIPO Center also assists regional domain name registries to develop dispute resolution policies in relation to regional domain names, so called ccTLDs.[21] The WIPO Center currently provides dispute resolution services for 62 ccTLDs worldwide.

C. Tailored ADR for Collecting societies

Another more recent area where WIPO tailored ADR services have been utilized is collecting societies.

1. *Why Tailored ADR for Collecting Societies*

Collecting societies collect royalties for certain copyright owners in different areas and use different collecting management systems for this purpose. A collecting society normally has members that can register their works with it and to which the collecting society redistributes the collected royalties. These members may get involved in disputes amongst each other over their entitlement to the amount collected by the collecting society.

Indeed, collecting societies are increasingly facing such conflicts for which effective dispute resolution mechanisms need to be developed. The WIPO Center has developed a specific arbitration procedure for AGICOA (as explained below) and is currently working with another collecting society based in Europe to establish a tailored ADR system.

20 On the UDRP, see www.wipo.int/amc/en/domains/gtld/.

21 On ccTLDs, see www.wipo.int/amc/en/domains/cctld/.

2. *WIPO Expedited Arbitration for AGICOA*

In 2008, the WIPO Center responded to a request by AGICOA (Association de Gestion Internationale Collective des Œuvres Audiovisuelles) by developing the « WIPO Expedited Arbitration Rules for AGICOA »[22], tailored to the specific needs of AGICOA right holders.

AGICOA is an international not-for-profit organization involved in the tracking and distribution of royalties on the retransmission of audiovisual works created by independent producers.[23] It appears that as of September 2009, AGICOA had collected and distributed over half a billion Euros in royalty payments for a portfolio of more than 700,000 audiovisual products since 2000.[24]

Conflicts arise when an AGICOA rights holder registers a work declaring the same rights, for the same territory, the same language version, or for the same television channel as another right holder, and with an overlapping percentage of rights.

This why a twofold dispute resolution process was put in place. In a first mandatory phase, AGICOA operates a conflict resolution procedure for disputes between AGICOA rights holders under AGICOA Conflict Rules. These provide for a settlement and recommendation phase conducted by AGICOA.[25] In the event AGICOA's final recommendation is rejected, parties can opt either to go to a national court or to initiate arbitration, for example under the specific WIPO Expedited Arbitration Rules for AGICOA.

The second optional phase under WIPO Expedited Arbitration Rules for AGICOA applies where right holders agree in an arbitration agreement to submit their dispute to arbitration under these Rules.

These Rules have been particularly customized to the needs in AGICOA conflicts. One of the specifically tailored provisions stipulates that parties may file submissions in English or French, subject to appropriate determination by the sole arbitrator. Also, the Rules provide for

22 See www.wipo.int/amc/en/arbitration/agicoa/.

23 For more information, see AGICOA's website at: www.agicoa.org.

24 See Catalina Saffon & Corinne Chantrier, Collective Management of Audiovisual Works: Facing the challenges, then and now, in WIPO Magazine, Issue 5, September 2009, www.wipo.int/wipo_magazine/en/2009/05/article_0007.html.

25 For more information on this procedure, see AGICOA's website at: www.agicoa.org/english/rightsholder/settle.html.

the direct implementation of the arbitration award by AGICOA, which updates the rights and releases the royalties accordingly.

Furthermore, a specific schedule of fees has been adopted to reflect the general amounts in dispute in AGICOA conflicts.

For AGICOA disputes, the WIPO Center has identified a special panel of copyright and entertainment law arbitrators from various jurisdictions, who can be appointed in cases filed under the WIPO Expedited Arbitration Rules for AGICOA.

D. WIPO Mediation and Expedited Arbitration for Film and Media

Responding to a need expressed in the film and media industry, the WIPO Center launched in December 2009 « WIPO Mediation and Expedited Arbitration for Film and Media ». This scheme has been tailored to the needs in film and media related disputes and aims to provide an international forum for neutral, cost and time effective dispute resolution in the film and media sector.[26]

The background to this system is a Memorandum of Understanding signed in July 2009 between WIPO and the Singaporean Ministry of Information, Communication and the Arts.[27] Under this Memorandum, the Media Development Authority of Singapore and a group of international film and media experts have been collaborating with the WIPO Center in the development of WIPO Mediation and Expedited Arbitration for Film and Media.

The WIPO Film and Media system includes a specific set of « WIPO Mediation and Expedited Arbitration Rules for Film and Media » (WIPO Film and Media Rules), as well as model contract dispute resolution clauses and submission agreements. Further, an international Panel of Film and Media Mediators, Arbitrators and Experts with experience in entertainment related disputes was established, from which appointments are made in cases filed under these Rules. Also, a specific and moderate Schedule of Fees applies to such cases.

The WIPO Film and Media Rules are particularly adapted for international disputes, which may relate to a variety of issues, such as production and co-production agreements, joint-ventures, copyright related

26 See www.wipo.int/amc/en/film.

27 See the related WIPO Press Release of July 28, 2009: www.wipo.int/pressroom/en/articles/2009/article_0027.html.

agreements, financing agreements, distribution agreements, broadcasting agreements, completion bond agreements, laboratory-access agreements, funding agreements, development agreements, licensing, music synchronization agreements, merchandising agreements, insurance agreements, artist and talent agreements, new media agreements, sponsorship agreements, co-ownership agreement, confidentiality and non-disclosure agreements, and TV and media formats.

As of April 2010, the WIPO Center and the Format Recognition and Protection Association (FRAPA) will collaborate in alternative dispute resolution in the area of TV program format disputes.[28] The WIPO Center has thereby taken on FRAPA's existing mediation activity and will administer TV format related disputes filed under the WIPO Mediation and Expedited Arbitration Rules for Film and Media.

1. *How Does the WIPO Film and Media Dispute Resolution Procedure Work ?*

Parties that opt for the WIPO Film and Media Rules can elect to have either a mediation or an expedited arbitration procedure, or a combination of both (i. e., in a first phase of mediation the parties would try to settle the case, and failing that, each party has the option to submit the case to binding expedited arbitration).

The WIPO Film and Media Rules provide for particularly reduced time lines in order to expedite the dispute resolution process.

A specific appointment procedure applies, whereby, and unless the parties have agreed on the person of the mediator or the sole arbitrator or on another appointment procedure, the WIPO Center will normally provide the parties with a list containing the names of specialized mediators and arbitrators with expertise in film and media. Parties can then agree on a person from that list or indicate their preferences. The WIPO Center will then appoint the agreed person, or if no person could be agreed upon, make the appointment taking into account these preferences. Disputes under the WIPO Film and Media Rules are decided by a sole arbitrator. If parties prefer to appoint a three-member arbitral tribunal, they are free to use the standard WIPO Arbitration Rules.

28 See the related WIPO press release of April 7, 2010: www.wipo.int/pressroom/en/articles/2010/article_0009.html.

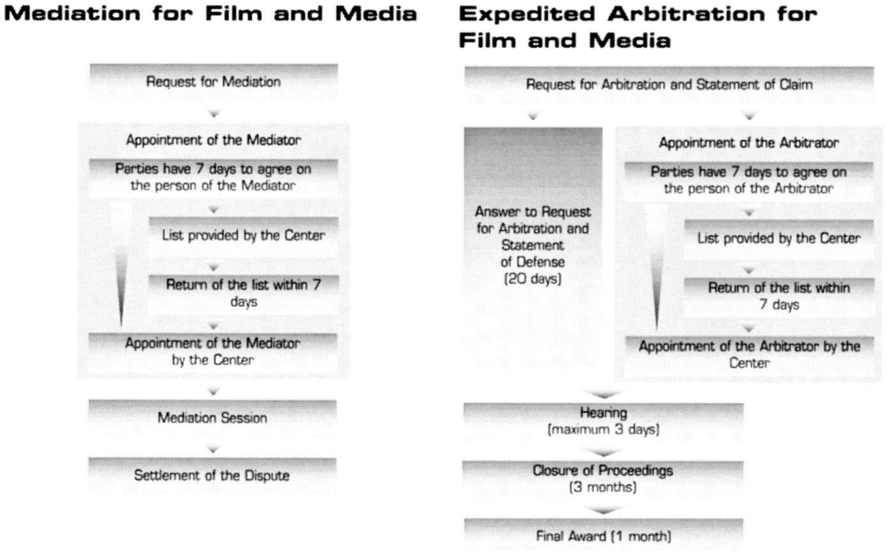

The diagram is taken from Berly Acosta-Lelievre, A Cost-Effective Alternative, WIPO Magazine, February 2010, www.wipo.int/wipo_magazine/en/2010/01/article_0008.html.

2. *Example: WIPO Arbitration of a TV Rights Distribution Dispute*

In a recent WIPO case, a European sports association granted to an Asian media company exclusive rights to broadcast an international sports competition in certain territories for a certain period of time. The broadcasting agreement included a WIPO Arbitration clause providing for a sole arbitrator. A dispute arose as to the scope and execution of the broadcasting agreement, following which the Asian company initiated the WIPO Arbitration proceeding. The WIPO Center submitted a list of qualified candidates to the parties, who agreed upon an arbitrator with expertise in sports and multimedia matters and dispute resolution experience.

E. Other Sectors of WIPO Center Involvement

The WIPO Center also collaborates with stakeholders in emerging IP-related areas, including biodiversity, traditional knowledge, traditional cultural expressions and access to health care, in order to develop adapted dispute resolution systems. For example, it currently advises the Secretariat of the International Treaty for Plant Genetic Resources for Food and Agriculture (ITPGRFA) on ADR guidelines in the context of the ITPGRFA and the related Standard Material Transfer Agreement. The WIPO Center is also involved in informal explorations of ADR's potential in the context of the Convention on Biological Diversity of June 5, 1992.

Also, the WIPO Center is particularly active in the area of technology transfer and research and development. Apart from administering mediations and arbitrations in this area, the WIPO Center collaborates with providers of model contracts, advises research associations in developing internal ADR mechanisms and provides procedural advice on ADR clauses in research and development and technology transfer agreements.[29]

Another area of WIPO Center involvement is art and cultural heritage.[30] In that sector the WIPO Center closely collaborates with WIPO's program in the area of traditional knowledge and traditional cultural expressions (also folklore), as well as WIPO's copyright program. The WIPO Center has identified a list of cultural heritage mediators and arbitrators that can be appointed in such cases. A number of art and culture related cases have been filed with the WIPO Center, involving for example an artist, galleries, a museum, an indigenous community, a producer of artistic performances.

29 For more information on this subject, see JUDITH SCHALLNAU, Alternative Dispute Resolution in Research & Development collaborations – the WIPO Arbitration and Mediation Center, in IPR Helpdesk, no. 41. January-March 2009; Mediation in Research & Development projects – the WIPO Arbitration and Mediation Center, in IPR Helpdesk, no. 42, April – June 2009; Arbitrating Disputes in International and Domestic R&D Collaborations, in IPR Helpdesk, no. 43 July – September 2009. All available at: www.ipr-helpdesk.org.

30 For more information, see SARAH THEURICH, Art and Cultural Heritage Dispute Resolution, in WIPO Magazine, Issue 4, July 2009, www.wipo.int/wipo_magazine/en/2009/04/article_0007.html.

intelle©tual p®operty - p®opriété intelle©tuelle
p®opriété intelle©tuelle - *intelle©tual p®operty*

Livres parus dans la collection

Books published in the series

Vol. 1 (2010):
Sport et propriété intellectuelle /
Sport and Intellectual Property
ISBN: 978-3-7255-6005-9

Vol. 2 (2010):
La résolution des litiges de propriété intellectuelle /
Resolution of Intellectual Property Disputes
ISBN: 978-3-7255-6154-4

www.pi-*ip*.ch